BIOLOGY
The Dynamics of Life

Reinforcement and Study Guide

Teacher Edition

Glencoe McGraw-Hill

New York, New York   Columbus, Ohio   Woodland Hills, California   Peoria, Illinois

A GLENCOE PROGRAM
BIOLOGY: THE DYNAMICS OF LIFE

Student Edition

Teacher Wraparound Edition

Laboratory Manual, SE and TE

Reinforcement and Study Guide, SE and TE

Content Mastery, SE and TE

Section Focus Transparencies and Masters

Reteaching Skills Transparencies and Masters

Basic Concepts Transparencies and Masters

BioLab and MiniLab Worksheets

Concept Mapping

Chapter Assessment

Critical Thinking/Problem Solving

Spanish Resources

Tech Prep Applications

Biology Projects

Computer Test Bank Software and Manual
WINDOWS/MACINTOSH

Lesson Plans

Block Scheduling

Inside Story Poster Package

Science and Technology Videodisc Series, Teacher Guide

English/Spanish Audiocassettes

MindJogger Videoquizzes

Interactive CD-ROM

Videodisc Program

Glencoe Science Professional Series:
Exploring Environmental Issues

Performance Assessment in the Biology Classroom

Alternate Assessment in the Science Classroom

Cooperative Learning in the Science Classroom

Send all inquiries to:
Glencoe/McGraw-Hill
936 Eastwind Drive
Westerville, OH 43081

ISBN 0-02-828248-5
Printed in the United States of America.
1 2 3 4 5 6 7 8 9 10   047   08 07 06 05 04 03 02 01 00 99

Contents

To the Teacher

This *Reinforcement and Study Guide* for **Biology: The Dynamics of Life** helps students understand, organize, and compare the main biology concepts in their textbook. The questions and activities in the study guide also help build strong study and reading skills. There are four study guide pages for each chapter in the textbook. Each BioDigest in the textbook has two study guide pages. Students will find the study guide easy to follow because the section titles match those in the textbook. Further, italicized sentences in the study guide direct students to the appropriate specific topics in the text.

The *Reinforcement and Study Guide* exercises employ a variety of formats including short-answer questions, multiple-choice, matching, true/false, ordering, labeling, completion, and short essay. The sheets allow writing space for students' responses, thus eliminating the need for notebooks or additional paper. The clear, easy-to-follow exercises and the self-pacing format is geared to build your students' confidence in understanding biology.

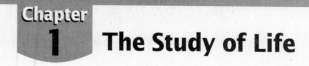

Chapter 1 The Study of Life

In your textbook, read about the science of biology.

Answer the following questions.

1. What is the primary focus of all biological studies?

_____

_____

2. What is meant by the statement, "Living things do not exist in isolation"?

_____

_____

In your textbook, read about why biologist study the diversity of life.

For each of the statements below, write _true_ or _false_.

_____   **3.** People study biology only if they are planning to become biologists.

_____   **4.** By studying biology, you can better appreciate the great diversity of species on Earth and the way each species fits into the dynamic pattern of life on the planet.

_____   **5.** The study of biology includes the investigation of interactions among species.

In your textbook, read about the characteristics of living things.

Complete each statement.

6. To be considered _____ , something must exhibit all of the _____ of life.

7. _____ is another word for "living thing."

8. Every living thing, from simple, single-celled organisms to complex, multicellular plants and animals, is made up of parts that function together in an orderly living _____ .

Read each of the following statements. If it describes the process of reproduction, write _yes_. If not, write _no_.

_____   **9.** New leaves appear on a tree in spring.

_____   **10.** An amoeba divides in half.

_____   **11.** A bean plant produces seeds in long pods.

_____   **12.** Pollen grains are released from a flower.

_____   **13.** A starfish produces a new arm after losing one to a predator.

Circle the letter of the choice that best completes the statement.

14. A species is defined as a group of similar-looking organisms that

  a. undergo similar developmental changes.   **b.** can interbreed.

  c. can interbreed and produce fertile offspring.   **d.** reproduce in the same way.

15. Every organism begins life as a(n)

  a. embryo.   **b.** single cell.   **c.** nucleus.   **d.** fertilized egg.

16. A corn plant producing ears of corn is an example of

  a. growth.   **b.** reproduction.   **c.** development.   **d.** all of these.

17. If members of a species fail to reproduce successfully, the species

  a. will eventually become extinct.   **b.** will not develop normally.

  c. will evolve into a new species.   **d.** will remain unchanged.

Complete the table below by checking the correct column for each example.

Example	Stimulus	Response
18. The recess bell ringing at an elementary school		
19. Your mouth watering at the sight of food on a plate		
20. A sudden drop in air temperature		
21. A flu virus entering your body		
22. Getting butterflies in your stomach before giving a speech		

Answer the following questions.

23. Explain the concept of homeostasis.

_____

_____

_____

24. What is an adaptation?

_____

_____

_____

25. What is evolution?

_____

_____

In your textbook, read about observing and hypothesizing.

Answer the following questions.

1. What is meant by *scientific methods*? _____

_____

2. What is a hypothesis? _____

_____

3. How is a hypothesis tested? _____

In your textbook, read about experimenting.

For each item in Column A, write the letter of the matching item in Column B.

Column A	Column B
_____ **4.** A procedure that tests a hypothesis by collecting information under controlled conditions	**a.** dependent variable
_____ **5.** In an experiment, the group in which all conditions are kept the same	**b.** experimental group
_____ **6.** In an experiment, the group in which all conditions are kept the same except for the one being tested	**c.** independent variable
_____ **7.** The condition that is changed by the experimenter	**d.** experiment
_____ **8.** The condition being observed or measured in an experiment	**e.** control group

Use each of the terms below just once to complete the passage.

experimental results	experiment(s)	hypothesis	laws
scientific journals	theory	valid	verify

When **(9)** _____ are reported in **(10)** _____ ,

other scientists may try to **(11)** _____ the results by repeating the

(12) _____ . Usually when a(n) **(13)** _____ is supported

by data from several scientists, it is considered **(14)** _____ . Over time, a hypothesis

that is supported by many observations and experiments becomes a **(15)** _____ .

Some well-established facts of nature, such as gravity, are recognized as **(16)** _____ .

In your textbook, read about kinds of research.

Complete the chart by checking the correct column for each example.

Example	Quantitative Research	Descriptive Research
1. Numerical data		
2. Field study of hunting behavior		
3. Thermometer, balance scale, stopwatch		
4. Testable hypothesis		
5. Measurements from controlled laboratory experiments		
6. Purely observational data		
7. Binoculars, tape recorder, camera		

Complete each statement.

8. In order for scientific research to be universally understood, scientists report measurements in the

_____ , a modern form of the metric system.

9. This system of measurement is abbreviated _____ .

10. This system is a _____ system in which measurements are expressed in

multiples of _____ or _____ of a basic unit.

In your textbook, read about science and society.

Determine if the following statement is true. If it is not, rewrite the italicized part to make it true.

11. Ideas about the value of knowledge gained through scientific research come from a society's *social,*

ethical, and *moral* concerns. _____

12. Pure science is scientific research carried out *primarily to solve a specific environmental problem.*

_____

13. *Technology* is the practical application of scientific research to improve human life and the world in

which we live. _____

14. A technological solution to a human problem can benefit humans but may also *cause a different, possibly*

serious, problem. _____

15. *Scientists* have the final say about how the results of scientific discoveries are applied.

_____

BioDigest 1

What Is Biology?

In your textbook, read about characteristics of life.

Complete the following statements.

Biology is the study of **(1)** _____ and the **(2)** _____ among them. Biologists use a variety of **(3)** _____ methods to study the details of life.

For each item in Column A, write the letter of the matching item in Column B.

Column A	Column B
_____ **4.** The basic unit is the cell.	**a.** development
_____ **5.** Maintenance of a stable internal environment	**b.** growth
_____ **6.** Reaction to a change in the environment	**c.** homeostasis
_____ **7.** Cell enlargement and division	**d.** organization
_____ **8.** Changes in an organism that take place over time	**e.** reproduction
_____ **9.** Transmission of heredity information from one generation to the next	**f.** response to stimulus

Using what you know about characteristics of life, determine if each of the following describes a living or nonliving thing.

_____ **10.** rust on a bucket

_____ **11.** an apple on a tree

_____ **12.** bacteria

_____ **13.** lightning

_____ **14.** a dinosaur fossil

_____ **15.** a wasp

BioDigest 1
What Is Biology, *continued*

In your textbook, read about scientific methods.

Decide if each of the following statements is true. If it is not, rewrite the italicized part to make it true.

16. Scientific methods include observation, hypothesis, experiment, and *theory.* _____

17. A statement that can be tested and presents a possible solution to a question is a *law.*

_____

18. In a controlled experiment, two groups are tested and all conditions except *two* are kept the same for

both groups. _____

19. A condition that remains the same for both groups is called the *independent variable.*

_____

20. A condition that is changed by the experimenter in one group and not the other is called the

dependent variable. _____

21. A scientific experiment can be conducted *only in a laboratory.* _____

22. A theory is a *law* that has been confirmed by many experiments. _____

Read each of the following statements. If it is a testable hypothesis, write <u>yes</u>. If it is not a testable hypothesis, write <u>no</u>.

_____ **23.** If a person exercises, his or her pulse rate will increase.

_____ **24.** Cats make better pets than dogs.

_____ **25.** When fertilizer is added to soil, plants grow taller.

Identify each of the two italicized items as either an independent or a dependent variable.

26. The *number of red blood cells* in a mouse's blood at *different levels of iron* in its diet

_____

27. The *amount of starch formed* in a plant leaf for *different times* of exposure to light

_____

Chapter 2 Principles of Ecology

In your textbook, read about what ecology is and about aspects of ecological study.

Use each of the terms below just once to complete the passage.

| ecology | biotic factors | nonliving | environments | atmosphere |
| humans | organisms | soil | biosphere | abiotic factors |

Living organisms in our world are connected to other **(1)** _____ in a

variety of ways. The branch of biology called **(2)** _____ is the scientific study of

interactions among organisms and their **(3)** _____ , including relationships

between living and **(4)** _____ things.

All living things on Earth can be found in the **(5)** _____ , the portion

of Earth that supports life. It extends from high in the **(6)** _____ to the bottom

of the oceans. Many different environments can be found in the biosphere. All living organisms found in

an environment are called **(7)** _____ . Nonliving parts of an environment are

called **(8)** _____ . For example, whales, trees, and **(9)** _____

are biotic factors. Ocean currents, temperature, and **(10)** _____ are abiotic factors.

In your textbook, read about levels of organization in ecology.

For each item in Column A, write the letter of the matching item in Column B.

	Column A	Column B
_____	**11.** A group of organisms of one species that interbreed and live in the same place at the same time	**a.** community
_____	**12.** A collection of interacting populations	**b.** competition
_____	**13.** Interactions among the populations and abiotic factors in a community	**c.** forest
_____	**14.** Occurs between organisms when resources are scarce	**d.** population
_____	**15.** A terrestrial ecosystem	**e.** ecosystem

In your textbook, read about organisms in ecosystems.

For each statement below, write <u>true</u> or <u>false</u>.

_____ **16.** A habitat is the role a species plays in a community.

_____ **17.** Habitats may change.

_____ **18.** A niche is the place where an organism lives its life.

_____ **19.** A habitat can include only one niche.

_____ **20.** A species' niche includes how the species meets its needs for food and shelter.

_____ **21.** The centipedes and worms that live under a certain log occupy the same habitat but have different niches.

_____ **22.** It is an advantage for two species to share the same niche.

_____ **23.** Competition between two species is reduced when the species have different niches.

Complete the table below by writing the kind of relationship described on the left.

Relationships Among Organisms	
Description of Relationship	**Kind of Relationship**
24. Organisms of different species live together in a close, permanent relationship.	
25. One species benefits and the other species is neither benefited nor harmed by the relationship.	
26. One species benefits from the relationship at the expense of the other species.	
27. Both species benefit from the relationship.	

Chapter 2 **Principles of Ecology,** *continued*

In your textbook, read about how organisms obtain energy and about matter and energy flow in ecosystems.

Answer the questions below. Use the diagram of a food web to answer questions 1–7.

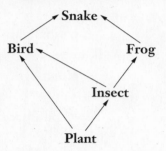

1. How many food chains make up the food web?

_____

2. Which organism is an herbivore?

_____

3. Which organism is an autotroph?

_____

4. Which organism is a third-order heterotroph? To what trophic level does that organism belong?

_____

5. Which organism is an omnivore?

_____

6. Which organisms belong to more than one food chain?

_____

7. Which organism belongs to more than one trophic level?

_____

8. What are decomposers? From which trophic levels are the organisms that decomposers feed on?

_____

_____

9. What does a pyramid of energy show about the amount of energy available at different trophic levels of a food chain?

_____

10. Why do different trophic levels have different amounts of energy?

_____

_____

In your textbook, read about cycles in nature.

Circle the letter of the choice that best completes the statement or answers the question.

11. Energy that is lost at each trophic level of an ecosystem is replenished by

  a. heat.   **b.** nutrients.   **c.** sunlight.   **d.** organisms.

12. Besides energy, what moves through the organisms at each trophic level of an ecosystem?

  a. organisms   **b.** nutrients   **c.** sunlight   **d.** cycles

13. Evaporation and condensation a part of the

  a. carbon cycle.   **b.** nitrogen cycle.   **c.** phosphorus cycle.   **d.** water cycle.

14. Plants lose water to the air through

  a. condensation.   **b.** photosynthesis.   **c.** their roots.   **d.** evaporation.

15. Animals lose water when they

  a. breathe in.   **b.** urinate.   **c.** breathe out.   **d.** both b and c.

16. The water in the atmosphere is returned to the earth by

  a. precipitation.   **b.** evaporation.   **c.** photosynthesis.   **d.** decomposition.

17. Autotrophs and heterotrophs use carbon molecules for energy and

  a. photosynthesis.   **b.** growth.   **c.** decomposition.   **d.** both a and b.

18. What do plants use in photosynthesis to make carbon molecules?

  a. carbon dioxide   **b.** carbohydrates   **c.** fertilizer   **d.** oxygen

19. Heterotrophs get carbon molecules by

  a. making the molecules themselves.   **b.** feeding on other organisms.

  c. decaying.   **d.** growing.

20. When decomposers break down the carbon molecules in dead organisms,

  a. the dead organisms are converted to coal.   **b.** oxygen is released.

  c. carbon dioxide is released.   **d.** carbon dioxide is converted to energy-rich carbon molecules.

21. Fertilizers provide plants with

  a. nitrogen.   **b.** carbon.   **c.** water.   **d.** oxygen.

22. Which of the following convert(s) nitrogen in the air into a form plants can use?

  a. bacteria   **b.** lightning   **c.** sunlight   **d.** both a and b

23. Plants use nitrogen to make

  a. carbohydrates.   **b.** nitrogen gas.   **c.** proteins.   **d.** both b and c.

24. An animal returns nitrogen to the environment when it

  a. breathes.   **b.** decomposes.   **c.** urinates.   **d.** both b and c.

25. Animals get phosphorus from

  a. the air.   **b.** eating plants.   **c.** water.   **d.** the soil.

26. Phosphorus in the soil comes from

  a. rocks.   **b.** decaying organisms.   **c.** the air.   **d.** both a and b.

Chapter 3 Communities and Biomes

In your textbook, read about living in a community.

Determine if the statement is true. If it is not, rewrite the italicized part to make it true.

1. The *interactions* of abiotic and biotic factors result in conditions that are suitable for some organisms but not for others. _____

2. Food availability and temperature can be *biotic factors* for a particular organism. _____

3. A limiting factor is any biotic or abiotic factor that *promotes* the existence, numbers, reproduction, or distribution of organisms. _____

4. At high elevations where the soil is thin, vegetation is limited to *large, deep-rooted* trees.

_____

5. Factors that limit one population in a community may also have *an indirect* effect on another population.

_____

6. *Tolerance* is the ability of an organism to withstand fluctuations in biotic and abiotic environmental factors. _____

7. A population of deer would become *larger* as conditions move away from optimal toward either extreme of the deer's range of tolerance. _____

8. Different species may have different ranges of tolerance. _____

In your textbook, read about succession: changes over time.

Use each of the terms below just once to complete the passage.

climax	primary	decades	succeed
pioneer	succession	species	slows down

The natural changes and **(9)** _____ replacements that take place in the communities

of ecosystems are know as **(10)** _____ . It can take **(11)** _____ or even centuries

for one community to **(12)** _____ , or replace, another. When new sites of land are formed, as

in a lava flow, the first organisms to colonize the new area are **(13)** _____ species. This colo-

nization is called **(14)** _____ succession. The species inhabiting the area gradually change.

Eventually, succession **(15)** _____ and the community becomes more stable. Finally, a mature

community that undergoes little or no change, called a **(16)** _____ community, develops.

For each item in Column A, write the letter of the matching item in Column B.

Column A

_____ **17.** Sequence of community changes where soil is formed, allowing small, weedy plants to inhabit the area

_____ **18.** Sequence of community changes occurring as a result of a natural disaster, such as a forest fire

_____ **19.** A stable, mature community with little or no succession occurring

_____ **20.** An example of a biotic limiting factor affecting a community of organisms

_____ **21.** An example of an abiotic limiting factor affecting a community of organisms

Column B

a. a severe drought

b. primary succession

c. amount of plant growth

d. secondary succession

e. climax community

The statements below describe the secondary succession that occurred within an area of Yellowstone National Park. Number the events in the order in which they occurred.

_____ **22.** Grasses, ferns, and pine seedlings inhabited the area.

_____ **23.** Annual wildflowers grew from the bare soil.

_____ **24.** A fire burned thousands of acres of land.

_____ **25.** A climax community of lodgepole pines developed.

_____ **26.** Bare soil covered the area.

In your textbook, read about aquatic biomes: life in the water.

Complete each statement.

1. A large group of ecosystems sharing the same type of _____ is

called a _____ .

2. Biomes located in bodies of _____ , such as oceans, lakes, and rivers, are called

_____ .

3. The water in marine biomes is _____ .

4. Oceans contain the largest amount of _____ , or living material, of any biome on Earth.

Yet, most of the organisms are so _____ that they cannot be seen without magnification.

5. The _____ is that part of marine biomes shallow enough to be penetrated by sunlight.

6. Deep-water regions of marine biomes receiving no sunlight make up the _____ .

Circle the letter of the response that best completes the statement.

7. If you followed the course of a river, it would eventually flow into
   a. a lake.   **b.** a stream.   **c.** an ocean or a sea.   **d.** a swamp.

8. The body of water where fresh water from a river mixes with salt water is called
   a. an estuary.   **b.** a shoreline.   **c.** a sandbar.   **d.** a sea.

9. Organisms living in intertidal zones have structures that protect them from
   a. the dark.   **b.** sunlight.   **c.** wave action.   **d.** temperature.

10. Life is abundant in photic zones because
   a. there are no waves.   **b.** the water is warm.
   c. the water is clean.   **d.** there are many nutrients.

11. The greatest number of organisms living in the photic zone of a marine biome are
   a. dolphins.   **b.** plankton.   **c.** plants.   **d.** sharks.

12. Few organisms live at the bottom of a deep lake because of the lack of
   a. sunlight.   **b.** space.   **c.** plankton.   **d.** bacteria.

In your textbook, read about terrestrial biomes.

Answer the following questions.

13. Which two abiotic factors generally determine the type of climax community that will develop in a particular part of the world?

_____

14. In which terrestrial biome is the ground permanently frozen?

_____

15. What are some adaptations that desert plants have developed?

_____

_____

_____

16. Describe the three layers of a tropical rain forest, including organisms that live in each layer.

_____

_____

_____

_____

Write the name of each major terrestrial biome next to its description.

_____ **17.** Arid land with sparse, drought-resistant plants

_____ **18.** Largest terrestrial biome that supports small plants and grasses, but few trees

_____ **19.** Treeless land where only small plants and grasses grow during the long summer days

_____ **20.** Warm, wet land that supports many species of organisms

_____ **21.** Land with coniferous forests, peat swamps, and long, harsh winters

_____ **22.** Land populated with broad-leaved hardwood trees that lose their leaves annually

Chapter

4 **Population Biology**

In your textbook, read about the principles of population growth.

Refer to Graphs A and B below. Answer the following questions.

Graph A

Size
of
Population

Time

Graph B

Size
of
Population

Time

1. What type of population growth is shown in Graph A? Explain this type of growth.

_____

_____

2. Which graph shows the most likely growth of a squirrel population living in a forest? _____

3. Which graph shows a population's growth under ideal conditions? _____

4. Why don't populations of organisms grow indefinitely?

_____

_____

_____

Use each of the terms below just once to complete the passage.

| grows | carrying capacity | below | births |
| above | under | deaths | exceed |

The number of organisms of one species that an environment can support is called its

(5) _____ . If the number of organisms in a population is **(6)** _____ the

environment's carrying capacity, births **(7)** _____ deaths and the population

(8) _____ . If the number of organisms rises **(9)** _____ the carrying capacity

of the environment, **(10)** _____ will exceed **(11)** _____ . This pattern will

continue until the population is once again at or **(12)** _____ the carrying capacity.

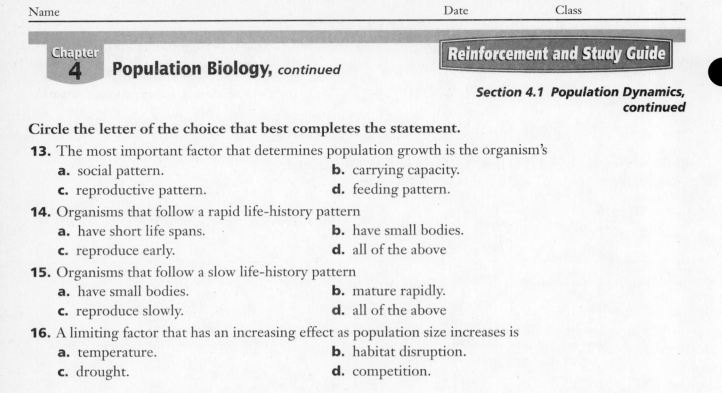

Circle the letter of the choice that best completes the statement.

13. The most important factor that determines population growth is the organism's
    a. social pattern.   **b.** carrying capacity.
    c. reproductive pattern.   **d.** feeding pattern.

14. Organisms that follow a rapid life-history pattern
    a. have short life spans.   **b.** have small bodies.
    c. reproduce early.   **d.** all of the above

15. Organisms that follow a slow life-history pattern
    a. have small bodies.   **b.** mature rapidly.
    c. reproduce slowly.   **d.** all of the above

16. A limiting factor that has an increasing effect as population size increases is
    a. temperature.   **b.** habitat disruption.
    c. drought.   **d.** competition.

In your textbook, read about how organism interactions limit population size.

Answer the following.

17. The snowshoe hare is a primary source of food for the Canadian lynx. Explain how the lynx
population size changes when the hare population increases.

_____

_____

18. Explain how the change in the lynx population size affects the hare population.

_____

_____

19. What is the relationship between the lynx and the hare called?

_____

_____

20. When does competition decrease the size of a population?

_____

_____

21. What can cause an organism to exhibit stress, and what symptoms of stress can lead to a decrease
in population size?

_____

_____

Chapter 4 Population Biology, *continued*

Reinforcement and Study Guide

Section 4.2 Human Population Growth

In your textbook, read about demographic trends.

Determine if the statement is true. If it is not, rewrite the italicized part to make it true.

1. Looking at *past* population trends is a good way to predict the future of human populations.

_____

2. Demography is the study of population *health* characteristics.

_____

3. Worldwide human populations have *decreased* exponentially over the past few centuries.

_____

4. Humans are able to *increase* environmental effects on the human population through controlling disease, eliminating competing organisms, and increasing food production.

_____

5. To tell whether a population is *growing*, you must know the difference between the birthrate and the death rate.

_____

6. The death rate is *decreasing* in the United States.

_____

7. The birthrate is *increasing* in the United States.

_____

8. *Birthrate* is the number of offspring a female produces during her reproductive years.

_____

9. In the United States, families are now *smaller* than in previous decades.

_____

10. Birthrates and death rates of countries around the world *are basically the same.*

_____

11. If a country has a high death rate, it *may also* have a high birthrate.

_____

12. If a country has a low death rate and a *high* birthrate, it will grow slowly, if at all.

_____

For each statement in Column A, write the letter of the item in Column B that completes the statement correctly.

Column A	Column B
_____ **13.** Population growth will change if the largest _____ of a population is in its post-reproductive years.	**a.** age structure
_____ **14.** The proportions of a population that are at different _____ make up its age structure.	**b.** stable
_____ **15.** If you know a population has a large group of individuals in their pre-reproductive years, you would predict that the population's growth will be _____ .	**c.** proportion
_____ **16.** If the proportions of a population at different age levels are fairly equal, the population will be _____ .	**d.** fertility
_____ **17.** The population growth of a country depends on its birthrate, death rate, and _____ rate.	**e.** rapid
_____ **18.** To make predictions about the growth of a population, demographers must know its _____ .	**f.** age levels

Complete each statement.

19. _____ is the movement into and out of populations.

20. _____ is the movement of humans into a population.

21. _____ is the movement of humans from a population.

22. Immigration and emigration of people have no effect on total _____ population.

23. Immigration and emigration of people affect _____ population growth rates.

24. Suburban growth due to _____ has placed stress on schools and various public services.

Chapter 5 Biological Diversity and Conservation

In your textbook, read about biological diversity.

Use the terms below just once to complete the passage. You will not use all the terms.

environments	variety	greater	space	species
biological diversity	equator	less	decrease	increase

(1) _____ refers to the **(2)** _____ of life in an

area. Another word for biological diversity is biodiversity. The simplest measure of biodiversity is the

number of **(3)** _____ that live in a certain area. The more species there are,

the **(4)** _____ is the biodiversity of the area. Biodiversity on land tends to

(5) _____ as you move toward the **(6)** _____ .

Biodiversity is greater on large islands than on small islands because large islands have more

(7) _____ and a greater variety of **(8)** _____ .

In your textbook, read about the importance of biodiversity.

For each statement below, write <u>true</u> or <u>false</u>.

_____ **9.** Biodiversity provides our world with beauty.

_____ **10.** The loss of a species from an ecosystem usually has no effect because of the presence of other species in the ecosystem.

_____ **11.** Biodiversity decreases the stability of ecosystems because more species are competing with each other.

_____ **12.** Increasing the biodiversity of an ecosystem may result in more niches.

_____ **13.** Diseases are more likely to spread in an ecosystem with high biodiversity than in an ecosystem with low biodiversity.

_____ **14.** A decrease in Earth's biodiversity may affect people's diets.

_____ **15.** Preserving diverse plant species may lead to the discovery of new drugs in the future.

Chapter 5 **Biological Diversity and Conservation,** *continued*

Section 5.1 Vanishing Species, *continued*

In your textbook, read about the loss of biodiversity.

For each item in Column A, write the letter of the matching item in Column B.

Column A	Column B
_____ **16.** The number of members of a species is so low that there is a possibility of extinction.	**a.** passenger pigeon
_____ **17.** This animal is an example of an endangered species.	**b.** threatened species
_____ **18.** The population of a species begins declining rapidly.	**c.** black rhinoceros
_____ **19.** This animal is an example of an extinct species.	**d.** African elephant
_____ **20.** All members of a species have died, so the species no longer exists.	**e.** extinct species
_____ **21.** This animal is an example of a threatened species.	**f.** endangered species

In your textbook, read about threats to biodiversity.

Complete the table by checking the correct column for each statement.

Statement	Habitat Loss	Habitat Fragmentation	Habitat Degradation
22. Animals have no migratory route.			
23. A rain forest is burned.			
24. A highway divides a forest.			
25. Acid precipitation leaches nutrients from the soil.			
26. Detergents and other chemicals pollute bodies of water.			
27. Coral is mined for building materials.			
28. The reduction of the ozone layer causes more ultraviolet radiation to reach Earth's surface.			

Chapter 5 Biological Diversity and Conservation, *continued*

Reinforcement and Study Guide

Section 5.1 Vanishing Species, continued

Circle the letter of the choice that best completes the statement.

29. When species lose their habitats, they may
   a. lack food.
   b. lack shelter.
   c. be in danger of becoming extinct.
   d. all of the above.

30. Habitat fragmentation often leads to
   a. increased species diversity within an area.
   b. larger habitats for species.
   c. decreased species diversity within an area.
   d. an increased food supply for species.

31. Different conditions along the boundaries of an ecosystem are called
   a. habitat fragmentation.
   b. edge effect.
   c. habitat loss.
   d. canopy effect.

32. The greatest source of air pollution is
   a. volcanic eruptions.
   b. forest fires.
   c. burning fossil fuels.
   d. CFCs.

33. Acid precipitation
   a. may decrease biodiversity on land.
   b. has no effect on biodiversity.
   c. may increase biodiversity in water.
   d. both a and c.

34. The reduction of the ozone layer is caused by
   a. burning fossil fuels.
   b. acid precipitation.
   c. heavy metals.
   d. CFCs.

35. Algal blooms in lakes
   a. are caused by acid precipitation.
   b. decrease the amount of oxygen in the lake when they decay.
   c. clog the gills of fish.
   d. both a and b.

36. When exotic species are introduced into an area, their populations may grow exponentially because the species
   a. are large.
   b. are predators.
   c. lack competitors and predators.
   d. are small.

37. The African elephant population was greatly reduced between 1970 and 1990 due to
   a. habitat degradation.
   b. excessive hunting.
   c. habitat loss.
   d. pollution.

Reinforcement and Study Guide

Section 5.2 Conservation of Biodiversity

In your textbook, read about strategies of conservation biology.

Answer the following questions.

1. What is conservation biology?

_____

_____

2. How does the U.S. Endangered Species Act protect biodiversity?

_____

_____

_____

3. How do nature preserves help protect biodiversity?

_____

_____

4. Why is it usually better to preserve one large area of land instead of a few smaller areas of land?

_____

_____

5. Why are habitat corridors used to connect different protected areas?

_____

6. What caused the steady decline of the black-footed ferret population in Wyoming?

_____

_____

7. What efforts were made to increase the size of the black-footed ferret population?

_____

_____

8. How are seed banks useful in protecting biodiversity?

_____

_____

_____

9. What are some problems of keeping endangered animals in captivity before reintroducing them to their original habitats?

_____

_____

Copyright © Glencoe/McGraw-Hill, a division of The McGraw-Hill Companies, Inc.

BioDigest
2 **Ecology**

In your textbook, read about ecosystems.

For each statement below, write <u>true</u> or <u>false</u>.

_____ 1. Organisms interact with the nonliving parts of their environments.

_____ 2. Relationships between organisms are abiotic factors in ecosystems.

_____ 3. In the carbon cycle, animals produce nutrients from carbon dioxide in the atmosphere.

_____ 4. Commensalism is a relationship in which one species benefits while the other species is neither helped nor harmed.

_____ 5. The temperature and precipitation in a certain land area influence the type of biome that is found there.

In your textbook, read about food for life.

Use the diagram on the right to answer questions 6–10.

6. Describe a food chain using organisms in the pyramid.

_____

_____

_____

_____

_____

7. Which organisms are carnivores?

_____

8. How many trophic levels are included in the pyramid?

_____

9. Which trophic level has the smallest biomass?

_____

10. How does the biomass of the autotrophs compare with the biomass of the herbivores?

_____

_____

_____

In your textbook, read about population size.

Use the terms below to complete the passage. You will not use all the terms.

carrying capacity	species	maximum	limit	competition
linear growth	minimum	exceeds	food	exponential growth

A population is the number of organisms of one **(11)** _____ that live in a

certain area. Under ideal conditions in which there are no factors that **(12)** _____

the size of a population, a population shows **(13)** _____ . However, in the

environment, the sizes of populations are influenced by various limiting factors, such as the availability

of **(14)** _____ , water, space, and other resources. As population size increases,

(15) _____ for the resources increases. The **(16)** _____ size of

a population that an environment can support is the environment's **(17)** _____

for that population. When a population **(18)** _____ the carrying capacity,

individuals are unable to meet all their needs and die.

In your textbook, read about succession and biodiversity.

Number the steps of succession below in the order in which they occur.

_____ **19.** Shade from grasses and shrubs provides protection for tree saplings.

_____ **20.** Pioneer species and other small plants are unable to grow in the shade and die.

_____ **21.** Grasses and bushes appear.

_____ **22.** A plot of farmland is abandoned.

_____ **23.** Tree saplings grow and increase the amount of shade in the area.

_____ **24.** Pioneer species, such as dandelions, take root in the soil.

Answer the following questions.

25. What effect does succession have on the biodiversity of ecosystems?

_____

26. What human actions decrease the biodiversity of ecosystems?

_____

_____

In your textbook, read about elements, atoms, and isotopes.

Determine if the statement is true. If it is not, rewrite the italicized part to make it true.

1. An element is a substance that *can be* broken down into simpler substances. _____

2. On Earth, *90* elements occur naturally. _____

3. Only four elements—*carbon, hydrogen, oxygen, and nitrogen*—make up more than 96 percent of the mass of a human. _____

4. Each element is abbreviated by a one- or two-letter *formula*. _____

5. Trace elements, such as iron and magnesium, are present in living things in *very large* amounts.
_____

6. The properties of elements are determined by *the structures of their atoms*. _____

Label the parts of the atom. Use these choices:

energy level   electron   neutron   proton   nucleus

e^- ———— **11.** _____

7. _____

p^+
n^0

10. _____

8. _____   **9.** _____

Answer the following questions.

12. What is the maximum number of electrons in each of the following energy levels: first, second, third?
_____
_____

13. Boron has two isotopes, boron-10 and boron-11. Boron-10 has five protons and five neutrons. How many protons and neutrons does boron-11 have? Explain.
_____
_____
_____
_____
_____

| Chapter 6 | The Chemistry of Life, continued | Reinforcement and Study Guide |

In your textbook, read about compounds and bonding, chemical reactions, and mixtures and solutions.

Write the type of substance described. Use these choices: compound, element.

_____ **14.** H_2O, a liquid that no longer resembles either hydrogen or oxygen gas

_____ **15.** A substance that can be broken down in a chemical reaction

_____ **16.** Carbon, the substance represented by the symbol C

Complete the table by checking the correct column for each description.

Statement	Ionic Bond(s)	Covalent Bond(s)
17. Found in the compound NaCl		
18. Increases the stability of atoms		
19. Results in the formation of a molecule		
20. Is formed when atoms share electrons		

Fill in the blanks with the correct number of molecules to balance the chemical equation. Then answer the questions.

$$C_6H_{12}O_6 + \underline{} O_2 \longrightarrow \underline{} CO_2 + \underline{} H_2O$$

21. Why must chemical equations always balance?

_____

_____

22. Which number indicates the number of atoms of each element in a molecule of a substance.

_____

23. When is a mixture not a solution?

_____

_____

24. What is the difference between an acid and a base?

_____

_____

Chapter 6 The Chemistry of Life, *continued*

Section 6.2 Water and Diffusion

In your textbook, read about water and its importance.

For each statement below, write <u>true</u> or <u>false</u>.

_____ **1.** In a water molecule, electrons are shared equally between the hydrogen atoms and oxygen atom.

_____ **2.** The attraction of opposite charges between hydrogen and oxygen forms a weak oxygen bond.

_____ **3.** Because of its polarity, water can move from the roots of a plant up to its leaves.

_____ **4.** Water changes temperature easily.

_____ **5.** Unlike most substances, water expands when it freezes.

Circle the letter of the choice that best completes the statement.

6. All objects in motion have
   a. potential energy.   **b.** heat energy.   **c.** kinetic energy.   **d.** random energy.

7. The first scientist to observe evidence of the random motion of molecules was
   a. Brown.   **b.** Darwin.   **c.** Mendel.   **d.** Hooke.

8. The net movement of particles from an area of higher concentration to an area of lower concentration is called
   a. dynamic equilibrium.   **b.** nonrandom movement.
   c. concentration gradient.   **d.** diffusion.

9. Diffusion occurs because of
   a. nonrandom movement of particles.   **b.** random movement of particles.
   c. a chemical reaction between particles.   **d.** chemical energy.

10. When a few drops of colored corn syrup are added to a beaker of pure corn syrup, the color will
   a. move from low concentration to high concentration.
   b. form a polar bond.
   c. start to diffuse.
   d. remain on the bottom of the beaker.

11. Diffusion can be accelerated by
   a. decreasing the pressure.   **b.** increasing the temperature.
   c. decreasing the movement of particles.   **d.** increasing the dynamic equilibrium.

12. When materials pass into and out of a cell at equal rates, there is no net change in concentration inside the cell. The cell is in a state of
   a. dynamic equilibrium.   **b.** metabolism.   **c.** imbalance.   **d.** inertia.

13. The difference in concentration of a substance across space is called
   a. dynamic equilibrium.   **b.** concentration gradient.
   c. diffusion.   **d.** Brownian movement.

Chapter 6 **The Chemistry of Life,** *continued*

In your textbook, read about the role of carbon in organisms.

For each of the following statements about carbon, write <u>true</u> or <u>false</u>.

_____ **1.** Carbon atoms can bond together in straight chains, branched chains, or rings.

_____ **2.** Large molecules containing carbon atoms are called micromolecules.

_____ **3.** Polymers are formed by hydrolysis.

_____ **4.** Cells use carbohydrates for energy.

Write each item below under the correct heading.

| sucrose | glucose | starch | $C_6H_{12}O_6$ |
| cellulose | glycogen | fructose | $C_{12}H_{22}O_{11}$ |

Monosaccharide
5.
6.
7.

Dissaccharide
8.
9.

Polysaccharide
10.
11.
12.

Complete the table by checking the correct column for each description.

Description	Lipids	Proteins	Nucleic Acids
13. Made up of nucleotides			
14. Most consist of three fatty acids bonded to a glycerol molecule			
15. DNA and RNA			
16. Contain peptide bonds			
17. Produce proteins			
18. Commonly called fats and oils			
19. Made up of amino acids			
20. Used for long-term energy storage, insulation, and protective coatings			
21. Contain carbon, hydrogen, oxygen, and nitrogen			

Chapter 7

A View of the Cell

In your textbook, read about the history of the cell theory.

For each statement in Column A, write the letter of the matching item in Column B.

Column A	Column B
_____ **1.** The first scientist to describe living cells as seen through a simple microscope	**a.** Schleiden
_____ **2.** Uses two or more glass lenses to magnify either living cells or prepared slides	**b.** compound light microscope
_____ **3.** A scientist who observed that cork was composed of tiny, hollow boxes that he called cells	**c.** electron microscope
_____ **4.** A scientist who concluded that all plants are composed of cells	**d.** Schwann
_____ **5.** A scientist who concluded that all animals are composed of cells	**e.** Hooke
_____ **6.** The microscope that allowed scientists to view molecules	**f.** Leeuwenhoek

In your textbook, read about the two basic cell types.

Complete the table by checking the correct column for each statement.

Statement	Prokaryotes	Eukaryotes
7. Organisms that have cells lacking internal membrane-bound structures		
8. Do not have a nucleus		
9. Are either single-celled or made up of many cells		
10. Generally are single-celled organisms		
11. Organisms that have cells containing organelles		

In your textbook, read about maintaining a balance.

Use each of the terms below just once to complete the passage.

| glucose | plasma membrane | homeostasis |
| organism | balance | selective permeability |

Living cells maintain a **(1)** _____ by controlling materials that enter and leave. Without this

ability, the cell cannot maintain **(2)** _____ and will die. The cell must regulate internal con-

centrations of water, **(3)** _____ , and other nutrients and must eliminate waste products.

Homeostasis in a cell is maintained by the **(4)** _____ , which allows only certain

particles to pass through and keeps other particles out. This property of a membrane is known as

(5) _____ . It allows different cells to carry on different activities within the

same **(6)** _____ .

In your textbook, read about the structure of the plasma membrane.

For each statement below, write <u>true</u> or <u>false</u>.

_____ **7.** The structure and properties of the cell wall allow it to be selective and maintain homeostasis.

_____ **8.** The plasma membrane is a bilayer of lipid molecules with protein molecules embedded in it.

_____ **9.** A phospholipid molecule has a nonpolar, water-insoluble head attached to a long polar, soluble tail.

_____ **10.** The fluid mosaic model describes the plasma membrane as a structure that is liquid and very rigid.

_____ **11.** Eukaryotic plasma membranes can contain cholesterol, which tends to make the membrane more stable.

_____ **12.** Transport proteins span the cell membrane, creating the selectively permeable membrane that regulates which molecules enter and leave a cell.

_____ **13.** Proteins at the inner surface of the plasma membrane attach the membrane to the cell's support structure, making the cell rigid.

Chapter 7 A View of the Cell, *continued*

Section 7.3 Eukaryotic Cell Structure

In your textbook, read about cellular boundaries; nucleus and cell control; assembly, transport, and storage in the cell; and energy transformers.

Complete the table by writing the name of the cell part beside its structure/function. A cell part may be used more than once.

Structure/Function	Cell Part
1. A membrane-bound, fluid-filled sac	
2. Closely stacked, flattened membrane sacs	
3. The sites of protein synthesis	
4. A folded membrane that forms a network of interconnected compartments in the cytoplasm	
5. The clear fluid inside the cell	
6. Organelle that manages cell functions in eukaryotic cell	
7. Contains chlorophyll, a green pigment that traps energy from sunlight and gives plants their green color	
8. Digest excess or worn-out cell part, food particles, and invading viruses or bacteria	
9. Small bumps located on the endoplasmic reticulum	
10. Provides temporary storage of food, enzymes, and waste products	
11. Firm, protective structure that gives the cell its shape in plants, fungi, most bacteria, and some protists	
12. Produce a usable form of energy for the cell	
13. Modifies proteins chemically, then repackages them	
14. Contains inner membranes arranged in stacks of membranous sacs called grana	
15. Plant organelles that store starches or lipids or that contain pigments	

Copyright © Glencoe/McGraw-Hill, a division of The McGraw-Hill Companies, Inc.

Chapter 7 — A View of the Cell, *continued*

In your textbook, read about structures for support and locomotion.

Determine if the statement is true. If it is not, rewrite the italicized part to make it true.

16. Cells have a support structure within the *cytoplasm* called the cytoskeleton.

_____

17. The *exoskeleton* is composed of thin, fibrous elements that form a framework for the cell.

_____

18. *Microtubules* of the cytoskeleton are thin, hollow cylinders made of protein.

_____

19. Cilia and flagella are cell surface structures that are adapted for *respiration*.

_____

20. *Flagella* are short, numerous, hairlike projections from the plasma membrane.

_____

21. Flagella are longer and *more* numerous than cilia.

_____

22. In *multicellular* organisms, cilia and flagella are the major means of locomotion.

_____

23. In *prokaryotic* cells, both cilia and flagella are composed of microtubules.

_____

Write titles for each of the generalized diagrams and then label the parts. Use these choices: plant cell, animal cell, plasma membrane, chloroplast, small vacuole, large vacuole, cell wall.

24. _____

25. _____

26. _____

27. _____

28. _____

29. _____

30. _____

Chapter 8 · Cellular Transport and the Cell Cycle

In your textbook, read about osmosis: diffusion of water.

Complete the table by checking the correct column for each statement.

Statement	Isotonic Solution	Hypotonic Solution	Hypertonic Solution
1. Causes a cell to swell			
2. Doesn't change the shape of a cell			
3. Causes osmosis			
4. Causes a cell to shrink			

In your textbook, read about passive transport and active transport.

For each item in Column A, write the letter of the matching item in Column B.

Column A

_____ **5.** Transport protein that provides a tubelike opening in the plasma membrane through which particles can diffuse

_____ **6.** Is used during active transport but not passive transport

_____ **7.** Process by which a cell takes in material by forming a vacuole around it

_____ **8.** Particle movement from an area of higher concentration to an area of lower concentration

_____ **9.** Process by which a cell expels wastes from a vacuole

_____ **10.** A form of passive transport that uses transport proteins

_____ **11.** Particle movement from an area of lower concentration to an area of higher concentration

_____ **12.** Transport protein that changes shape when a particle binds with it

Column B

a. energy

b. facilitated diffusion

c. endocytosis

d. passive transport

e. active transport

f. exocytosis

g. carrier protein

h. channel protein

Reinforcement and Study Guide

Section 8.2 Cellular Growth and Reproduction

In your textbook, read about cell size limitations.

Determine if the statement is true. If it is not, rewrite the italicized part to make it true.

1. Most *living cells* are between 2 and 200 µm in diameter. _____

2. Diffusion of materials over long distance is *fast*. _____

3. If a cell doesn't have enough *DNA* to make all the proteins it needs, the cell cannot live.

_____

4. As a cell's size increases, its volume increases much *slower* than its surface area.

_____

5. If a cell's diameter doubled, the cell would require *two* times more nutrients and would have *two*

times more wastes to excrete. _____

In your textbook, read about cell reproduction.

Use each of the terms below just once to complete the passage.

nucleus	genetic material	chromosomes	packed
identical	chromatin	vanish	cell division

    The process by which two cells are produced from one cell is called **(6)** _____ .

The two cells are **(7)** _____ to the original cell. Early biologists observed that just

before cell division, several short, stringy structures appeared in the **(8)** _____ .

These structures seemed to **(9)** _____ soon after cell division. These structures,

which contain DNA and became darkly colored when stained, are now called **(10)** _____ .

Scientists eventually learned that chromosomes carry **(11)** _____ , which

is copied and passed on from generation to generation. Chromosomes normally exist as

(12) _____ , long strands of DNA wrapped around proteins. However, before

a cell divides, the chromatin becomes tightly **(13)** _____ .

Chapter 8 **Cellular Transport and the Cell Cycle,** *continued*

Section 8.2 Cellular Growth and Reproduction, continued

In your textbook, read about the cell cycle and interphase.

Complete the table by checking the correct column for each statement.

Statement	Interphase	Mitosis
14. Cell growth occurs.		
15. Nuclear division occurs.		
16. Chromosomes are distributed equally to daughter cells.		
17. Protein production is high.		
18. Chromosomes are duplicated.		
19. DNA synthesis occurs.		
20. Cytoplasm divides immediately after this period.		
21. Mitochondria and other organelles are manufactured.		

In your textbook, read about the phases of mitosis.

Identify the following phases of mitosis. Use these choices: telophase, metaphase, anaphase, prophase. Then label the diagrams. Use these choices: sister chromatids, centromere, spindle fibers, centrioles.

22. _____   23. _____   24. _____   25. _____

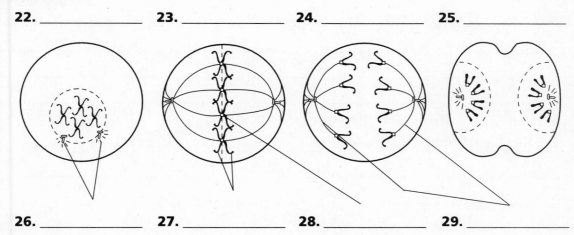

26. _____   27. _____   28. _____   29. _____

Answer the question.

30. How does mitosis result in tissues and organs?

_____

_____

In your textbook, read about normal control of the cell cycle and cancer.

Answer the following questions.

1. In what ways do enzymes control the cell cycle?

_____

_____

2. What directs the production of these enzymes?

_____

_____

3. What can cause the cell cycle to become uncontrolled?

_____

_____

_____

4. What can result when the cell cycle becomes uncontrolled?

_____

_____

5. What is the relationship between environmental factors and cancer?

_____

_____

_____

_____

6. What is a tumor? Describe the final stages of cancer.

_____

_____

_____

_____

7. Cancer is the second leading cause of death in the United States. What four types of cancer are the most prevalent?

_____

_____

_____

Chapter 9 Energy in a Cell

Reinforcement and Study Guide

Section 9.1 ATP in a Molecule

In your textbook, read about cell energy.

Use each of the terms below just once to complete the passage.

energy	phosphate	adenosine	charged
ATP	chemical bonds	work	ribose

To do biological **(1)** _____ , cells require energy. A quick source

of energy that cells use is the molecule **(2)** _____ . The **(3)** _____

in this molecule is stored in its **(4)** _____ . ATP is composed of a(n)

(5) _____ molecule bonded to a(n) **(6)** _____ sugar.

Three **(7)** _____ molecules called **(8)** _____ groups

are attached to the sugar.

In your textbook, read about forming and breaking down ATP and the uses of cell energy.

Examine the diagram below. Then answer the questions.

Energy from food → ATP → ADP + P$_i$ → E n e r g y

9. How is energy stored and released by ATP?

_____

_____

_____

_____

10. How do cells use the energy released from ATP?

_____

_____

_____

In your textbook, read about trapping the sun's energy.

Determine if the statement is true. If it is not, rewrite the italicized part to make it true.

1. Photosynthesis is the process plants use to trap the sun's energy to make *glucose*.

_____

2. ATP molecules are made during the *light-independent* reactions of photosynthesis.

_____

3. *Carbon dioxide* gas is produced during photosynthesis.

_____

4. The light-dependent reactions of photosynthesis take place in the membranes of the thylakoid discs in *mitochondria*.

_____

5. The thylakoid membranes contain chlorophyll and other pigments that *absorb* sunlight.

_____

In your textbook, read about the light-dependent reactions of photosynthesis.

Number the following steps of the light-dependent reactions in the order in which they occur.

_____ **6.** The energy lost by electrons as they pass through the electron transport chain is used to make ATP.

_____ **7.** The electrons pass from the chlorophyll to an electron transport chain.

_____ **8.** Sunlight strikes the chlorophyll molecules in the thylakoid membranes.

_____ **9.** $NADP^+$ molecules change to NADPH as they carry the electrons to the stroma of the chloroplast.

_____ **10.** The sunlight's energy is transferred to the chlorophyll's electrons.

_____ **11.** The electrons are passed down a second electron transport chain.

Answer the following questions.

12. How are the electrons that are lost by the chlorophyll molecules replaced?

_____

_____

13. How do plants produce oxygen during photosynthesis?

_____

_____

In your textbook, read about the light-independent reactions.

Circle the letter of the choice that best completes the statement or answers the question.

14. The Calvin cycle includes
    a. the light-dependent reactions.   **b.** an electron transport chain.
    c. the light-independent reactions.   **d.** photolysis.

15. The Calvin cycle takes place in the
    a. mitochondria.   **b.** stroma.
    c. nucleus.   **c.** thylakoid membrane.

16. What product of the light-dependent reactions is used in the Calvin cycle?
    a. oxygen   **b.** carbon dioxide   **c.** NADPH   **d.** chlorophyll

17. What gas is used in the first step of the Calvin cycle?
    a. oxygen   **b.** carbon dioxide   **c.** hydrogen   **d.** water

18. A carbon atom from carbon dioxide is used to change the five-carbon sugar RuBP into
    a. ATP.   **b.** two molecules.   **c.** PGA.   **d.** a six-carbon sugar.

19. How many molecules of the three-carbon sugar PGA are formed?
    a. two   **b.** one   **c.** six   **d.** three

20. ATP, NADPH, and hydrogen ions are used to convert PGA into
    a. PGAL.   **b.** glucose.   **c.** RuBP.   **d.** carbon dioxide.

21. How many rounds of the Calvin cycle are needed to form one glucose molecule?
    a. one   **b.** six   **c.** two   **d.** three

22. What two molecules leave the Calvin cycle and are combined to form glucose?
    a. RuBP   **b.** PGA   **c.** PGAL   **d.** CO_2

23. Which molecule from the Calvin cycle is used to replenish the five-carbon sugar, RuBP, which is used at the beginning of the cycle?
    a. NADP   **b.** CO_2 **c.** PGA   **d.** PGAL

In your textbook, read about the cellular respiration and fermentation.

Fill in the names of the molecules to complete the glycolysis reaction. Use these choices: 2PGAL, 4ATP, glucose, 2ADP, 2 pyruvic acid, 2NADH + 2H⁺. Then answer the questions.

Glycolysis

7. What happens to pyruvic acid before entering the citric acid cycle?

_____

8. What happens to the electrons carried by the NADH and $FADH_2$ molecules produced during the citric acid cycle?

_____

_____

9. During which stages of cellular respiration are ATP molecules formed?

_____

10. Why is oxygen necessary for cellular respiration?

_____

11. How is fermentation different from cellular respiration?

_____

_____

In your textbook, read about comparing photosynthesis and cellular respiration.

Answer the following question.

12. Describe two ways in which cellular respiration is the opposite of photosynthesis.

_____

_____

_____

_____

3 The Life of a Cell

In your textbook, read about the chemistry of life.

Label the diagram below, using these choices:

atom   electron   molecule   neutron   nucleus   proton

1. _____

2. _____

3. _____

4. _____

5. _____

6. _____

In your textbook, read about eukaryotes, prokaryotes, and organelles.

Complete each statement.

7. Every cell is surrounded by a plasma _____ .

8. _____ are organisms with cells that contain membrane-bound structures called organelles within the cell.

9. Organisms having cells without internal membrane-bound structures are called

_____ .

10. The plasma membrane is composed of a _____ with embedded proteins.

11. The _____ controls cell functions.

12. Ribosomes are organelles found in the cytoplasm that produce _____ .

13. The _____ and Golgi apparatus transport and modify proteins.

14. Plant cells contain _____ that capture the sun's light energy so that it can be transformed into usable chemical energy.

15. A network of microfilaments and microtubules attached to the cell membrane give the cell

_____ .

16. _____ are long projections from the surface of the plasma membrane and move in a whiplike fashion to propel a cell.

BioDigest 3 **The Life of a Cell,** *continued*

Reinforcement and Study Guide

In your textbook, read about diffusion and osmosis.

Answer the following questions.

17. What is diffusion? _____

_____

18. What is osmosis? _____

_____

19. What is active transport? _____

_____

In your textbook, read about mitosis.

For each item in Column A, write the letter of the matching item in Column B.

Column A	Column B
_____ **20.** Duplicated chromosomes condense and mitotic spindles form on the two opposite ends of the cell.	**a.** anaphase
_____ **21.** Chromosomes slowly separate to opposite ends of cells.	**b.** interphase
_____ **22.** Chromosomes uncoil, spindle breaks down, and nuclear envelope forms around each set of chromosomes.	**c.** metaphase
_____ **23.** Cells experience a period of intense metabolic activity prior to mitosis.	**d.** prophase
_____ **24.** Chromosomes line up in center of cell.	**e.** telophase

In your textbook, read about energy in a cell.

Decide if each of the following statements is true. If it is not, rewrite the italicized part to make it true.

_____ **25.** Adenosine triphosphate (ATP) is the most commonly used source of *protein* in a cell.

_____ **26.** *Light-dependent* reactions convert energy into starch through the Calvin cycle.

_____ **27.** *Mitochondria* convert food energy to ATP through a series of chemical reactions.

_____ **28.** Glycolysis produces a net gain of two ATP for *every two molecules* of glucose.

Chapter
10 **Mendel and Meiosis**

Section 10.1 Mendel's Laws of Heredity

In your textbook, read why Mendel succeeded.

Complete each statement.

1. Mendel was the first person to succeed in predicting how traits are _____ from generation to generation.

2. Mendel used _____ plants in his experiments.

3. In peas, both male and female sex cells—_____—are in the same flower.

4. _____ occurs when the male gamete fuses with the female gamete.

5. Mendel used the process called _____ when he wanted to breed one plant with another.

6. Mendel carefully _____ his experiments and the peas he used.

7. Mendel studied only one _____ at a time and analyzed his data mathematically.

In your textbook, read about Mendel's monohybrid crosses.

Refer to the table of pea-plant traits on the right. Then complete the table on the left by filling in the missing information for each cross. The first one is done for you.

Parent Plants	F₁ generation	
	Offspring	Appearance
8. round × wrinkled RR × rr	Rr	round
9. yellow × green YY × yy		
10. axial × terminal AA × _____	Aa	
11. tall × short _____ × _____	Tt	
12. inflated × constricted _____ × ii		

Pea-Plant Traits		
Trait	Dominant	Recessive
seed shape	round (R)	wrinkled (r)
seed color	yellow (Y)	green (y)
flower position	axial (A)	terminal (a)
plant height	tall (T)	short (t)
pod shape	inflated (I)	constricted (i)

In your textbook, read about phenotypes and genotypes and Mendel's dihybrid crosses.

Determine if the statement is true. If it is not, rewrite the underlined part to make it true.

13. A pea plant with the genotype *TT* has the same phenotype as a pea plant with genotype *tt*. _____

14. When Mendel crossed true-breeding pea plants that had round yellow seeds with true-breeding pea plants that had wrinkled green seeds, <u>some</u> of the offspring had round yellow seeds because round and yellow were the dominant forms of the traits. _____

15. When Mendel allowed heterozygous F_1 plants that had round yellow seed to self-pollinate, he found that <u>some</u> of the F_2 plants had wrinkled green seeds. _____

16. The law of independent assortment states that <u>genes</u> for different traits are inherited independently of each other. _____

In your textbook, read about Punnett squares and probability.

The Punnett square below is for a dihybrid cross between pea plants that are heterozygous for seed shape (*Rr*) and seed color (*Yy*). Complete the Punnett square by recording the expected genotypes of the offspring. Then answer the questions.

	RY	*Ry*	*rY*	*ry*
RY				
Ry				
rY				
ry				

17. Use the chart on the previous page to determine the phenotypes of the offspring. Record the phenotypes below the genotypes in the Punnett square. Is an offspring produced by the cross more likely to have wrinkled seeds or round seeds? _____

18. What is the probability that an offspring will have wrinkled yellow seeds? _____

Chapter 10 Mendel and Meiosis, *continued*

In your textbook, read about genes, chromosomes, and numbers.

Examine the table. Then answer the questions.

Chromosome Numbers of Some Common Organisms

Organism	Body Cell (*2n*)	Gamete (*n*)
Human	46	23
Garden pea	14	7
Fruit fly	8	4
Tomato	24	12
Dog	78	39
Chimpanzee	48	24
Leopard frog	26	13
Corn	20	10

1. What is the diploid number of chromosomes in corn?

   _____

2. What is the haploid number of chromosomes in corn?

   _____

3. Is the chromosome number related to the complexity of the organism?

   _____

4. How many pairs of chromosomes do humans have?

   _____

5. What process maintains a constant number of chromosomes within a species?

   _____

In your textbook, read about the phases of meiosis.

Label the diagrams below. Use these choices: Metaphase I, Metaphase II, Interphase, Telophase I, Telophase II, Anaphase I, Anaphase II, Prophase I, Prophase II.

6. _____ 7. _____ 8. _____ 9. _____ 10. _____

11. _____ 12. _____ 13. _____ 14. _____

The following statements describe interphase and and meiosis I. Identify each phase. Then place them in sequential order using the numbers 1 through 5. Use 1 for the phase that occurs first and 5 for the phase that occurs last.

Statement	Name of Phase	Sequence
15. Homologous chromosomes line up at the equator in pairs.		
16. The cell replicates its chromosomes.		
17. Homologous chromosomes separate and move to opposite ends of the cell.		
18. The spindle forms, and chromosomes coil up and come together in a tetrad; crossing over may occur.		
19. Events occur in the reverse order from the events of prophase I. Each cell has only half the genetic information; however, another cell division is needed because each chromosome is still doubled.		

In your textbook, read about how meiosis provides for genetic variation and about mistakes in meiosis.

For each statement below, write <u>true</u> or <u>false</u>.

_____ **20.** Reassortment of chromosomes can occur during meiosis by crossing over or by independent segregation of homologous chromosomes.

_____ **21.** Genetic recombination is a major source of variation among organisms.

_____ **22.** The random segregation of chromosomes during meiosis explains Mendel's observation that genes for different traits are inherited independently of each other.

_____ **23.** Nondisjunction always results in a zygote with an extra chromosome.

_____ **24.** Down syndrome is a result of polyploidy.

_____ **25.** Mistakes in meiosis can occasionally be beneficial.

Chapter 11 DNA and Genes

In your textbook, read about what DNA is and the replication of DNA.

Label the diagram. Use these choices: nucleotide, deoxyribose, phosphate group, nitrogen base, hydrogen bonds, base pair.

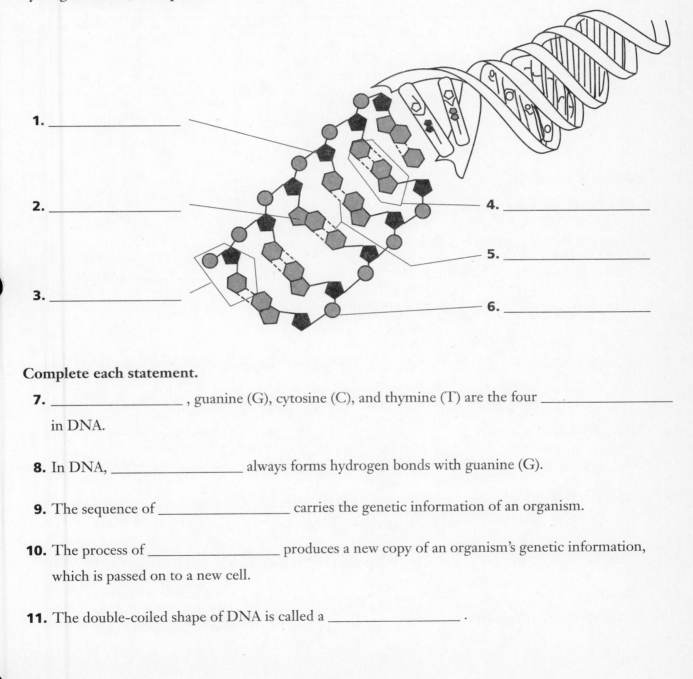

1. _____

2. _____

3. _____

4. _____

5. _____

6. _____

Complete each statement.

7. _____ , guanine (G), cytosine (C), and thymine (T) are the four _____ in DNA.

8. In DNA, _____ always forms hydrogen bonds with guanine (G).

9. The sequence of _____ carries the genetic information of an organism.

10. The process of _____ produces a new copy of an organism's genetic information, which is passed on to a new cell.

11. The double-coiled shape of DNA is called a _____ .

DNA and Genes, *continued*

In your textbook, read about genes and proteins and RNA.

Complete the chart on the three chemical differences between DNA and RNA.

Structure	DNA	RNA
1. strand of nucleotides		
2. sugar		
3. nitrogen base		

In your textbook, read about the genetic code.

Complete each statement.

4. Proteins are made up of _____ .

5. There are twenty different types of _____ .

6. The message of the DNA code is information for building _____ .

7. Each set of three nitrogen bases that codes for an amino acid is known as a

_____ .

8. The amino acid _____ is represented by the mRNA codon ACA.

9. _____ and _____ are mRNA codons for phenylalanine.

10. There can be more than one _____ for the same amino acid.

11. For any one codon, there can be only one _____ .

12. The genetic code is said to be universal because a codon represents the same

_____ in almost all organisms.

13. _____ , _____ , and _____ are stop codons.

14. _____ and _____ are amino acids that are each

represented by only one codon.

Section 11.2 From DNA to Protein,
continued

In your textbook, read about transcription from DNA to mRNA.

Complete each statement.

15. Proteins are made in the cytoplasm of a cell, whereas DNA is found only in the

_____ .

16. The process of making RNA from DNA is called _____ .

17. The process of transcription is similar to the process of DNA _____ .

18. _____ carries information from the DNA in the nucleus out into the cyto-

plasm of the cell.

19. mRNA carries the information for making proteins to the _____ .

In your textbook, read about translation from mRNA to protein.

Label the diagram. Use these choices: transfer RNA (tRNA), amino acid, amino acid chain, codon, anticodon, messenger RNA (mRNA), ribosome.

20. _____

21. _____

22. _____

23. _____

24. _____

25. _____

26. _____

Chapter 11 DNA and Genes, continued

Reinforcement and Study Guide

Section 11.3 Genetic Changes

In your textbook, read about mutation: a change in DNA.

Circle the letter of the choice that best completes the statement.

1. A mutation is any mistake or change in the
   a. cell.   **b.** DNA sequence.   **c.** ribosomes.   **d.** nucleus.

2. A point mutation is a change in
   a. several bases in mRNA.   **b.** several bases in tRNA.
   c. a single base pair in DNA.   **d.** several base pairs in DNA.

3. A mutation in which a single base is added or deleted from DNA is called
   a. a frame shift mutation.   **b.** a point mutation.   **c.** translocation.   **d.** nondisjunction.

4. Chromosomal mutations are especially common in
   a. humans.   **b.** animals.   **c.** bacteria.   **d.** plants.

5. Few chromosome mutations are passed on to the next generation because
   a. the zygote usually dies.
   b. the mature organism is sterile.
   c. the mature organism is often incapable of producing offspring.
   d. all of the above.

6. When part of one chromosome breaks off and is added to a different chromosome, the result is a(n)
   a. translocation.   **b.** insertion.   **c.** inversion.   **d.** deletion.

7. Many chromosome mutations result when chromosomes fail to separate properly during
   a. mitosis.   **b.** meiosis.   **c.** crossing over.   **d.** linkage.

8. The failure of homologous chromosomes to separate properly is called
   a. translocation.   **b.** disjunction.   **c.** nondisjunction.   **d.** deletion.

9. Mutations that occur at random are called
   a. spontaneous mutations.   **b.** nonspontaneous mutations.
   c. nonrandom mutations.   **d.** environmental mutations.

10. An agent that can cause a change in DNA is called a(n)
   a. zygote.   **b.** inversion.
   c. mutagen.   **d.** mutation.

11. Mutations in body cells can sometimes result in
   a. new species.   **b.** cancer.
   c. sterile offspring.   **d.** hybrids.

Chapter 12 Patterns of Heredity and Human Genetics

Reinforcement and Study Guide

Section 12.1 Mendelian Inheritance of Human Traits

In your textbook, read about making a pedigree.

Examine the pedigree to the right. Then answer the following questions.

1. Is the trait being studied in the pedigree recessive or dominant? How do you know?

   _____

   _____

   _____

   _____

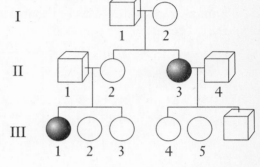

2. Are II-1 and II-2 carriers of the trait? How do you know?

   _____

   _____

   _____

3. What is the probability that II-1 and II-2 will produce an individual with the trait being studied? Draw a Punnett square to show your work.

   _____

   _____

   _____

   _____

4. What is the likely genotype of II-4 for the trait being studied in the pedigree?

   _____

In your textbook, read about simple recessive heredity and simple dominant heredity.

For each item in Column A, write the letter of the matching item from Column B.

Column A	Column B
_____ **5.** Recessive disorder that results from the absence of an enzyme required to break lipids down	**a.** cystic fibrosis
_____ **6.** Lethal genetic disorder caused by a dominant allele	**b.** simple dominant traits
_____ **7.** Most common genetic disorder among white Americans	**c.** Tay-Sachs disease
_____ **8.** Recessive disorder that results from the absence of an enzyme that converts one amino acid into another one	**d.** Huntington's disease
_____ **9.** Tongue curling and Hapsburg lip	**e.** phenylketonuria

**Patterns of Heredity and
Human Genetics,** *continued*

In your textbook, read about complex patterns of inheritance.

Answer the following questions.

1. Complete the Punnett square for a cross between a homozygous red-flowered snapdragon (*RR*) and a homozygous white-flowered snapdragon (*R'R'*). Give the genotype and phenotype of the offspring in the F$_1$ generation.

<u>Key</u>
RR - red
R'R' - white   F$_1$
RR' - pink

genotype: _____

phenotype: _____

2. When traits are inherited in an incomplete dominance pattern, what is true of the phenotype of the heterozygotes?

_____

3. Complete the Punnett square for a cross between two pink-flowered (*RR'*) F$_1$ plants. Give the phenotype ratio of the offspring in the F$_2$ generation.

F$_2$

phenotype ratio: _____

4. In what type of inheritance are both alleles expressed equally?

_____

5. Complete the Punnett square for a cross between a black chicken (*BB*) and a white chicken (*WW*). Give the phenotype of the offspring in the F$_1$ generation.

<u>Key</u>
BB - black
WW - white   F$_1$
BW - checkered

phenotype: _____

Copyright © Glencoe/McGraw-Hill, a division of The McGraw-Hill Companies, Inc.

Copyright © Glencoe/McGraw-Hill, a division of The McGraw-Hill Companies, Inc.

Chapter 12 Patterns of Heredity and Human Genetics, *continued*

For each statement below, write <u>true</u> or <u>false</u>.

_____ **6.** Traits controlled by more than two alleles are said to have multiple alleles.

_____ **7.** Multiple alleles can be studied only in individuals.

_____ **8.** In humans, there are 23 pairs of matching homologous chromosomes called autosomes.

_____ **9.** Two chromosomes called the sex chromosomes determine the sex of an individual.

_____ **10.** The sex chromosomes of a human male are XX, and the sex chromosomes of a human female are XY.

_____ **11.** Traits controlled by genes located on sex chromosomes are called sex-linked traits.

_____ **12.** The first known example of sex-linked inheritance was discovered in pea plants.

In your textbook, read about environmental influences.

Answer the following questions.

13. What characteristics of an organism can affect gene function?

_____

_____

14. Do the internal environments of males and females differ? Explain.

_____

_____

15. What are some environmental factors that can influence gene expression?

_____

_____

16. Give two examples of how an environmental factor can affect the expression of a phenotype.

_____

_____

Reinforcement and Study Guide

Section 12.3 Complex Inheritance of Human Traits

In your textbook, read about multiple alleles in humans.

Complete the table by filling in the missing information.

Genotypes	Human Blood Groups Surface Molecules	Phenotypes
1. $I^A I^A$ or $I^A i$	A	
2. $I^B I^B$ or $I^B i$		B
3.	A and B	AB
4.	none	

Complete each statement.

5. Blood groups are a classic example of _____ inheritance in humans.

6. The alleles _____ are always both expressed.

7. The alleles I^A and I^B are _____ , meaning they are always both expressed.

8. I^A and I^B are dominant to _____ .

9. Blood typing is necessary before a person can receive a _____ .

10. A child who inherits I^A from his mother and I^B from his father will have type _____ blood.

11. A child whose parents both have type O blood will have type _____ blood.

12. If a woman with blood type A has a baby with blood type AB, a man with blood type O _____ be the father.

13. Blood tests _____ be used to prove that a certain man is the father of a child.

Chapter 13 Genetic Technology

In your textbook, read about selective breeding and determining genotypes.

Complete each statement.

1. Organisms that are homozygous dominant and those that are _____ for a trait controlled by Mendelian inheritance have the same phenotype.

2. A _____ determines whether an organism is heterozygous or homozygous dominant for a trait.

3. Usually the parent with the known genotype is _____ for the trait in question.

4. When two cultivars are crossed, their offspring will be _____ .

Answer the following.

5. A breeder performs a testcross to determine whether an Alaskan malamute is homozygous dominant (*DD*) or heterozygous (*Dd*) for a recessive dwarf allele. Half the offspring appear dwarf. What is the genotype of the unknown dog? Complete the Punnett square to verify your answer.

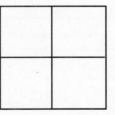

_____

6. What results would be expected if the unknown dog was homozygous dominant (*DD*)? Complete the Punnett square to verify your answer.

_____

_____

Reinforcement and Study Guide

Section 13.2 Recombinant DNA Technology

In your textbook, read about gene engineering.

For each item in Column A, write the letter of the matching item in Column B.

Column A	Column B
_____ **1.** Bacterial proteins that have the ability to cut both strands of the DNA molecule at certain points	**a.** recombinant DNA
_____ **2.** Contain foreign DNA	**b.** vector
_____ **3.** Is made by connecting segments of DNA from different sources	**c.** restriction enzymes
_____ **4.** General term for a vehicle used to transfer a foreign DNA fragment into a host cell	**d.** plasmid
_____ **5.** A small ring of DNA found in a bacterial cell	**e.** transgenic organisms
_____ **6.** The procedure for cleaving DNA from an organism into small segments, and inserting the segments into another organism	**f.** genetic engineering or recombinant DNA technology

Complete the table by checking the correct column for each vector.

Vectors	Mechanical	Biological
7. Viruses		
8. Micropipette		
9. Metal bullets		
10. Plasmids		

Chapter 13 **Genetic Technology,** *continued*

Section 13.2 Recombinant DNA Technology, continued

In your textbook, read about applications of DNA technology.

Complete the table by checking the correct column for each statement.

Statement	Bacteria	Transgenic Plant(s)	Animal(s)
11. Employed in the production of growth hormone to treat dwarfism and insulin to treat diabetes			
12. Difficult to produce because of thick cell walls and few biological vectors			
13. Some can be made using a bacterium that normally causes tumor-like galls.			
14. Contain many genes common to humans			
15. Have been engineered to break down pollutants into harmless products			
16. The first patented organism			
17. Produced using mechanical vectors such as the gene gun			
18. Produce phenylalanine, an amino acid needed to make artificial sweeteners			
19. In the future, they will be more nutritious and be able to grow in unfavorable conditions.			
20. Helps scientists to learn about human diseases			
21. Produce insulin, a hormone used in treating diabetes			
22. Produced by using a micropipette to inject DNA into unfertilized eggs			
23. Contain foreign genes that slow down the process of spoilage			

Chapter 13 **Genetic Technology,** *continued*

In your textbook, read about mapping and sequencing the human genome and applications of the Human Genome Project.

Determine if the statement is true. If it is not, rewrite the italicized part to make it true.

1. The human genome consists of approximately *1000* genes located on 46 chromosomes.

_____

2. Scientists *have* determined the exact chromosomal location of all genes.

_____

3. The genetic map that shows the location of genes on a chromosome is called a *pedigree map*.

_____

4. Instead of examining actual offspring, scientists examine *egg* cells to create linkage maps.

_____

5. Gene therapy is being performed on patients suffering from *sickle-cell anemia*.

_____

6. *Electrolysis* can be used to separate DNA fragments.

_____

Answer the following questions.

7. What is the Human Genome Project?

_____

_____

8. Why is mapping by linkage data extremely inefficient in humans?

_____

_____

9. What are the three areas of current research that utilize chromosome maps?

_____

_____

10. Why is DNA fingerprinting reliable?

_____

_____

_____

BioDigest
4 **Genetics**

In your textbook, read about simple Mendelian inheritance and meiosis.

Complete each statement.

1. A trait is _____ if only one allele is needed for that trait to be expressed. If both alleles are needed for the trait to be expressed, the trait is _____ .

2. When a *TT* tall pea plant is crossed with a *tt* short pea plant, there is a 100% probability that all offspring will be _____ and have the genotype _____ .

3. Unlike mitosis, _____ produces cells that contain only one copy of each _____ .

4. _____ and the rearrangement of alleles during _____ provide mechanisms for genetic variability.

In your textbook, read about producing physical traits and complex inheritance patterns.

Predict the outcome of the following crosses. Use Punnett squares to support your answers.

5. Homozygous short × Homozygous short

_____

6. Heterozygous for purple flowers × Heterozygous for purple flowers

_____

_____

_____

7. Heterozygous pink snapdragon × Heterozygous pink snapdragon

_____

_____

_____

_____

Sequence the steps in protein synthesis from 1 to 4.

_____ **8.** Amino acids bond together to form a protein.

_____ **9.** Sequence of bases in DNA is copied into mRNA.

_____ **10.** tRNA molecules bring appropriate amino acids to the mRNA on the ribosome.

_____ **11.** mRNA leaves the cell nucleus.

For each item in Column A, write the letter of the matching item in Column B.

Column A	Column B
_____ **12.** Results in an mRNA copy of DNA	**a.** incomplete dominance
_____ **13.** Sequence of three bases in mRNA	**b.** X-linked trait
_____ **14.** Site of translation	**c.** ribosome
_____ **15.** Governed by several genes	**d.** transcription
_____ **16.** Heterozygote has an intermediate phenotype.	**e.** translation
_____ **17.** Double-stranded molecule that stores and transmits genetic information	**f.** codon
_____ **18.** More likely to appear in males than in females	**g.** polygenic inheritance
_____ **19.** Results in a sequence of amino acids	**h.** DNA

In your textbook, read about recombinant DNA technology and gene therapy.

Sequence the steps to making recombinant DNA from 1 to 5.

_____ **20.** The plasmid becomes part of a host cell's chromosome.

_____ **21.** A DNA fragment is inserted into a plasmid.

_____ **22.** The DNA fragment replicates during cell division.

_____ **23.** The plasmid enters a host bacterial cell.

_____ **24.** A host cell produces a protein that it would not have produced naturally.

Answer the following questions.

25. What is gene therapy?

_____

_____

26. What are clones?

_____

27. What is a vector? Give two examples of vectors.

_____

_____

Chapter
14 **The History of Life**

In your textbook, read about the early history of Earth.

For each statement below, write true or false.

_____ **1.** Earth is thought to have formed about 4.6 billion years ago.

_____ **2.** The conditions on primitive Earth were very suitable for life.

_____ **3.** Geological events on Earth set up conditions that would play a major role in the evolution of life on Earth.

_____ **4.** Violent rainstorms beginning 3.9 million years ago formed Earth's oceans.

_____ **5.** The first organisms appeared on land between 3.9 and 3.5 billion years ago.

In your textbook, read about a history in the rocks.

For each statement in Column A, write the letter of the matching item in Column B.

Column A	Column B
_____ **6.** A footprint, trail, or burrow, providing evidence of animal activity	**a.** petrified fossil
_____ **7.** A fossil embedded in tree sap, valuable because the organism is preserved intact	**b.** imprint
_____ **8.** An exact stone copy of an original organism, the hard parts of which have been penetrated and replaced by minerals	**c.** trace fossil
_____ **9.** Any evidence of an organism that lived long ago	**d.** cast
_____ **10.** The fossil of a thin object, such as a leaf or feather, that falls into sediments and leaves an outline when the sediments hardened	**e.** amber-preserved
_____ **11.** An empty space left in rock, showing the exact shape of the organism that was buried and decayed there	**f.** fossil
_____ **12.** An object formed when a mold is filled in by minerals from the surrounding rock	**g.** mold

In your textbook, read about the age of a fossil.

Answer the following questions.

13. Explain how relative dating works.

_____

_____

_____

14. What is the limitation of relative dating?

_____

15. What dating technique is often used by paleontologists to determine the specific age of a fossil?

_____

16. How do scientists use this dating technique to determine the ages of rocks or fossils?

_____

_____

In your textbook, read about a trip through geologic time.

Complete the table by checking the correct column for each statement.

Statement	Era			
	Pre-Cambrian	Paleozoic	Mesozoic	Cenozoic
17. The first photosynthetic bacteria form dome-shaped structures called stromatolites.				
18. Primates evolve and diversify.				
19. Divided into three periods: Triassic, Jurassic, and Cretaceous				
20. An explosion of life, characterized by the appearance of many types of invertebrates and plant phyla				
21. Mammals appear.				
22. Dinosaurs roam Earth, and the ancestors of modern birds evolve.				
23. Flowering plants appear.				
24. Amphibians and reptiles appear.				

In your textbook, read about origins: the early ideas.

Use each of the terms below just once to complete the passage.

microorganisms	vital force	Louis Pasteur	biogenesis
nonliving matter	S-shaped	disproved	Francesco Redi
organisms	broth	microscope	spontaneous generation
spontaneously	air		

Early scientists believed that life arose from **(1)** _____ through a process they called **(2)** _____ . In 1668, the Italian physician **(3)** _____ conducted an experiment with flies that **(4)** _____ this idea. At about the same time, biologists began to use an important new research tool, the **(5)** _____ . They soon discovered the vast world of **(6)** _____ . The number and diversity of these organisms was so great that scientists were led to believe once again that these organisms must have arisen **(7)** _____ . By the mid-1800s, however, **(8)** _____ was able to disprove this hypothesis once and for all. He set up an experiment, using flasks with unique **(9)** _____ necks. These flasks allowed **(10)** _____ , but no organisms, to come into contact with a broth containing nutrients. If some **(11)** _____ existed, as had been suggested, it would be able to get into the **(12)** _____ through the open neck of the flask. His experiment proved that organisms arise only from other **(13)** _____ . This idea, called **(14)** _____ , is one of the cornerstones of biology today.

Determine if the statement is true. If it is not, rewrite the italicized part to make it true.

15. Biogenesis *explains* how life began on Earth.

_____

16. For life to begin, simple *inorganic* molecules had to be formed and then organized into complex molecules.

_____

17. Several billion years ago, Earth's atmosphere had no free *methane.*

_____

18. Primitive Earth's atmosphere may have been composed of water vapor, hydrogen, methane, and

ammonia. _____

19. In the early 1900s, Alexander Oparin proposed a widely accepted hypothesis that life began *on land*.

_____

20. *Pasteur* hypothesized that many chemical reactions occurring in the atmosphere resulted in the for-

mation of a primordial soup. _____

21. In 1953, Miller and Urey tested Oparin's hypothesis by simulating the conditions of *modern* Earth in

the laboratory. _____

22. Miller and Urey showed that organic compounds, including *nucleic acids* and sugars, could be formed

in the laboratory, just as had been predicted. _____

23. This "life-in-a-test-tube" experiment of Miller and Urey provides support for some modern hypothe-

ses of *biogenesis*. _____

24. Sidney Fox took Miller and Urey's experiment further and showed how amino acids could cluster to

form *protocells*. _____

In your textbook, read about the evolution of cells.

Answer the following questions.

25. Describe the likely characteristics of the first organisms on Earth.

_____

_____

_____

26. What is an autotroph? What factors helped them thrive on Earth?

_____

_____

_____

27. What present-day organisms may be similar to the first autotrophs? Why?

_____

28. What change occurred in Earth's atmosphere after the evolution of photosynthesizing prokaryotes?
Why?

_____

_____

Chapter 15 — The Theory of Evolution

Section 15.1 Natural Selection and the Evidence for Evolution

In your textbook, read about Charles Darwin and natural selection.

For each statement, write <u>true</u> or <u>false</u>.

_____ **1.** H.M.S. *Beagle*, upon which Charles Darwin served as naturalist, set sail on a collecting and mapping expedition in 1831.

_____ **2.** The environments that Darwin studied exhibited little biological diversity.

_____ **3.** By careful anatomical study, Darwin found that the many species of plants and animals on the Galapagos Islands were unique and bore no relation to species seen in other parts of the world.

_____ **4.** The tortoises of the Galapagos Islands are among the largest on Earth.

_____ **5.** After returning to England, Darwin studied his collections for 10 years.

_____ **6.** Darwin named the process by which evolution proceeds *artificial selection*.

You are a naturalist who traveled to the Galapagos Islands. Below are excerpts from field notes. Next to each set of notes, write a heading. Use these choices: Overproduction of Offspring, Natural Selection, Struggle for Existence, Variation.

7.
> **Field Notes**
>
> Female finches found on the Galapagos Islands lay enormous numbers of eggs.
>
> _____

8.
> **Field Notes**
>
> These finches compete for a particular species of insect that inhabits the small holes found in tree bark.
>
> _____

9.
> **Field Notes**
>
> Some finches' beaks are long, some are short. The finches with long beaks are better adapted to remove the insects from the bark.
>
> _____

10.
> **Field Notes**
>
> The finches with the long beaks survive and produce greater numbers of offspring with long beaks.
>
> _____

Chapter 15   **The Theory of Evolution,** continued

Section 15.1 Natural Selection and the Evidence for Evolution, continued

In your textbook, read about natural selection and adaptations.

Identify the type of structural adaptation that the statement describes. If the statement applies to both, write <u>both</u>. Use these choices: mimicry, camouflage, both.

_____ **11.** Enable(s) an organism to blend in with its surroundings

_____ **12.** Provide(s) protection for an organism by copying the appearance of another species

_____ **13.** The coloration of a flounder that allows the fish to avoid predators

_____ **14.** Involve(s) changes to the external appearance of an organism

_____ **15.** A flower that looks like a female bee

In your textbook, read about evidence for evolution.

Complete the chart by checking the kind of evidence described.

Evidence	Type of Evidence				
	Homologous Structure	**Analogous Structure**	**Vestigial Structure**	**Embryological Development**	**Genetic Comparisons**
16. A modified structure seen among different groups of descendants					
17. In the earliest stages of development, a tail and gill slits can be seen in fish, birds, rabbits, and mammals.					
18. Exemplified by forelimbs of bats, penguins, lizards, and monkeys					
19. The forelimbs of flightless birds					
20. DNA and RNA comparisons may lead to evolutionary trees.					
21. Bird and butterfly wings have same function but different structures					
22. A body structure reduced in function but may have been used in an ancestor					

Chapter 15 The Theory of Evolution, continued

Reinforcement and Study Guide

Section 15.2 Mechanisms of Evolution

In your textbook, read about population genetics and evolution.

Determine if the statement is true. If it is not, rewrite the italicized part to make it true.

1. *Adaptations* of species are determined by the genes contained in the DNA code. _____

2. When Charles *Mendel* developed the theory of natural selection in the 1800s, he did not include a genetic explanation. _____

3. Natural selection can act upon an individual's *genotype*, the external expression of genes. _____

4. Natural selection operates on *an individual* over many generations. _____

5. The entire collection of genes among a population is its *gene frequency*. _____

6. If you know the *phenotypes* of all the organisms in a population, you can calculate the allelic frequency of the population. _____

7. A population in which frequency of alleles *changes* from generation to generation is said to be in genetic equilibrium. _____

8. A population that is in *genetic equilibrium* is not evolving. _____

9. Any factor that affects *phenotype* can change allelic frequencies, thereby disrupting the genetic equilibrium of populations. _____

10. Many *migrations* are caused by factors in the environment, such as radiation or chemicals, but others happen by chance. _____

11. Mutations are *important* in evolution because they result in genetic changes in the gene pool. _____

12. Genetic *equilibrium* is the alteration of allelic frequencies by chance processes. _____

13. Genetic drift is more likely to occur in *large* populations. _____

14. The factor that causes the greatest change in gene pools is *mutation*. _____

15. The type of natural selection by which one of the extreme forms of a trait is favored is called *disruptive selection*. _____

Chapter
15 **The Theory of Evolution,** *continued*

In your textbook, read about the evolution of species.

Complete each statement.

16. _____ can occur only when either interbreeding or the production of fertile offspring is prevented among members of a population.

17. _____ occurs when formerly interbreeding organisms are prevented from producing fertile offspring.

18. Polyploid speciation is perhaps the fastest form of speciation because it results in immediate

_____ .

19. The hypothesis that species originate through a slow buildup of new adaptations is known as

_____ .

20. This hypothesis is supported by evidence from the _____ record.

21. The hypothesis of _____ states that speciation may occur rapidly.

In your textbook, read about patterns of evolution.

Answer the following questions.

22. What happened to the ancestor of the honey creeper when it left the mainland and encountered the diverse niches of Hawaii?

_____

_____

23. What is adaptive radiation?

_____

_____

24. Adaptive radiation is one example of divergent evolution. When does divergent evolution occur?

_____

_____

_____

25. When will convergent evolution occur?

_____

_____

Chapter 16 Primate Evolution

Section 16.1 Primate Adaptation and Evolution

In your textbook, read about the characteristics of a primate.

Complete the chart by checking those structures or functions that are characteristic of primates.

Structure/Function	Primate
1. Round head	
2. Flattened face	
3. Small head	
4. Large relative brain size	
5. Highly developed vision	
6. Poor vision	
7. Binocular vision	
8. Color vision	
9. Color-blind	
10. Vision the dominant sense	
11. Smell the dominant sense	
12. Immobile joints	
13. Flexible shoulder joints	
14. Skeleton adapted for movement among trees	
15. Skeleton adapted for swimming	
16. Hands and feet equipped with claws	
17. Hands and feet equipped with nails	
18. Eyes face to the side	
19. Feet constructed for grasping	
20. Opposable thumbs	

In your textbook, read about primate origins.

For each statement below, write <u>true</u> or <u>false</u>.

_____ **21.** Scientists believe that primates evolved about 66,000 years ago.

_____ **22.** The earliest primate may have been a prosimianlike animal called *Purgatorius*.

_____ **23.** Anthropoids are a group of small-bodied primates.

_____ **24.** Prosimians include lemurs and tarsiers.

_____ **25.** Prosimians can be found in the tropical forests of South America.

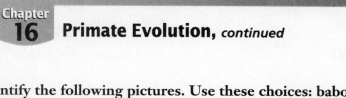

Chapter 16 **Primate Evolution,** *continued*

Identify the following pictures. Use these choices: baboon, tarsier, spider monkey. Then on the second line write the group that is represented by the picture. Use these choices: New World monkey, Old World monkey, prosimian.

26. _____

_____

27. _____

_____

28. _____

_____

Answer the following questions.

29. What do similarities among monkeys, apes, and humans indicate about their evolution?

_____

_____

30. According to the fossil record, what were the first modern anthropoids to evolve and about when did they evolve?

_____

_____

31. What is the evolutionary history of primates based on?

_____

_____

32. What may have led to the eventual speciation of baboons and other ground-living monkeys?

_____

_____

33. What does DNA analysis of modern hominoids suggest about their evolutionary history?

_____

_____

Chapter 16 **Primate Evolution,** *continued*

Section 16.2 Human Ancestry

In your textbook, read about hominids.

Answer the following questions.

1. What is an australopithecine? _____

2. What fossil skull did Raymond Dart discover in Africa in 1924? _____

3. Why was *A. africanus* unlike any primate fossil skull that Dart had ever seen? _____

_____

4. What did the position of the foramen magnum indicate to Dart? _____

_____

Label the following skulls. Use these choices: chimpanzee, human, *A. afarensis*

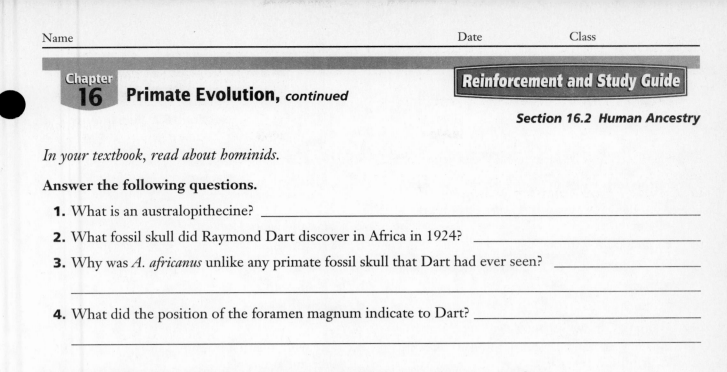

5. _____   6. _____   7. _____

For each statement below, write <u>true</u> or <u>false</u>.

_____ 8. Much of what scientists know about australopithecines comes from the "Lucy" skeleton.

_____ 9. "Lucy" is 3.5 billion years old.

_____ 10. "Lucy" is classified as *A. africanus*.

_____ 11. *A. afarensis* is the earliest known hominid species.

_____ 12. *A. afarensis* walked on all four legs and had a humanlike brain.

_____ 13. Australopithecines are alive today and can be found in southern Africa and Asia.

_____ 14. Australopithecines probably played a role in the evolution of modern hominids.

In your textbook, read about the emergence of modern humans.

Circle the letter of the choice that best completes the statement or answers the question.

15. The first skull of *Homo habilis* was discovered by
  a. Raymond Dart.
  b. Louis and Mary Leakey.
  c. Donald Johanson.
  d. Gert Terblance.

16. When compared to an australopithecine skull, the *Homo habilis* skull is
  a. more humanlike.
  b. less humanlike.
  c. more apelike.
  d. exactly the same.

17. Which of the following is *not* true about *Homo habilis*?
  a. They existed between 1.5 and 2 million years ago.
  b. They were the first hominids to make and use tools.
  c. They were probably scavengers of their food.
  d. They gave rise to *A. africanus*.

18. *Homo habilis* means
  a. "handy human."
  b. "tool-using human."
  c. "upright human."
  d. "talking human."

19. Of the primates below, which has the largest brain?
  a. *Homo habilis*
  b. *Homo erectus*
  c. an ape
  d. an australopithecine

20. Which of the following is *not* true about *Homo erectus*?
  a. They probably hunted.
  b. They were the first hominids to use fire.
  c. They may have given rise to hominids that resemble modern humans.
  d. They were found only in Africa.

21. *Homo sapiens* includes
  a. Neanderthals.
  b. australopithecines.
  c. *A. africanus*.
  d. *A. afarensis*.

Determine whether each statement below best describes Neanderthals, Cro-Magnons, or both.

_____ **22.** They lived in caves during the ice ages.

_____ **23.** They are identical to modern humans in height, skull, and teeth structure.

_____ **24.** They may have been the first hominids to develop religious views.

_____ **25.** They may have used language.

_____ **26.** They were talented toolmakers and artists.

Chapter 17 **Organizing Life's Diversity**

Section 17.1 Classification

In your textbook, read about how classification began and about biological classification.

For each item in Column A, write the letter of the matching item in Column B.

Column A	Column B
_____ **1.** Grouping objects or information based on similarities	**a.** Aristotle
_____ **2.** Naming system that gives each organism a two-word name	**b.** Linnaeus
_____ **3.** Developed the first system of classification	**c.** genus
_____ **4.** Branch of biology that groups and names organisms	**d.** classification
_____ **5.** Designed a system of classifying organisms based on their physical and structural similarities	**e.** taxonomy
_____ **6.** Consists of a group of similar species	**f.** binomial nomenclature

Determine if the statement is true. If it is not, rewrite the italicized part to make it true.

7. The scientific name of a species consists of a *family* name and a descriptive name.

_____

8. The scientific name of modern humans is *Homo sapiens*.

_____

9. *Latin* is the language of scientific names.

_____

10. The *scientific* names of organisms can be misleading.

_____

11. Taxonomists try to identify the *evolutionary relationships* among organisms.

_____

12. Besides comparing the structures of organisms, taxonomists also compare the organisms' geographic distribution and *chemical makeup*.

_____

13. Similarities between living species and extinct species *cannot* be used to determine their relationship to each other.

_____

14. Because the bones of some dinosaurs have large internal spaces, some scientists think dinosaurs are more closely related to *amphibians* than to reptiles.

_____

15. Classification can be useful in identifying the *characteristics* of an unknown organism.

In your textbook, read about how living things are classified.

Examine the table showing the classification of four organisms. Then answer the questions.

Taxon	Green Frog	Mountain Lion	Domestic Dog	Human
Kingdom	Animalia	Animalia	Animalia	Animalia
Phylum	Chordata	Chordata	Chordata	Chordata
Class	Amphibia	Mammalia	Mammalia	Mammalia
Order	Anura	Carnivora	Carnivora	Primates
Family	Ranidae	Felidae	Canidae	Hominidae
Genus	*Rana*	*Felis*	*Canis*	*Homo*
Species	*Rana clamitans*	*Felis concolor*	*Canis familiaris*	*Homo sapiens*

16. Which taxon includes the most specific characteristics? _____

17. Which taxon includes the broadest characteristics? _____

18. Which taxon includes more species, an order or a family? _____

19. Which taxon includes only organisms that can successfully interbreed? _____

20. If two organisms belong to the same family, what other taxonomic groups do the organisms have in common.

_____

21. Which two organisms in the chart are most closely related? Explain.

_____

_____

_____

22. To which taxa do all four organisms belong?

_____

23. Which class does not include animals that have hair or fur? _____

24. What is the order, family, and genus of a human?

_____

25. Using the information in the chart, what can you conclude about the classification taxa of an organism with the scientific name *Rana temporaria?*

_____

_____

_____

Chapter 17 **Organizing LIfe's Diversity,** continued

In your textbook, read about how evolutionary relationships are determined.

Explain how scientists use each item below to determine the evolutionary relationships among organisms.

1. structural similarities: _____

_____

2. breeding behavior: _____

_____

3. geographical distribution: _____

_____

4. chromosome comparisons: _____

_____

5. biochemistry: _____

_____

In your textbook, read about phylogenetic classification: models.

Use the cladogram to answer the questions.

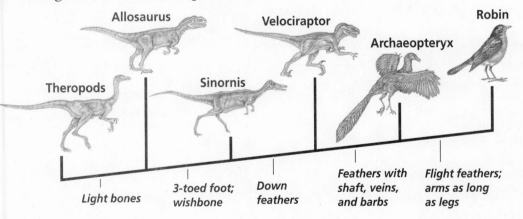

6. What five probable ancestors of the modern bird (robin) are shown on the cladogram?

_____

7. Which dinosaur is probably the most recent common ancestor of *Velociraptor* and *Archaeopteryx*?

_____

8. Which traits shown on the cladogram are shared by *Archaeopteryx* and modern birds?

_____

_____

Chapter 17 **Organizing LIfe's Diversity,** *continued*

Reinforcement and Study Guide

Section 17.2 The Six Kingdoms,
continued

Use the fanlike phylogenetic diagram to answer the questions.

9. How does the fanlike diagram differ from a cladogram?

_____

_____

10. Which group of plants evolved most recently? _____

11. To which group are starfishes more closely related, arthropods or jellyfishes? _____

12. Which group of animals includes the fewest species? _____

13. About how long ago did plants evolve? _____

In your textbook, read about the six kingdoms of organisms.

Circle the letter of the choice that best completes the statement or answers the question.

14. Organisms that do not have a nucleus bounded by a membrane are
    a. multicellular.   **b.** eukaryotes.   **c.** protists.   **d.** prokaryotes.

15. Fungi obtain food by
    a. photosynthesis.   **b.** chemosynthesis.
    c. endocytosis.   **d.** absorbing nutrients from organic materials.

16. Animals are
    a. autotrophs.   **b.** heterotrophs.   **c.** prokaryotes.   **d.** stationary.

BioDigest
5 **Change Through Time**

In your textbook, read about the Geologic Time Scale.

Complete the table.

Era	Time period	Biologic event
1.	4.6 billion–600 million years ago	**2.**
3.	600 million–245 million years ago	**4.**
5.	245 million–66 million years ago	**6.**
7.	66 million years ago–present	**8.**

In your textbook, read about origin of life theories.

Complete each statement.

9. Spontaneous generation assumes that life arises spontaneously from _____ .

10. Francesco Redi and Louis Pasteur designed _____ to disprove spontaneous generation.

11. The theory of _____ states that life comes only from pre-existing life.

12. Clusters of organic molecules might have formed _____ , which may have evolved into the first true cells.

Order the evolutionary development of the following organisms from 1 to 4.

_____ **13.** chemosynthetic prokaryotes   _____ **15.** heterotrophic prokaryotes

_____ **14.** eukaryotes   _____ **16.** oxygen-producing photosyn-
                                                                    thetic prokaryotes

In your textbook, read about the evidence and mechanics of evolution.

Answer the following questions.

17. What assumption is made in the relative dating of fossils? _____

_____

18. What are homologous structures? _____

_____

For each statement below, write <u>true</u> or <u>false</u>.

_____ **19.** Evolution occurs when a population's genetic equilibrium remains unchanged.

_____ **20.** Mutations, genetic drift, and migration may disrupt the genetic equilibrium of populations.

_____ **21.** Stabilizing selection favors the survival of a population's average individuals for a feature.

_____ **22.** Disruptive selection occurs when an extreme feature is naturally selected.

_____ **23.** Adaptive radiation occurs when species that once were similar to an ancestral species become increasingly distinct due to natural selection pressures.

In your textbook, read about primate evolution.

For each item in Column A, write the letter of the matching item in Column B.

Column A	Column B
_____ **24.** Primate adaptation	**a.** anthropoids
_____ **25.** Primate category that includes humans and apes	**b.** Australopithecines
_____ **26.** Characteristic of New World monkeys	**c.** genus *Homo*
_____ **27.** Appearing in fossil record about 2 million years ago along with stone tools	**d.** opposable thumb
_____ **28.** Possible human ancestors dating from 5 to 8 million years ago	**e.** prehensile tail

In your textbook, read about organizing life's diversity.

Look at the taxonomic classification of a bobcat shown below. Answer the questions.

29. What is the largest taxon in this classification system?

_____

30. What is the scientific name of a bobcat?

_____

Taxon	Name
Kingdom	*Animalia*
Phylum	*Chordata*
Class	*Mammalia*
Order	*Carnivora*
Family	*Felidae*
Genus	*Lynx*
Species	*rufus*

Chapter 18 Viruses and Bacteria

Reinforcement and Study Guide

Section 18.1 Viruses

In your textbook, read about the characteristics of a virus.

For each item in Column A, write the letter of the matching item in Column B.

Column A	Column B
_____ **1.** Genetic material of a virus	**a.** virus
_____ **2.** Where a virus attaches to a host cell	**b.** T4 phage
_____ **3.** Nonliving particle that replicates inside a living cell	**c.** DNA or RNA
_____ **4.** A virus's protein coat	**d.** capsid
_____ **5.** Interlocks with a molecular shape in a host cell's plasma membrane	**e.** receptor site
_____ **6.** Layer that surrounds the capsid of some viruses	**f.** envelope
_____ **7.** A virus that infects *E. coli* bacteria	**g.** host
_____ **8.** A cell in which a virus replicates	**h.** attachment protein

In your textbook, read about viral replication cycles.

Complete the table by checking the correct column for each statement.

Statement	Lytic Cycle	Lysogenic Cycle
9. Viral genes are expressed immediately after the virus infects the host cell.		
10. Many new viruses are assembled.		
11. This cycle is preceded by a virus entering a host cell.		
12. Viral DNA is integrated into the host cell's chromosome.		
13. Viruses are released from the host cell by lysis or exocytosis.		
14. Reverse transcriptase is used to make DNA from the RNA of a retrovirus.		
15. A provirus is replicated along with the host cell's chromosome.		

Chapter 18 Viruses and Bacteria, *continued*

Use each of the terms below just once to complete the passage.

DNA	white blood cells	lysogenic
lytic	AIDS	proviruses

Many disease-causing viruses have both lytic and **(16)** _____ cycles. For example,

when HIVs infect **(17)** _____ , the viruses enter a lysogenic cycle. Their genetic

material becomes incorporated into the **(18)** _____ of the white blood cells, forming

(19) _____ . When this happens, the white blood cells still function normally, and the

person may not appear ill. Eventually, the proviruses enter a **(20)** _____ cycle, killing

the white blood cells. As a result, the person loses the ability to fight diseases and develops

(21) _____ .

In your textbook, read about viruses and cancer, plant viruses, and the origin of viruses.

Determine if the statement is true. If it is not, rewrite the italicized part to make it true.

_____ **22.** Some viruses can change normal cells to *tumor* cells.

_____ **23.** Retroviruses and the papilloma virus, which causes *hepatitis B*,
                          are examples of tumor viruses.

_____ **24.** *All* plant viruses cause diseases in plants.

_____ **25.** The first virus ever identified was the plant virus called *tobacco mosaic virus*.

_____ **26.** The patterns of color in some flowers are caused by *tumor* viruses.

_____ **27.** Tumor viruses contain genes that are found in *normal* cells.

_____ **28.** Scientists think viruses originated from *their host cells*.

Chapter 18 Viruses and Bacteria, *continued*

Section 18.2 Archaebacteria and Eubacteria

In your textbook, read about the diversity of prokaryotes and about the characteristics of bacteria.

Answer the following questions.

1. What are three types of environments in which archaebacteria are found? _____

_____

2. In what three ways do eubacteria obtain nutrients? _____

_____

3. How does a bacterium's cell wall protect it? _____

_____

4. Where is the genetic material of a bacterium found? _____

_____

5. What structure do some bacteria use to move? _____

6. What is the difference between gram-positive bacteria and gram-negative bacteria? _____

_____

_____

_____

7. What are three different shapes of bacteria? _____

8. Describe the three growth patterns of bacteria and state the prefix used to identify each growth pattern.

_____

_____

_____

Identify the type of bacterial reproduction described. Use these choices: binary fission, conjugation.

_____ **9.** Bacterium with a new genetic makeup is produced.

_____ **10.** Circular chromosome is copied.

_____ **11.** Genetic material is transferred through a pilus.

_____ **12.** Two identical cells are produced.

_____ **13.** Sexual reproduction occurs.

Chapter 18 **Viruses and Bacteria,** continued

In your textbook, read about adaptations in bacteria and the importance of bacteria.

Circle the letter of the choice that best completes the statement.

14. Scientists think the first bacteria on Earth were

   a. aerobic.   **b.** anaerobic.   **c.** fatal.   **d.** oxygen-dependent.

15. Bacteria that are obligate anaerobes release energy from food by

   a. cellular respiration.   **b.** using oxygen.

   c. using nitrogen.   **d.** fermentation.

16. As an endospore, a bacterium

   a. produces toxins.   **b.** dries out.   **c.** causes diseases.   **d.** is protected.

17. Botulism is caused by endospores of *C. botulinum* that have

   a. been killed.   **b.** produced toxins.

   c. germinated.   **d.** reproduced.

18. Nitrogen is important because all organisms need it to make

   a. proteins.   **b.** ATP.   **c.** DNA.   **d.** all of these.

19. The process by which bacteria use enzymes to convert nitrogen gas into ammonia is called

   a. nitrogenation.   **b.** atmospheric separation.

   c. nitrogen fixation.   **d.** eutrophication.

20. Bacteria return nutrients to the environment by breaking down

   a. dead organic matter.   **b.** inorganic materials.

   c. enzymes and sugar.   **d.** nitrogen in legumes.

21. Bacteria are *not* used to make

   a. vinegar.   **b.** jams.   **c.** cheese.   **d.** yogurt.

22. Bacteria are responsible for the following diseases:

   a. strep throat and tetanus.   **b.** gonorrhea and syphilis.

   c. tuberculosis and diphtheria.   **d.** all of these.

23. Due to reduced death rates from bacterial diseases and improved sanitation and living conditions, the average person born in the United States today will live to be about

   a. 25 years old.   **b.** 50 years old.

   c. 75 years old.   **d.** 90 years old.

Reinforcement and Study Guide

Section 19.1 The World of Protists

In your textbook, read about what a protist is.

Determine if the statement is true. If it is not, rewrite the italicized part to make it true.

1. The kingdom *Protista* is the most diverse of all six kingdoms. _____

2. Protists can be grouped into three general types—*animal-like*, *plantlike*, and *viruslike*.

_____

3. All protists are *eukaryotes* that carry on most of their metabolic processes in membrane-bound

organelles. _____

In your textbook, read about the characteristics and diversity of protozoans.

Complete each statement.

4. The _____ -like protists are all unicellular heterotrophs known as protozoans.

5. Amoebas move and change their body shape by forming extensions of their plasma membranes called

_____ .

6. Amoebas use _____ to pump out excess water from their cytoplasm.

7. Most amoebas reproduce by _____ in which a parent produces one or more

identical offspring by dividing into two cells.

8. One group of protozoans are called _____ because they move by whipping

one or more flagella from side to side.

9. A paramecium moves by beating thousands of hairlike _____ .

10. When food supplies are low, paramecia may reproduce by undergoing a form of

_____ .

11. Parasitic protozoans called _____ live inside their hosts and may reproduce

by means of a spore.

12. Malaria is caused by protozoans of the genus _____ .

13. The insect that is responsible for transmitting malaria-causing protozoans to humans is the

_____ .

Chapter 19 **Protists,** *continued*

In your textbook, read about what algae are and about their diversity.

For each item in Column A, write the letter of the item in Column B that completes the statement correctly.

Column A	Column B

_____ **1.** The euglenoids, diatoms, and dinoflagellates are _____ .

a. algae

_____ **2.** Unicellular protists that are major producers of oxygen in aquatic ecosystems are _____ .

b. phyla

_____ **3.** Unicellular and multicellular photosynthetic protists are _____ .

c. pigments

_____ **4.** Most green, red, and brown algae are _____ algae.

d. phytoplankton

_____ **5.** Photosynthetic _____ are used to classify algae.

e. unicellular

_____ **6.** Algae are classified into six _____ .

f. multicellular

Identify the phylum of the alga shown below and label its parts. Use these choices: flagellum, mitochondrion, pellicle, chloroplast, nucleus, eyespot, contractile vacuole, Euglenophyta.

7. Phylum _____

8. _____

9. _____

10. _____

11. _____

12. _____

13. _____

14. _____

Circle the letter of the choice that best completes the statement.

15. When diatoms that have been reproducing asexually reach about one-fourth of their original size, they

    a. die.

    b. triple in size.

    c. reproduce sexually.

    d. all of these.

16. Dinoflagellates are unicellular algae that

    a. have two flagella.

    b. create red tides.

    c. have thick cellulose plates.

    d. all of these.

17. Red algae are a kind of seaweed having pigments that absorb green, violet, and blue light waves, which allows the algae to

    a. live only in fresh water.

    b. photosynthesize in limited light.

    c. live only in salt water.

    d. both a and b.

18. The air bladders of brown algae allow the algae to

    a. breathe.

    b. reproduce.

    c. float near the water's surface.

    d. live in salt water.

19. A green alga that forms colonies is

    a. Spirogyra.

    b. Ulva.

    c. Chlamydomonas.

    d. Volvox.

In your textbook, read about alternation of generations.

Use each of the terms below just once to complete the passage.

diploid	gametophyte	alternation of generations	meiosis
haploid	sporophyte	spores	zygote

Some algae have a life cycle that has a pattern called **(20)** _____ .

These algae alternate between a(n) **(21)** _____ form that is called the

(22) _____ because it produces gametes, and a(n)

(23) _____ form called the **(24)** _____ . When the

haploid gametes fuse, they form a(n) **(25)** _____ from which the sporophyte

develops. Certain cells in the sporophyte undergo **(26)** _____ to form haploid

(27) _____ that develop into gametophytes.

Chapter 19   **Protists,** continued

In your textbook, read about the different kinds of funguslike protists.

Use all the terms in the list below at least once to complete the concept map for funguslike protists.

cell division   three phyla   spores   cellular slime molds

plasmodial slime molds   water molds and mildew   flagellated reproductive cells

In your textbook, read about the origin of protists.

Answer the following question.

8. What does scientific evidence show is the relationship between protists and other groups of organisms?

_____

_____

_____

_____

Chapter 20 Fungi

In your textbook, read about the general characteristics of fungi.

Answer the following questions.

1. What are the threadlike filaments in a multicellular fungus called? What do they form?

   _____

   _____

   _____

2. Some hyphae are divided into individual cells by cross walls with pores in them. What are these cross walls called? What purpose do the pores serve?

   _____

   _____

   _____

3. What is one way that fungi are like plants and one way they are unlike plants?

   _____

   _____

   _____

   _____

In your textbook, read about adaptations in fungi.

Determine if the statement is true. If it is not, rewrite the italicized part to make it true.

4. Many fungi are decomposers, which *break down organic substances* into raw materials that can be used by other organisms. _____

5. Fungi use *cellular digestion* to obtain nutrients. _____

6. Hyphae release *digestive enzymes* that break down molecules in their food source.

   _____

7. *Mutualistic* fungi are decomposers. _____

8. *Parasitic fungi grow spores* into host cells and absorb the cell's nutrients.

   _____

In your textbook, read about reproduction in fungi.

Complete each statement.

9. Fungi reproduce _____ by fragmentation, budding, or producing spores.

10. In _____ , pieces of hyphae grow into new mycelia.

11. The process of a parent cell undergoing mitosis and producing a new individual that pinches off, matures, and separates from the parent is called _____ .

12. When environmental conditions are right, a _____ may germinate and produce a threadlike _____ that will grow into a mycelium.

13. Some hyphae grow away from the mycelium to produce a spore-containing structure called a _____ .

14. In most fungi, the structures that support _____ are the only part of the fungus that can be seen.

15. Fungi may produce spores by _____ or _____ .

16. Many adaptations of fungi for survival involve _____ .

17. _____ protect spores and keep them from from drying out until they are released.

18. A single puffball may produce a cloud containing as many as _____ spores.

19. Producing a large number of spores increases a species' chances of _____ .

20. Fungal spores can be dispersed by _____ , _____ , and _____ .

Chapter 20 Fungi, *continued*

Section 20.2 The Diversity of Fungi

In your textbook, read about zygomycotes.

Order the steps of growth and reproduction in zygomycotes from 1 to 5.

_____ **1.** Hyphae called rhizoids penetrate the food, anchor the mycelium, and absorb nutrients.

_____ **2.** An asexual spore germinates on a food source and hyphae begin to grow.

_____ **3.** Spores are released and another asexual cycle begins.

_____ **4.** Hyphae called stolons grow across the surface of the food source and form a mycelium.

_____ **5.** Special hyphae grow upward to form sporangia that are filled with asexual spores.

Use each of the terms below just once to complete the passage.

yeasts	conidia	multicellular	conidiophores	yeast cells
sac fungi	ascospores	unicellular	vaccine	ascus

Ascomycotes are also called **(6)** _____ because they produce sexual spores,

called **(7)** _____ , in a saclike structure, called a(n) **(8)** _____ .

During asexual reproduction, ascomycotes produce spores called **(9)** _____ .

These asexual spores are produced in chains or clusters at the tips of structures called

(10) _____ , which are elongated hyphae.

Morels and truffles are **(11)** _____ ascomycotes that are edible. Yeasts are

(12) _____ ascomycotes. **(13)** _____ are used to make

beer, wine, and bread. They are also used in genetic research. A(n) **(14)** _____

for the disease hepatitis B is produced from rapidly growing **(15)** _____ , which

contain spliced human genes.

Chapter 20 **Fungi,** *continued*

In your textbook, read about basidiomycotes.

Answer the following questions about the life of a mushroom.

16. What are basidia and where are they found?

_____

_____

_____

17. What happens when mycelia of two different mating strains meet?

_____

18. What does a mycelium with two nuclei in its cells form?

_____

19. What does a diploid cell inside a basidium produce as a result of meiosis?

_____

_____

In your textbook, read about deuteromycotes, the mutualistic relationships of mycorrhizae and lichens, and the origins of fungi.

Write the letter of the item in Column B that best completes each statement in Column A.

Column A	Column B
_____ **20.** _____ is an example of a deuteromycote.	**a.** basidiomycotes
_____ **21.** A mycorrhiza is a mutualistic relationship between a fungus and a(n) _____ .	**b.** mycorrhizae
_____ **22.** _____ is an antibiotic produced by a deuteromycote.	**c.** alga
_____ **23.** Plants that have _____ associated with their roots grow larger.	**d.** *Penicillium*
_____ **24.** _____ make up a division of fungi that have no known sexual stage.	**e.** pioneer species
_____ **25.** A lichen is a mutualistic relationship between a fungus and a(n) _____ or cyanobacterium.	**f.** deuteromycotes
_____ **26.** Lichens are _____ in all parts of the world.	**g.** penicillin
_____ **27.** Scientists think that ascomycotes and _____ evolved from a common ancestor.	**h.** plant

BioDigest 6 — Viruses, Bacteria, Protists, and Fungi

In your textbook, read about viruses.

Label the parts of a virus.

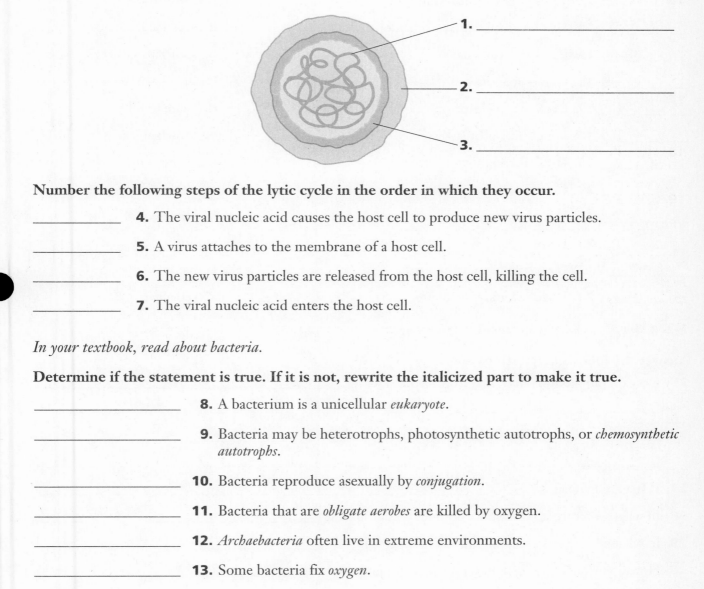

1. _____

2. _____

3. _____

Number the following steps of the lytic cycle in the order in which they occur.

_____ **4.** The viral nucleic acid causes the host cell to produce new virus particles.

_____ **5.** A virus attaches to the membrane of a host cell.

_____ **6.** The new virus particles are released from the host cell, killing the cell.

_____ **7.** The viral nucleic acid enters the host cell.

In your textbook, read about bacteria.

Determine if the statement is true. If it is not, rewrite the italicized part to make it true.

_____ **8.** A bacterium is a unicellular *eukaryote*.

_____ **9.** Bacteria may be heterotrophs, photosynthetic autotrophs, or *chemosynthetic autotrophs*.

_____ **10.** Bacteria reproduce asexually by *conjugation*.

_____ **11.** Bacteria that are *obligate aerobes* are killed by oxygen.

_____ **12.** *Archaebacteria* often live in extreme environments.

_____ **13.** Some bacteria fix *oxygen*.

BioDigest 6 — Viruses, Bacteria, Protists, and Fungi, *continued*

In your textbook, read about protists.

Write the letter of the item in Column B that best matches the item in Column A.

Column A	Column B
_____ **14.** Can be unicellular, colonial, or multicellular	**a.** green algae
_____ **15.** Parasitic protozoans	**b.** sporozoans
_____ **16.** Causes malaria	**c.** amoeba
_____ **17.** Can be both autotrophic and heterotrophic	**d.** slime mold
_____ **18.** Funguslike protist	**e.** brown algae
_____ **19.** Uses cilia to move	**f.** *Plasmodium*
_____ **20.** Contain carotenoids	**g.** euglenas
_____ **21.** Have hard, armorlike plates	**h.** *Paramecium*
_____ **22.** Kelps	**i.** dinoflagellates
_____ **23.** Uses pseudopodia to move	**j.** diatoms
_____ **24.** Have red and blue pigments	**k.** red algae

In your textbook, read about fungi.

Answer the following questions.

25. How do fungi obtain nutrients from a food source? _____

_____

26. How do fungi play a role in recycling nutrients on Earth? _____

_____

27. What are hyphae? _____

28. In what structure do club fungi produce sexual spores? _____

29. In what structure do sac fungi produce sexual spores? _____

30. How do mycorrhizae benefit both the plants and the fungi? _____

_____

_____

_____

31. What is a lichen? _____

_____

Chapter
21   **What Is a Plant?**

In your textbook, read about the origins and adaptations of plants.

For each answer given below, write an appropriate question.

1.   **Answer:** Multicellular eukaryotes having thick cell walls made of cellulose, a protective, waterproof covering, and that can produce its own food in the form of glucose through photosynthesis

     Question: _____

2.   **Answer:** The earliest known plant fossils

     Question: _____

3.   **Answer:** Protective, waxy layers that cover most fruits, leaves, and stems

     Question: _____

4.   **Answer:** The organ of a plant that traps light energy for photosynthesis, and is supported by a stem

     Question: _____

5.   **Answer:** The organ that works like an anchor, transports nutrients, and absorbs water and minerals

     Question: _____

In your textbook, read about alternation of generations.

Use each of the terms below just once to complete the passage.

diploid   generations   meiosis
gametes   haploid   sporophyte

The lives of all plants consist of two alternating stages, or **(6)** _____ . The

gametophyte generation of a plant is responsible for the development of **(7)** _____ .

All seeds of the gametophyte, including the gametes, are **(8)** _____ . The

(9) _____ generation is responsible for the production of spores. All cells of the

sporophyte are **(10)** _____ . The spores are produced by the sporophyte plant

body by **(11)** _____ and are, therefore, haploid.

Chapter 21 **What Is a Plant?,** *continued*

In your textbook, read about the origin and adaptations of plants.

Circle the letter of the choice that best completes the statement.

12. The lives of _____ plants include two generations that alternate.
   a. non-seed producing
   b. seed
   c. all
   d. most

13. The generation of a plant responsible for producing gametes is the
   a. alternation of generations.
   b. gametophyte generation.
   c. sporophyte generation.
   d. seed-producing generation.

14. All gametophyte spores are _____ and all sporophyte tissue cells are _____ .
   a. haploid/diploid.
   b. diploid/haploid.
   c. haploid/haploid.
   d. diploid/diploid.

15. Non-seed plants _____ that grow into gametophytes.
   a. release spores into the environment
   b. retain spores in the parent plant
   c. release seeds into the environment
   d. retain seeds in the parent plant

Answer the following questions.

16. What is the difference between vascular and nonvascular plants?

_____

_____

_____

_____

17. Some land plants produce seeds. What is their function? How do they differ from spores?

_____

_____

_____

_____

18. How do algae and land plants get nutrients?

_____

_____

_____

_____

Chapter 21 **What Is a Plant?,** *continued*

Section 21.2 Survey of the Plant Kingdom

In your textbook, read about non-seed plants.

For each item in Column A, write the letter of the matching item in Column B.

Column A	Column B
_____ **1.** Leaves that are found on ferns	**a.** leafy liverworts
_____ **2.** Scaly structures that support male or female reproductive structures	**b.** thallose liverworts
_____ **3.** Plants with a broad, flattened body that resembles a lobed leaf	**c.** fronds
_____ **4.** Plants with three flattened rows of thin leaves	**d.** hornworts
_____ **5.** Nonvascular plants that grow in damp, shady habitats and whose sporophytes resemble horns	**e.** cones

Complete the chart below by marking the appropriate columns for each division of plants.

Division	Vascular	Nonvascular	Non-seed Plants	Seeds in Fruits	Seeds in Cones
6. Hepatophyta					
7. Anthocerophyta					
8. Bryophyta					
9. Psilophyta					
10. Lycophyta					
11. Sphenophyta					
12. Pterophyta					
13. Cycadophyta					
14. Gnetophyta					
15. Ginkgophyta					
16. Coniferophyta					
17. Anthophyta					

In your textbook, read about non-seed plants.

For each answer given below, write an appropriate question.

18.   **Answer:** Vascular plants that have neither roots nor leaves

   Question: _____

19.   **Answer:** Vascular plants that have hollow, jointed stems surrounded by whorls of scalelike leaves, whose cells contain large deposits of silica

   Question: _____

20.   **Answer:** Plants that may be the ancestors of all plants

   Question: _____

21.   **Answer:** Hard-walled reproductive cells found in non-seed plants

   Question: _____

22.   **Answer:** Nonvascular plants that rely on osmosis and diffusion to transport water and nutrients, although some members have elongated cells that conduct water and sugars

   Question: _____

In your textbook, read about seed plants.

Use each of the terms below just once to complete the passage.

Anthophyta   Cycadophyta   Gnetophyta
Coniferophyta   Ginkgophyta

Seed plants are classified into five divisions. Plants from the **(23)** _____ division are

palmlike trees with scaly trunks and are often mistaken for ferns or small palm trees. There is only one

living species in the **(24)** _____ division. The members of the **(25)** _____

division are the largest, most diverse group of seed plant on Earth and are commonly known as the flow-

ering plants. Three distinct genera make up the plant division called **(26)** _____ . Species

of the **(27)** _____ division can be identified by the characteristics of their needlelike or

scaly leaves.

Chapter
22 The Diversity of Plants

In your textbook, read about nonvascular plants—bryophyta, hepatophyta, and anthocerophyta.

Complete each statement.

1. Nonvascular plants are successful in habitats with adequate _____ .

2. The _____ generation is dominant in nonvascular plants.

3. Sperm are produced in male reproductive structures called _____ , and eggs are produced in female reproductive structures called _____ .

4. Mosses have colorless multicellular structures called _____ , which help anchor the stem to the soil.

5. Most liverworts have _____ that helps reduce evaporation of water from the plant's tissues.

6. Liverworts occur in many environments and include two groups: the _____ liverworts and the _____ liverworts.

7. One unique feature of hornworts is the presence of a(n) _____ in each cell.

8. The common names for the nonvascular plants, Bryophyta, Hepatophyta, and Anthocerophyta are _____ , _____ , and _____ .

Circle the letter of the response that best completes the statement.

9. Nonvascular plants are not as common or as widespread as vascular plants because
   a. nonvascular plants are small.
   b. the life functions of nonvascular plants require a close association with water.
   c. nonvascular plants are limited to dry habitats.
   d. none of the above.

10. The life cycle of nonvascular plants includes an alternation of generations between a
    a. diploid sporophyte and a diploid gametophyte.
    b. haploid sporophyte and a haploid gametophyte.
    c. diploid sporophyte and a haploid gametophyte.
    d. haploid sporophyte and a diploid gametophyte.

11. Fossil and genetic evidence suggests that the first land plants were
    a. mosses.
    b. sphagnum moss.
    c. liverworts.
    d. hornworts.

In your textbook, read about the alternation of generations of non-seed vascular plants and lycophyta.

Use each of the terms below just once to complete the passage.

antheridia	leaves	sporophyte
archegonia	prothallus	strobilus
egg	reproductive cells	zygote
fertilization	sperm	

Unlike nonvascular plants, the spore-producing **(1)** _____ is the dominant generation

in vascular plants. A major advance in vascular plants was the adaptation of **(2)** _____ to

form structures that protect the developing **(3)** _____ . In some non-seed vascular

plants, spore-bearing leaves form a compact cluster called a(n) **(4)** _____. Spores are

released from this compact cluster. These spores then grow to form the gametophyte, called a(n)

(5) _____ . This structure is relatively small and lives in or on soil. The prothallus then

forms **(6)** _____ , male reproductive structures, and **(7)** _____ , female

reproductive structures. **(8)** _____ are released from the antheridium and swim through a

film of water to the **(9)** _____ in the archegonium. **(10)** _____ occurs and

a large, dominant sporophyte plant develops from the fertilized **(11)** _____ .

For each statement below, write <u>true</u> or <u>false</u>.

_____ **12.** The leafy stems of lycophytes resemble clubs, and their reproductive structures are moss shaped.

_____ **13.** The leaves of lycophytes occur as pairs, whorls, or spirals along the stem.

_____ **14.** Lycophytes are simple vascular plants with creeping leaves.

_____ **15.** The club moss is commonly called ground pine because it is evergreen and resembles a miniature pine tree.

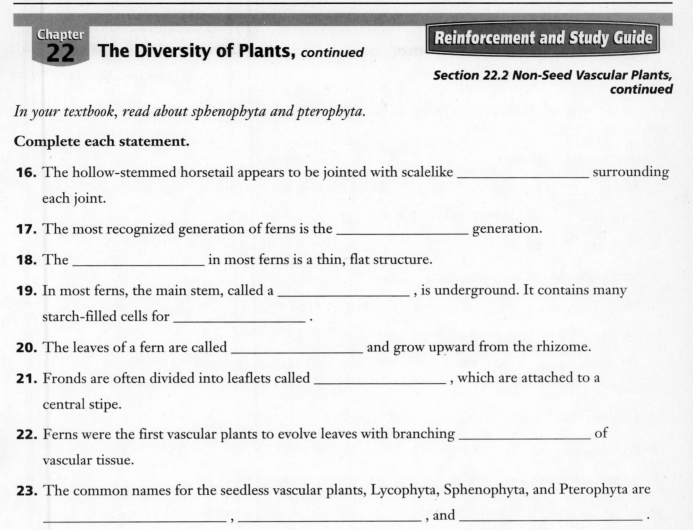

Chapter 22 **The Diversity of Plants,** *continued*

Section 22.2 Non-Seed Vascular Plants,
continued

In your textbook, read about sphenophyta and pterophyta.

Complete each statement.

16. The hollow-stemmed horsetail appears to be jointed with scalelike _____ surrounding each joint.

17. The most recognized generation of ferns is the _____ generation.

18. The _____ in most ferns is a thin, flat structure.

19. In most ferns, the main stem, called a _____ , is underground. It contains many starch-filled cells for _____ .

20. The leaves of a fern are called _____ and grow upward from the rhizome.

21. Fronds are often divided into leaflets called _____ , which are attached to a central stipe.

22. Ferns were the first vascular plants to evolve leaves with branching _____ of vascular tissue.

23. The common names for the seedless vascular plants, Lycophyta, Sphenophyta, and Pterophyta are _____ , _____ , and _____ .

Answer the following questions on the lines provided.

24. Why are sphenophytes, or horsetails, sometimes referred to as scouring rushes?

_____

_____

_____

25. Why might you be more familiar with ferns than with club mosses and horsetails?

_____

_____

_____

_____

Chapter 22 **The Diversity of Plants,** continued

In your textbook, read about the seed plants—cycadophyta, gingkophyta, gnetophyta, coniferophyta, and anthophyta.

Complete each statement.

1. An _____ , or young diploid sporophyte, has food-storage organs called _____ , which develop into leaves.

2. Vascular plants that produce _____ in cones are sometimes called _____ .

3. Seed plants do not require _____ for _____ .

4. The male gametophyte develops inside a structure called a(n) _____ that includes sperm cells, nutrients, and a protective outer covering.

5. The female gametophyte, which produces the egg cell, is contained within a sporophyte structure called a(n) _____ .

6. Biennials develop large storage roots and live for _____ .

7. Perennials produce flowers and seeds periodically for _____ .

8. Annual plants live for _____ .

9. _____ have one seed leaf; _____ have two seed leaves.

For each statement below, write _true_ or _false_.

_____ 10. Cycads are related to palm trees but their leaves unfurl like fern fronds.

_____ 11. There is only one species of ginkgo tree alive today.

_____ 12. Most gnetophytes today are found in the deserts or mountains of Africa, Asia, North America, and Central or South America.

_____ 13. Most conifers are evergreen plants that lose their needlelike leaves all at once and only grow in nutrient-rich soil.

_____ 14. Dropping leaves is an adaptation in deciduous plants to reduce water loss when it is less available during winter.

_____ 15. Anthophytes are unique in that they are the only division of plants that produce fruits.

Chapter 23 Plant Structure and Function

In your textbook, read about plant cells and tissues.

Match the definitions in Column 1 with the terms in describes from Column 2. Place the letter from Column 2 in the spaces under Column 1.

Column 1	Column 2
_____ **1.** The most abundant kind of plant cells	**a.** apical meristem
_____ **2.** Long cells with unevenly thickened cell walls. This type of cell wall allows the cells to grow.	**b.** collenchyma
_____ **3.** Cells with walls that are very thick and rigid. At maturity, these cells often die, leaving the cell walls to provide support for the plant.	**c.** companion cell
	d. cork cambium
_____ **4.** Dermal tissue that is composed of flattened parenchyma cells that cover all parts of the plant	**e.** epidermis
_____ **5.** Openings in the cuticle of the leaf that control the exchange of gases	**f.** guard cells
_____ **6.** Cells that control the opening and closing of the stomata.	**g.** meristem
_____ **7.** Hairlike projections that extend from the epidermis	
_____ **8.** Plant tissue composed of tubular cells that transports water and minerals from the roots to the rest of the plant	**h.** parenchyma
_____ **9.** Tubular cells, with tapered ends, which transport water throughout a plant	**i.** phloem
_____ **10.** Lateral meristem that produces a tough covering for the surface of stems and roots	**j.** sclerenchyma
_____ **11.** Vascular tissue that transport sugars from the leaves to all parts of the plant	**k.** sieve tube member
_____ **12.** Long, cylindrical phloem cells through which sugars and organic compounds flow	**l.** stomata
_____ **13.** Nucleated cells that help manage the transport of sugars and other organic compounds through the sieve cells of the phloem	**m.** tracheids
	n. trichomes
_____ **14.** Areas where new cells are produced	**o.** vascular cambium
_____ **15.** Growth tissue found at or near the tips of roots and stems	
_____ **16.** Tubular cells that transport water throughout the plant. These cells are wider and shorter than tracheids.	**p.** vessel element
_____ **17.** Lateral meristem that produces new xylem and phloem cells in the stems and roots	**q.** xylem

Chapter 23 **Plant Structure and Function,** *continued*

Section 23.2 Roots, Stems, and Leaves

In your textbook, read about roots and stems.

Label the parts of the dicot root. Use these choices:

cortex   phloem   epidermis   endodermis   xylem

Dicot Root

1. _____

2. _____

3. _____

4. _____

5. _____

For each statement below, write <u>true</u> or <u>false</u>.

_____ **6.** A root hair is a small extension of an epidermal, or outermost, cell layer of a dicot root.

_____ **7.** Layers of parenchyma cells make up the cortex of a dicot root and the central pith of a monocot root.

_____ **8.** Outside the endodermis is a tissue called the pericycle that develops vertical roots.

_____ **9.** Vascular cambium cells found at the center of a root grow more xylem and phloem cells that increase the size of the root.

_____ **10.** Behind the root tip are cell-producing growth tissues called the root cap.

_____ **11.** The difference between roots and stems lies in the way they transport water.

_____ **12.** Primary growth in a stem occurs in the apical meristem.

REINFORCEMENT AND STUDY GUIDE

Chapter 23 **Plant Structure and Function,** *continued*

Reinforcement and Study Guide

Section 23.2 Roots, Stems, and Leaves,
continued

In your textbook, read about stems and leaves.

Circle the letter of the response that best completes the statement.

13. Many wildflowers with soft, green stems are plants that have
    a. woody stems.
    b. herbaceous stems.
    c. woody roots.
    d. all of the above.

14. The functions of a plant's stem include
    a. transporting sugar.
    b. supporting the plant.
    c. transporting water and minerals.
    d. all of the above.

15. Any portion of the plant that stores sugars is called a
    a. petiole.
    b. mesophyll.
    c. root cap.
    d. sink.

16. The movement of sugars from the leaves through the phloem is called
    a. photosynthesis.
    b. transpiration.
    c. translocation.
    d. food storage.

In your textbook, read about the leaves of a plant.

Use each of the terms below just once to complete the passage.

stomata	extend	cuticle	transpiration	epidermis
veins	stem	petiole	photosynthesis	mesophyll

There are many parts to a leaf. Grass leaves grow right out of the **(17)** _____ ,

but other leaves are connected to the stem by a stalk called the **(18)** _____ .

The petiole is made of vascular tissues that **(19)** _____ up into the leaf to form

(20) _____ .

The outer surface of a leaf has a **(21)** _____ that covers the epidermis.

Inside the epidermis are two layers of photosynthetic cells that make up the

(22) _____ . Cells in the palisade layer have many chloroplasts and

carry out most of the leaf's **(23)** _____ . Leaves have a(n)

(24) _____ with a waxy cuticle and **(25)** _____ help

prevent water loss. The loss of water through the stomata is called **(26)** _____ .

Chapter 23 **Plant Structure and Function,** *continued*

In your textbook, read about plant hormones and plant responses.

Complete each statement.

1. A _____ is a chemical that is produced in one part of an organism and transported to another part, where it causes a physiological change.

2. The group of plant hormones called _____ promote cell elongation. Indoleacetic acid (IAA) is an example of this group of hormones.

3. The group of growth hormones that cause plants to grow taller because, like auxins, they stimulate cell elongation, are called _____ .

4. The hormones called _____ are so named because they stimulate cell division by stimulating the production of proteins needed for mitosis.

5. The plant hormone called _____ is a simple, gaseous compound composed of carbon and hydrogen that speeds the ripening of fruits.

6. A plant's response to an external stimulus that comes from a particular direction is called a _____ .

7. A responsive movement of a plant that is not dependent on the direction of the stimulus is called a _____ .

Determine if the statement is true. If it is not, rewrite the italicized part to make it true.

8. A *large* amount of hormone is needed to make physiological changes in a plant.

_____

9. If gibberellins are applied to the tip of a dwarf plant, it will grow *taller*.

_____

10. The growth of a plant towards light is caused by an unequal distribution of *ethylene* in the plant's stem.

_____

11. If a tropism is *negative*, the plant grows toward the stimulus.

_____

12. The growth of a plant toward light is called *phototropism*.

_____

13. *Gravitropism* is the direction of plant growth in response to gravity.

_____

14. A plant's response to touch is called *cytokinin*.

_____

Copyright © Glencoe/McGraw-Hill, a division of The McGraw-Hill Companies, Inc.

Chapter
24 Reproduction in Plants

Reinforcement and Study Guide

Section 24.1 Life Cycles of Mosses, Ferns, and Conifers

In your textbook, read about alternation of generations and the life cycles of mosses and ferns.

Use each of the terms below just once to complete the following statements.

diploid	meiosis	sporophyte
dominant	mitosis	vegetative reproduction
egg	protonema	
gametophyte	sperm	

1. The two phases of the plant life are the _____ stage and

the _____ stage.

2. The cells of the sporophyte are all _____ .

3. The female gamete is the _____ , and the male gamete is the _____ .

4. Some plants reproduce asexually by a process called _____ , in which a new

plant is produced from an existing vegetative structure.

5. Mosses belong to one of the few plant divisions in which the gametophyte plant is the

_____ generation.

6. A small, green filament of moss cells that develops into either a male or female moss gametophyte is

known as a(n) _____ .

7. The moss diploid zygote divides by _____ to form a new sporophyte in the

form of a stalk and capsule.

8. Spores are produced by _____ in the capsule of the moss sporophyte.

**Number each description to order the stages from spore release of the life cycle
of a fern, from 1 to 7.**

_____ **9.** A spore germinates and grows into a heart-shaped gametophyte called a prothallus.

_____ **10.** After fertilization, the diploid zygote grows into a sporophyte.

_____ **11.** As the sporophyte grows, roots and fronds grow out from the rhizome.

_____ **12.** Sperm swim through a film of water on the prothallus to reach and fertilize an egg in
the archegonium.

_____ **13.** In each sporangium, spores are produced by meiosis, and the cycle begins again as the
spores are dispersed by the wind.

_____ **14.** Sori, or clusters of sporangia, grow on the pinnae.

_____ **15.** A sporangium bursts, releasing haploid spores.

In your textbook, read about the life cycle of conifers.

Answer the following questions.

1. What is the dominant stage in conifers?

_____

2. What does the adult conifer produce on its branches?

_____

_____

3. What is a megaspore?

_____

_____

4. What are microspores and how are they produced?

_____

_____

5. What do the microspores develop into?

_____

6. What is a micropyle?

_____

7. How does fertilization take place?

_____

_____

_____

_____

8. After fertilization, a zygote develops inside the ovule into an embryo with several cotyledons. What happens to the ovule?

_____

_____

9. What happens to the seeds when the female cone opens and falls to the ground?

_____

_____

10. What will the seedling become?

_____

_____

Chapter 24 **Reproduction in Plants,** *continued*

Section 24.2 Flowers and Flowering

In your textbook, read about the structure of a flower.

Determine if the statement is true. If it is not, rewrite the italicized part to make it true.

1. In flowering plants, sexual reproduction takes place in the *seed*, which has several parts.

_____

2. The structure of a flower includes four kinds of organs: *sepals, petals, stamens, and ovaries*.

_____

3. *Petals* are usually colorful, leaflike structures that encircle the flower stem.

_____

4. The male reproductive structure located inside the petals of a flower is a *stamen*. Sperm-containing pollen is produced in the *anther* at the tip of the stamen.

_____

5. The female reproductive structure at the center of a flower is the *ovary*. Eggs are formed in the *pistil*, which is located in the bottom portion of the *ovary*.

_____

Label the parts of the flower. Use these choices:

sepal	**petal**	**stigma**	**ovule**
anther	**ovary**	**filament**	

6. _____

8. _____

10. _____

11. _____

7. _____

9. _____

12. _____

Chapter 24 **Reproduction in Plants,** *continued*

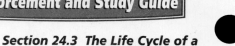
In your textbook, read about the life cycle of a flowering plant.

For each item in Column A, write the letter of the matching item from Column B.

<table>
<tr><td colspan="2" align="center">**Column A**</td><td align="center">**Column B**</td></tr>
<tr><td>_____</td><td>**1.** Two nuclei in one cell at the center of the embryo sac</td><td>**a.** dormancy</td></tr>
<tr><td>_____</td><td>**2.** A process in which one sperm fertilizes the egg and the other sperm joins with the central cell</td><td>**b.** double fertilization</td></tr>
<tr><td>_____</td><td>**3.** Food-storing tissue that develops from the triploid central cell and supports the development of the embryo</td><td>**c.** endosperm</td></tr>
<tr><td>_____</td><td>**4.** A period of inactivity in which seeds of some plant species remain until conditions are favorable for growth and development</td><td>**d.** germination</td></tr>
<tr><td>_____</td><td>**5.** The beginning of the development of the embryo into a new plant</td><td>**e.** hypocotyl</td></tr>
<tr><td>_____</td><td>**6.** This embryonic root is the first part of the embryo to appear from the seed</td><td>**f.** polar nuclei</td></tr>
<tr><td>_____</td><td>**7.** The portion of the stem near the seed</td><td>**g.** radicle</td></tr>
</table>

Answer the following questions.

8. How do anthophytes attract animal pollinators?

_____

_____

_____

9. How do seeds form after fertilization takes place?

_____

_____

_____

_____

10. Name three ways seeds are dispersed.

_____

_____

_____

_____

_____

BioDigest
7 Plants

In your textbook, read about plants.

Study the following diagram of alternation of generations in plants. Then answer the questions.

1. Is the sporophyte generation a haploid or diploid generation? _____

2. Is the gametophyte generation a haploid or diploid generation? _____

3. Is a spore haploid or diploid? _____

4. Is a gamete haploid or diploid? _____

5. Does a spore produce a gametophyte without fertilization? _____

6. Does a gamete produce a sporophyte without fertilization? _____

7. Which generation—sporophyte or gametophyte—produces a generation that is diploid?

_____

Seed Plants

Explain how these adaptations enable conifers to survive in cold or dry climates.

8. *Needles* _____

_____

9. *Stems* _____

_____

10. *Flexible leaves and branches* _____

_____

_____

BioDigest 7 **Plants,** *continued*

Flowering Plants

Fill in the following blanks to explain the function of a flower.

11. A flower has two major reproductive structures. The _____ is the

_____ reproductive organ. At the base of the pistil is the

_____ , which houses ovules, the female _____

generation of the plant. In each ovule, female gametes, or _____ , form.

12. The _____ and anther form the _____ reproductive

organ. The male _____ generation of the plant is _____ .

Within it, the male gametes are formed.

13. When pollination occurs, a _____ extends from the pollen grain to the

ovary, and two _____ travel down the tube to fertilize the eggs in the ovule.

14. Some flowers are colorful and showy. Others are small and inconspicuous. Explain how these two
flower types are adapted to different pollinators.

_____

_____

_____

15. Discuss three ways that seeds may be spread through the environment.

a. _____

b. _____

c. _____

Chapter
25 **What Is an Animal?**

In your textbook, read about the characteristics of animals.

Answer the following questions.

1. You have just discovered a new organism that you think is an animal. In order to be classified as an animal, what characteristics must it have?

_____

_____

2. What is one important factor that influences how an animal obtains its food?

_____

3. How might an animal be free-moving at one stage in its life and sessile at another? Give an example.

_____

_____

4. How do sessile, aquatic animals get their food?

_____

_____

If the animal described below is a sessile organism, write <u>yes</u>. If it is not, write <u>no</u>.

_____ **5.** Barnacles attached to a ship's hull

_____ **6.** A spider lying in wait in the center of its web

_____ **7.** Coral larvae drifting in a tropical ocean

_____ **8.** Sponges growing on the outside of a crab's shell

Complete each statement.

9. Digestion in a sponge takes place in _____ _____ , while digestion in a
more complex animal like a tiger takes place in a(n) _____ _____ .

10. Some of the food you had for breakfast has been stored as _____ or
_____ , ready to be used if it's a long time until your next meal.

Chapter 25 **What Is an Animal?,** *continued*

Section 25.1 Typical Animal Characteristics, *continued*

In your textbook, read about the development of animals.

Determine if the statement is true. If it is not, rewrite the italicized part to make it true.

11. Most animals develop from a single, fertilized egg called a *blastula*. _____

12. A zygote divides by a process known as *cleavage*. _____

13. The blastula is a *solid ball of cells*. _____

_____

Label the parts of the gastrula shown here. Use these choices:

ectoderm   endoderm   mesoderm   opening in gastrula

14. _____

15. _____

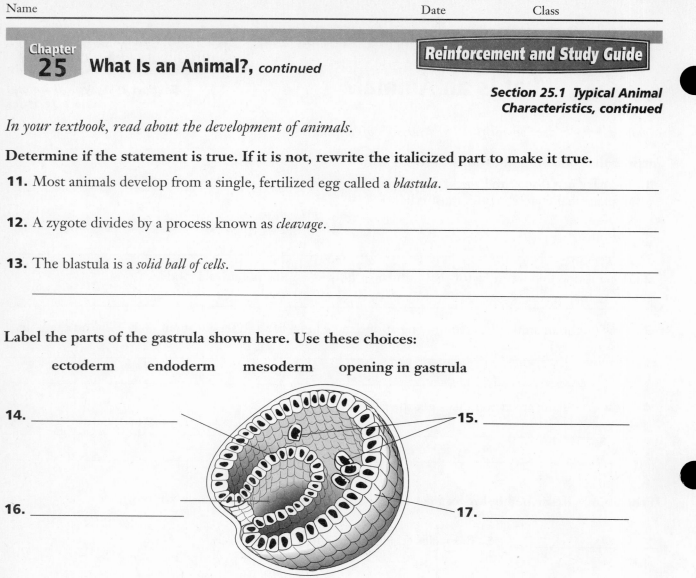

16. _____

17. _____

Complete the chart by checking the correct column for each description.

Description	Endoderm	Ectoderm	Mesoderm
18. Gives rise to digestive tract			
19. Continues to grow and divide			
20. Lines the inner surface of gastrula			
21. Gives rise to muscles			
22. Develops into skin and nervous tissue			
23. Forms from cells that break off endoderm			

REINFORCEMENT AND STUDY GUIDE

Chapter
25 What Is an Animal?, *continued*

Section 25.2 Body Plans and Adaptations

In your textbook, read about kinds of symmetry in animals.

Circle the letter of the choice that best completes the statement or answers the question.

1. Different kinds of symmetry make it possible for animals to
- **a.** grow very large.
- **b.** survive when cut into pieces.
- **c.** move and find food in different ways.
- **d.** live a long time.

2. The irregularly shaped body of a sponge is an example of
- **a.** asymmetry.
- **b.** gastrulation.
- **c.** symmetry.
- **d.** balance.

3. A sponge's body has how many layers of cells?
- **a.** one
- **b.** two
- **c.** three
- **d.** four

4. The embryonic development of a sponge does *not* include which of the following?
- **a.** formation of endoderm
- **b.** formation of mesoderm
- **c.** a gastrula stage
- **d.** a, b, and c

5. If you divided a radially symmetrical animal along any plane through its central axis, you would end up with
- **a.** roughly equal halves.
- **b.** front and back halves.
- **c.** top and bottom halves.
- **d.** three pieces.

6. Which of the following animals is *not* radially symmetrical?
- **a.** a hydra
- **b.** a sea urchin
- **c.** a spider
- **d.** a starfish

7. An organism with bilateral symmetry can be divided lengthwise into right and left halves that are
- **a.** asymmetrical.
- **b.** mirror images of each other.
- **c.** made up of two cell layers.
- **d.** flattened.

Identify each of the following body parts as being either dorsal or ventral on the animal's body.

_____ **8.** the navel of a killer whale

_____ **9.** the sail fin on an iguana

_____ **10.** the back of your neck

_____ **11.** the mouth of a shark

_____ **12.** the pouch of a kangaroo

Chapter
25 **What Is an Animal?,** *continued*

In your textbook, read about bilateral symmetry and body plans.

Answer the following questions.

13. In what ways was the development of a body cavity, or coelom, an advantage for bilaterally symmetrical animals?

_____

_____

14. Describe an acoelomate animal's body plan.

_____

_____

15. How do nutrients get to the cells in a flatworm's solid, acoelomate body?

_____

Use each of the terms below just once to complete the passage.

coelom	completely	double	internal organs
mesoderm	partly	pseudocoelom	

A roundworm has a **(16)** _____ , a fluid-filled body cavity that is **(17)** _____

lined with **(18)** _____ . Coelomate animals have a **(19)** _____ , a body

cavity that is **(20)** _____ surrounded by mesoderm and in which complex

(21) _____ are suspended by **(22)** _____ layers of mesoderm tissue.

In your textbook, read about animal protection and support.

For each statement below, write <u>true</u> or <u>false</u>.

_____ **23.** During the course of evolution, animal body plans have decreased in complexity.

_____ **24.** An exoskeleton provides protection and support on the outside of an animal's body, as well as a place for muscle attachment.

_____ **25.** An endoskeleton is a support framework housed within the body, a protective enclosure for internal organs, and a brace for muscles to pull against.

_____ **26.** An invertebrate is an animal with a backbone.

REINFORCEMENT AND STUDY GUIDE

Chapter 26 Sponges, Cnidarians, Flatworms, and Roundworms

In your textbook, read about sponges.

Answer the following questions.

1. How does the name *Porifera* relate to the structure of a sponge?

_____

_____

2. How do sponges obtain food from their environment?

_____

_____

3. Describe a sponge's body plan.

_____

_____

Complete the table by writing a cell type or structure in sponges that fits each description.

Type of Cell or Structure	Description
4.	Aid in reproduction and nutrient transport Help produce spicules
5.	Form the outside surface of body Contract to close pores
6.	Line interior of sponge's body Use flagella to draw water through pores
7.	Found in jellylike substance between layers Make up sponge's support system

Use each of the terms below just once to complete the passage.

external buds   eggs   hermaphroditic   internal fertilization

larvae   sexual   sperm

Sponges sometimes reproduce asexually by forming **(8)** _____ . Being

(9) _____ , a sponge can also produce both **(10)** _____ and sperm. During

(11) _____ reproduction, **(12)** _____ from one sponge fertilize the eggs

of another. Fertilization can be external, but **(13)** _____ is more common.

Free-swimming **(14)** _____ settle and develop into sessile adults.

In your textbook, read about cnidarians.

Identify each of the following descriptions as either the <u>polyp</u> or <u>medusa</u> form of a cnidarian.

_____ **1.** Reef-building corals on the Great Barrier Reef

_____ **2.** *Aurelia*, the moon jellyfish

_____ **3.** Deep sea anemones with meter-long tentacles

_____ **4.** The asexual phase in a jellyfish's life cycle

Answer the following questions.

5. Nematocysts are characteristic of cnidarians. How does a nematocyst work?

_____

_____

6. Compare and contrast how food is digested in a sponge and in a cnidarian.

_____

_____

7. How does a nerve net function?

_____

_____

Order the following steps in the life cycle of a jellyfish from A to F, beginning with the release of eggs and sperm.

_____ **8.** A polyp grows and buds repeatedly.

_____ **9.** External fertilization takes place in the sea.

_____ **10.** A zygote develops into a blastula, which develops into a larva.

_____ **11.** Male and female medusae release sperm and eggs, respectively.

_____ **12.** A cilia-covered larva settles onto a surface.

_____ **13.** A tiny medusa breaks free from its sessile parent and drifts away.

Chapter 26 **Sponges, Cnidarians, Flatworms, and Roundworms,** *continued*

Section 26.3 Flatworms

In your textbook, read about flatworms.

For each statement below, write <u>true</u> or <u>false</u>.

_____ 1. Flatworms are bilaterally symmetrical and have a clearly defined head.

_____ 2. Adult planarians can focus well enough with their eyespots to form images of objects in their environment.

_____ 3. Flame cells play an important role in maintaining water balance in planaria.

_____ 4. A planarian uses its pharynx to locate food.

_____ 5. Planarians reproduce sexually by producing encapsulated zygotes that hatch into free-swimming larvae.

In part C of the illustration below, draw in what you think will happen to the two halves of the cut planarian. Then, answer the question.

6.

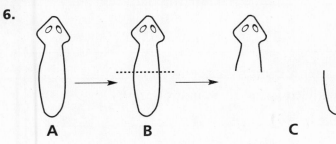

A   B   C

7. How is regeneration adaptive for survival in planarians?

_____

_____

_____

_____

Complete the table by checking the correct column for each description.

Description	Planarian	Tapeworm	Fluke
8. Lives parasitically within a host			
9. Body made up of proglottids			
10. Body is thin and solid			
11. Free-living in aquatic environments			
12. Attaches to host's intestine with scolex			
13. Extends a pharnyx to suck up food			
14. May live in host's blood vessels			

Chapter 26 **Sponges, Cnidarians, Flatworms, and Roundworms,** *continued*

In your textbook, read about roundworms.

Answer the following questions.

1. What impact do parasitic roundworms have on other organisms?

   _____

   _____

2. List three ways in which roundworms differ from flatworms.

   _____

   _____

3. What accounts for the characteristic wriggling movement of roundworms?

   _____

   _____

4. What are four of the most common parasitic roundworms that infect humans?

   _____

   _____

5. Can roundworms cause plant diseases? Explain.

   _____

   _____

6. What parts of plants are most commonly susceptible to parasitic roundworms?

   _____

   _____

Below are two medical reports. After reading each report, give a preliminary diagnosis of what you think might be causing the problem.

7.
┌─────────────────────────────────┐
│   **MEDICAL REPORT**   │
│   │
│ Patient is an active 5-year-old girl. │
│ Complains about a constant itching │
│ around the anal area, especially at │
│ night.   │
│   │
│ Preliminary Diagnosis: │
│   │
│ _____ │
└─────────────────────────────────┘

8.
┌─────────────────────────────────┐
│   **MEDICAL REPORT**   │
│   │
│ Patient is a 29-year-old female Peace │
│ Corps volunteer. Lived with remote │
│ tribe whose primary food is pigs. │
│ Complains of muscle pain.   │
│   │
│ Preliminary Diagnosis: │
│   │
│ _____ │
└─────────────────────────────────┘

Chapter 27
Mollusks and Segmented Worms

In your textbook, read about what a mollusk is.

The phylum *Mollusca* is a very diverse group of animals. Complete the table by checking the correct column for each characteristic.

Characteristic	Exhibited In:	
	All Mollusks	**Some Mollusks**
1. Possess a hard, external shell		
2. Bilaterally symmetrical		
3. Have a mantle		
4. Live on land		
5. Digestive tract has two openings.		
6. Inhabit aquatic environments		
7. Share similar developmental patterns		
8. Are slow-moving		
9. Have a coelom		

In your textbook, read about diversity of mollusks.

Identify each mollusk shown below. Write the name of the class to which it belongs and briefly describe where it lives.

10.

11.

12.

_____

_____

_____

_____

Chapter 27 **Mollusks and Segmented Worms,** *continued*

In your textbook, read about a mollusk's body systems and the diversity of mollusks.

Complete each statement.

13. Gastropods have either a(n) _____ shell or _____ shell.

14. Most mollusks have a(n) _____ circulatory system in which blood flows through

_____ into open _____ around tissues and organs.

15. Most mollusks use _____ for respiration, while a garden slug uses a primitive

_____ for gas exchange.

16. _____ are involved in removing wastes from a mollusk's body.

17. Fertilization in most aquatic mollusks takes place _____ .

For each statement below, write <u>true</u> or <u>false</u>.

_____ **18.** All shelled gastropods are predators.

_____ **19.** When a snail is disturbed, it pulls its body inside its shell for protection.

_____ **20.** Without a shell, terrestrial slugs and sea slugs (nudibranchs) have no protection against predators.

_____ **21.** The two shells of bivalve mollusks are held together by the mantle.

Determine whether each of the statements below best describes bivalves, gastropods, or both.

_____ **22.** Nearly all feed by filtering particles from the water around them.

_____ **23.** Most have a large muscular foot.

_____ **24.** They use a radula for feeding.

_____ **25.** Water flows through their bodies via well-developed incurrent and excurrent siphons.

Chapter 27 **Mollusks and Segmented Worms,** continued

Section 27.1 Mollusks, continued

In your textbook, read about cephalopods.

Answer the following questions.

26. Describe the "head-foot" region of a cephalopod.

_____

_____

_____

27. What would you expect to find on the interior surfaces of a squid's many arms?

_____

28. How does the intelligence of an octopus compare to that of a clam?

_____

_____

_____

Using what you know about the three major classes of mollusks, complete the chart below by checking the correct column(s) for each characteristic.

Characteristics	Type of Mollusk		
	Gastropods	**Bivalves**	**Cephalopods**
29. Intelligent, with a well-developed nervous system			
30. Have no distinct head			
31. Have an open circulatory system			
32. External shells present in some species			
33. All species are carnivorous predators.			
34. Use a radula in feeding			
35. All use gills for both respiration and food collection.			
36. Bite prey with a beak			

Chapter 27 Mollusks and
Segmented Worms, *continued*

In your textbook, read about segmented worms, including the Inside Story about earthworms.

Use each of the terms below just once to complete the passage:

Annelida	bristleworms	earthworms	muscles
parapodia	segments	setae	

Members of the phylum **(1)** _____ all have bodies made up of multiple

(2) _____ . Each segment has its own **(3)** _____ that function to lengthen

and shorten the worm's body. When present, bristlelike **(4)** _____ act as anchors while the

worm is moving along. In **(5)** _____ , each segment has a pair of **(6)** _____ .

The most familiar annelids are probably **(7)** _____ .

Determine if the statement is true. If it is not, rewrite the italicized part to make it true.

8. Earthworms have a *mouth with tiny teeth* in which food particles are ground up before entering

the digestive tract. _____

9. Blood is pumped throughout an earthworm's closed circulatory system by *an elongated,*

four-chambered heart. _____

10. Some body segments in annelids are *specialized for reproduction.* _____

**Below are the field notes of a biologist studying several newly collected annelid worms. Write the
type of annelid—<u>earthworm</u>, <u>bristleworm</u>, or <u>leech</u>—being described.**

11. Collected in rain forest of Papua, New Guinea;
very active; flattened, with 32 body segments;
has suckers on the ends of its body; no setae

Type of annelid: _____

12. Found crawling over corals on a reef;
contains only eggs; no male reproductive
organs; well-developed parapodia

Type of annelid: _____

13. Uncovered in top layer of moist soil;
body has minute setae on ventral
surface of each segment;
hermaphroditic

Type of annelid: _____

REINFORCEMENT AND STUDY GUIDE

Chapter 28 Arthropods

In your textbook, read about what an arthropod is and exoskeletons.

Answer the following questions.

1. What is the most distinguishing arthropod characteristic?

_____

2. Explain the advantage of having appendages with joints.

_____

_____

_____

3. List three functions of an arthropod exoskeleton.

_____

_____

_____

In your textbook, read about molting, segmentation, and gas exchange.

Complete each statement.

4. Prior to molting, a new exoskeleton forms _____ the old one.

5. Many arthropods have three distinct body sections: a(n) _____ ,

a(n) _____ , and a(n) _____ .

6. In arthropods that have a _____ , the head and thorax are fused.

Complete the table by checking the correct column to indicate the respiratory structure you would expect to find in each example.

Example	Type of Respiratory Structure		
	Book Lungs	**Gills**	**Tracheal Tubes**
7. freshwater crayfish			
8. tarantula			
9. hissing cockroach			
10. swallowtail butterfly			

Chapter 28 Arthropods, *continued*

In your textbook, read about arthropods' senses, body systems, and reproduction.

Identify the following as characteristics of either simple or compound eyes.

_____ **11.** have multiple lenses

_____ **12.** well-adapted for detecting slight movements

_____ **13.** have a single, focusing-type lens

_____ **14.** produce an image made up of thousands of parts

Determine if the statement is true. If it is not, rewrite the italicized part to make it true.

15. Animals produce pheromones, or *low frequency sounds*, that affect the behavior of others.

_____

16. In many arthropods, large, fused ganglia act as nervous system control centers *for the entire body*.

_____

17. Arthropods have an open circulatory system, in which blood leaves vessels and *comes in direct contact*

with body tissues. _____

18. *Respiration* occurs in arthropods via the Malpighian tubules. _____

19. During parthenogenesis, *fertilized eggs* develop into offspring. _____

In your textbook, read about arthropod origins.

Answer the following questions.

20. What are the major reasons for the widespread success of arthropods?

_____

_____

21. From what animal group did arthropods probably evolve?

_____

22. List three adaptations that have evolved in arthropods.

_____

_____

_____

Chapter 28 Arthropods, continued

Section 28.2 Diversity of Arthropods

In your textbook, read about arachnids.

Circle the letter of the response that best completes the statement.

1. An animal that is *not* a member of the class Arachnida is

  a. a spider.   **b.** a deer tick.   **c.** a walking stick.   **d.** a dust mite.

2. In spiders, chelicerae are highly modified appendages that are adapted for

  a. holding food and injecting poison.   **b.** spinning silk and weaving webs.

  c. chewing food.   **d.** mating and reproduction.

3. The appendages of a spider that function as sense organs are

  a. its chelicerae.   **b.** its pedipalps.   **c.** its legs.   **d.** its spinnerets.

4. After catching their prey and injecting it with poison, spiders

  a. eat the prey whole.

  b. lay their eggs in the prey.

  c. chew the prey into small pieces.

  d. suck up the prey's contents, which have been liquified with enzymes.

5. In ticks and mites, the head, thorax, and abdomen

  a. are absent.   **b.** are well-defined.

  c. are fused into one section.   **d.** are all the same size.

6. The fact that horseshoe crabs have remained relatively unchanged for 500 million years indicates that

  a. natural selection has not taken place.   **b.** they must reproduce by parthenogenesis.

  c. they have very little genetic diversity.   **d.** their environment has changed very little.

In your textbook, read about crustaceans, centipedes, and millipedes.

Determine if each statement is <u>true</u> or <u>false</u>.

_____ **7.** Having compound eyes on movable stalks is an advantage for aquatic crustaceans whose potential predators could attack from almost any direction.

_____ **8.** The legs of most crustaceans are unspecialized and used only for walking.

_____ **9.** You might be more likely to see pill bugs moving around out in the open on a rainy day than on a sunny one.

_____ **10.** Both centipedes and millipedes have book lungs for gas exchange.

Chapter 28 **Arthropods,** continued

In your textbook, read about insects.

Using the choices below, label the diagram of a honeybee.

antennae   compound eye   legs   mandibles   spiracles   wings

11. _____

12. _____

13. _____

14. _____

15. _____

16. _____

Complete the table by checking the correct column for each statement.

Description	Type of Metamorphosis	
	Complete	Incomplete
17. Insect begins life as a fertilized egg.		
18. Larva hatches from an egg.		
19. Nymph repeatedly molts and increases in size.		
20. Nymph hatches from an egg.		
21. Pupa undergoes changes while encased in cocoon.		
22. Adults and young usually eat the same food.		
23. Adults are the only sexually mature form.		

REINFORCEMENT AND STUDY GUIDE

Chapter 29 Echinoderms and Invertebrate Chordates

In your textbook, read about echinoderms' internal skeleton, radial symmetry, and the water vascular system.

Answer the following questions.

1. Describe the "spiny skin" that is a characteristic of echinoderms.

_____

_____

2. In what way is being radially symmetrical an advantage for adult echinoderms?

_____

_____

_____

_____

For each item in Column A, write the letter of the matching item in Column B.

Column A	Column B
_____ **3.** Has a flattened, immovable endoskeleton made up of fused plates	**a.** brittle star
_____ **4.** Has thin, flexible rays made up of small, overlapping, calcified plates	**b.** sea star
_____ **5.** Has a flexible endoskeleton divided into rather long, tapering rays	**c.** sand dollar
_____ **6.** Has tiny, calcified plates embedded in fleshy skin	**d.** sea lily
_____ **7.** Has feathery, branching rays made up of tiny, calcified plates	**e.** sea cucumber

Complete the following sentences.

8. Tube feet are part of an echinoderm's _____ _____ _____ , which is involved not only in locomotion, but also in _____ _____ , _____ , and food collecting.

9. In a sea star, water enters and exits the water vascular system through a structure called the _____ , a sievelike, disc-shaped opening on the _____ side of the body.

In your textbook, read about sea star structure, echinoderm larvae, nutrition, nervous systems, and origins.

Label this drawing of a sea star and of a cross section of one of its rays. Use these choices:

| ampulla | eyespot | madreporite | pedicellariae | tube foot |

10. _____

11. _____

12. _____

13. _____

14. _____

Identify each of the following as describing either larva or an adult echinoderm.

_____ **15.** free-swimming   _____ **16.** bilaterally symmetrical

_____ **17.** radially symmetrical   _____ **18.** moves with tube feet

Determine if each of the following statements is <u>true</u> or <u>false</u>.

_____ **19.** If a sea urchin population underwent a population explosion, you might expect to see a rapid decline in the amount of algal life in the area.

_____ **20.** Sea stars and brittle stars both eat suspended organic particles.

_____ **21.** Most echinoderms have highly developed sense organs.

_____ **22.** The fact that echinoderms have bilaterally symmetrical larvae and deuterostome development is strong evidence that they are most closely related to chordates.

Chapter 29 **Echinoderms and Invertebrate Chordates,** *continued*

In your textbook, read about the diversity of echinoderms.

Answer the following questions.

23. List the five classes of living echinoderms and the types of animals in each class.

_____

_____

_____

24. How is the ability to regenerate lost body parts adaptive for most echinoderms?

_____

_____

_____

Complete the table by checking the column(s) that best fit(s) each description.

Description	Asteroidea	Ophiuroidea	Echinoidea	Holothuroidea	Crinoidea
25. Have multiple rays					
26. May rupture and release internal organs when threatened					
27. Some members of the class are sessile					
28. Burrow into rock or sand					
29. Use mucus-coated tentacles for feeding					
30. Some members of the class can actively swim from place to place					
31. Use rays, not tube feet, for locomotion					
32. The most inflexible type of echinoderm					
33. Use long, feathery arms to trap food particles drifting past					
34. Eat bivalves and other small animals					

In your textbook, read about invertebrate chordates.

Complete the following sentences.

1. At some time in their life, all chordates possess a _____ , a dorsal hollow _____ _____ , _____ _____ , and muscle blocks.

2. During your early development, your notochord became your _____ , and your gill slits disappeared.

3. The _____ _____ is derived from the _____ portion of the dorsal nerve cord, whereas the _____ is derived from the anterior portion.

4. At some time during their lives, all chordates have a muscular _____ .

In your textbook, read about tunicates and lancelets.

Trace the path of water through a tunicate, starting with water entering the animal's body, by numbering the following statements from 1 to 5.

_____ **5.** Water leaves the pharynx region.

_____ **6.** Water passes through the gill slits, which filter food out of the water.

_____ **7.** Water is drawn into the body through the incurrent siphon.

_____ **8.** Water passes out of the body via the excurrent siphon.

_____ **9.** Water enters the pharynx, where the gill slits are located.

Complete the table by checking the correct column(s) for each description.

Description	Tunicates	Lancelets
10. Only larval forms have a tail		
11. Are filter feeders		
12. Retain all chordate traits throughout life		
13. Blood flow is continually reversed in the adult body		
14. Capable of actively swimming as adults		

BioDigest 8 Invertebrates

In your textbook, read about invertebrates.

Study the definitions on the next page and write the terms in the appropriate spaces in the cross-word puzzle below. All terms are important in the Biodigest.

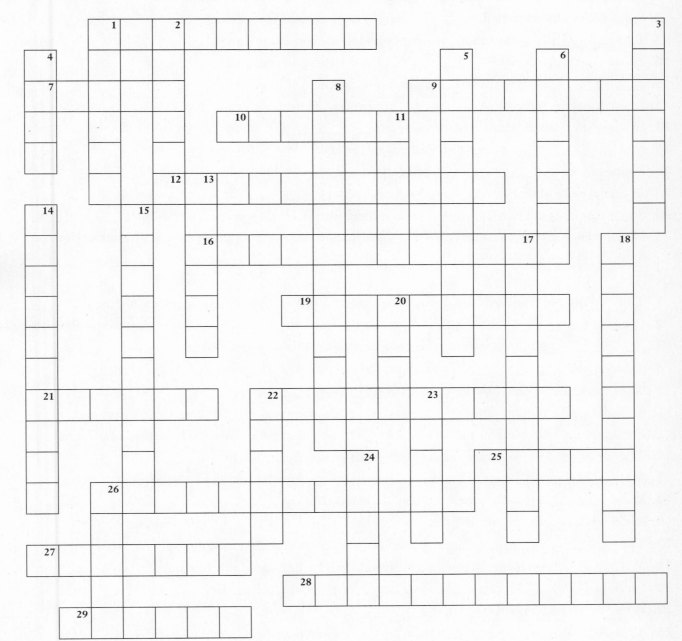

BioDigest 8 **Invertebrates,** *continued*

ACROSS

1. In a animal with _____ symmetry, the right and left sides are mirrors of each other.

7. An echinoderm has an inner skeleton; its _____ covering is called the epidermis.

9. Bivalves, gastropods, and cephalopods are _____ .

10. Some echinoderms have long _____ that are used for locomotion.

12. The _____ have radial symmetry and a water vascular system.

16. Because arthropods have _____ , fossil arthropods are frequently found.

19. _____ such as planaria have no body cavity.

21. In earthworms, internal _____ are suspended from the mesoderm.

22. In some invertebrates, an exoskeleton offers _____ and support for internal tissues.

25. A(n) _____ belongs to the phylum Cnidaria.

26. Sponges have a(n) _____ body shape.

27. In earthworms and other segmented worms, each _____ has its own muscles.

28. Some segments in chordates have been modified into stacked layers called (2 words) _____ .

29. In arthropods like grasshoppers, a set of jointed appendages called antennae are adapted to give the insect acute _____ .

DOWN

1. The mouthparts of an arthropod may be adapted for such things as chewing, lapping, or _____ .

2. Echinoderm _____ have bilateral symmetry, which suggests a close relationship to the chordates.

3. _____ go through metamorphosis during their life cycles.

4. A dorsal nerve _____ is a hollow, fluid-filled canal lying above the notochord.

5. Setae, or small bristles, help earthworms with _____ .

6. Mesoderm differentiates into _____ , circulatory vessels, and reproductive organs.

8. Echinoderms have a supporting _____ , which is inside of the body instead of outside.

11. The _____ of a mollusk such as a clam is secreted by the mantle.

13. A(n) _____ functions as a watery skeleton against which muscles can work.

14. Many _____ are parasitic, such as *Trichinella*.

15. Arthropods are characterized by having a wide variety of _____ for feeding.

17. The _____ of a cnidarian is found in a highly specialized stinging cell.

18. _____ are made up of two cell layers and have only one body opening.

20. Special _____ feet enable sea stars to move from place to place.

22. Water enters a sponge through _____ .

23. A jellyfish, a(n) _____ , and an anemone are types of cnidarians.

24. Bivalves acquire food by filtering water through their _____ .

26. A radula is a tonguelike organ used by snails to scrape _____ from surfaces.

Copyright © Glencoe/McGraw-Hill, a division of The McGraw-Hill Companies, Inc.

Chapter
30 Fishes and Amphibians

In your textbook, read about what is a fish.

Complete each statement.

1. All vertebrates are in the phylum _____ , and fish, amphibians, reptiles, birds, and mammals are in the subphylum _____ .

2. Vertebrates are bilaterally symmetrical, coelomate animals with endoskeletons, closed _____ systems, complex _____ , and efficient _____ systems.

3. If you compared the number of fish species to the number of all other vertebrate species combined, there would be more species of _____ .

Complete the table below to compare the three different kinds of fishes.

Class	Kind of Fish	Jaws?	Skeleton	Fertilization
4. _____	Lamprey and Hagfish	**5.** _____	**6.** _____	**7.** _____
Chondrichthyes	**8.** _____	**9.** _____	Cartilage	**10.** _____
11. _____	**12.** _____	Yes	**13.** _____	External and Internal

Answer the following questions.

14. How does a fish breathe through its gills?

_____

_____

_____

15. What two adaptations of cartilaginous and bony fishes help them to locate food?

_____

_____

_____

Copyright © Glencoe/McGraw-Hill, a division of The McGraw-Hill Companies, Inc.

Chapter 30 **Fishes and Amphibians,** continued

In your textbook, read about bony fishes.

Determine if the statement is true. If it is not, rewrite the italicized part to make it true.

16. While spawning, a female bony fish may lay *millions of eggs* to be fertilized externally by the male, but only a few will survive. _____

17. The development of *bone* was an important event in the evolution of vertebrates because it eventually allowed them to move onto land and support their body weight. _____

18. The backbone, comprised of separate *gills*, was a major evolutionary event for fishes because it provided support as well as flexibility, which helped to propel them through the water. _____

19. The *swim bladder*, an organ found in bony fishes, allows fish to control their depth in water.

_____

In your textbook, read about origins of fishes.

Examine the phylogenetic tree below. Then answer the question that follows.

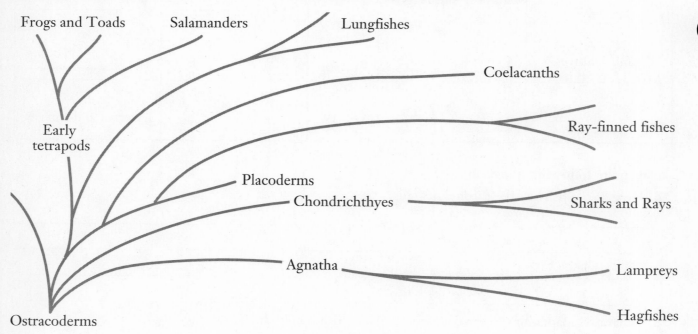

20. Which group of fishes do you think are most closely related to ancestral amphibians? Why?

_____

_____

_____

Chapter 30 **Fishes and Amphibians,** *continued*

Section 30.2 Amphibians

In your textbook, read about what is an amphibian.

Answer the following questions.

1. What three orders make up the class Amphibia?

_____

_____

_____

2. Why do amphibian eggs need to be laid in water?

_____

_____

_____

3. Where does an amphibian heart pump oxygen-rich blood, and where does it pump oxygen-poor blood?

_____

_____

_____

_____

For each item in Column A, write the letter of the matching item in Column B.

Column A	Column B
_____ **4.** Adult frogs and toads have legs, lungs, and a _____ heart.	**a.** two-chambered
_____ **5.** Tadpoles have gills, fins, and a _____ heart.	**b.** three-chambered
_____ **6.** Amphibians are _____ , animals whose body temperature changes with the temperature of their surroundings.	**c.** skin
_____ **7.** Fertilized amphibian eggs hatch into _____ during the aquatic phase of their life.	**d.** tadpoles
_____ **8.** Some salamanders have no lungs and breathe through their _____ .	**e.** ectotherms

Name _____ Date _____ Class _____

Chapter
30 **Fishes and Amphibians,** continued

Reinforcement and Study Guide

*Section 30.2 Amphibians,
continued*

In your textbook, read about the characteristics and diversity of amphibians.

Circle the letter of the response that best completes the statement.

9. Early amphibians needed large amounts of food and oxygen to
   a. walk on land.   **b.** breathe on land.
   c. become dormant in cold weather.   **d.** all of these.

10. In many amphibians, the most important organ for gas exchange is the
    a. blood.   **b.** skin.   **c.** lungs.   **d.** circulatory system.

11. Many frogs and toads use _____ as a defense against predators.
    a. toxins   **b.** electricity
    c. sharp claws   **d.** all of these

12. Frogs and toads have sound-producing bands of tissues in their throat called
    a. tongues.   **b.** vocal cords.
    c. vocal tissue.   **d.** none of these.

13. Salamanders are unlike frogs and toads because they have
    a. long, slender bodies.   **b.** tails.
    c. necks.   **d.** all of these.

14. Caecilians are amphibians that have no
    a. eyes.   **b.** skin.
    c. limbs.   **d.** heart.

In your textbook, read about the origins of amphibians.

For each statement below, write <u>true</u> or <u>false</u>.

_____ 15. Ancestral amphibians appeared on Earth about the same time as ancestral fishes.

_____ 16. Amphibians probably evolved from tetrapods during the Paleozoic Era.

_____ 17. Because the climate was hot and dry when amphibians first appeared on Earth, they had to stay near water.

_____ 18. Like modern-day salamanders, early amphibians probably had legs set at right angles to the body.

_____ 19. Because amphibians were a transitional group, they never were the dominant vertebrates on land.

Chapter 31 Reptiles and Birds

In your textbook, read about what is a reptile and the amniotic egg.

Complete the following table about reptilian adaptations and their advantages by writing in the missing information in each case.

Adaptation	Advantage
1.	In crocodilians, oxygenated and deoxygenated blood kept separate; higher level of energy production
2. Thick, scaly skin	
3.	Water not necessary for fertilization
4. Legs positioned for walking and running on land	
5.	Water not necessary for reproduction; young not overly vulnerable to aquatic predators; prevents injury or dehydration of embryo

Label the diagram below, using these choices:

albumen   allantois   amnion   chorion   embryo   shell   yolk sac

6. _____

7. _____

8. _____

9. _____

10. _____

11. _____

12. _____

Chapter 31 **Reptiles and Birds,** *continued*

Section 31.1 Reptiles,
continued

In your textbook, read about the diversity of reptiles and the origins of reptiles.

Complete the chart by checking the correct column(s) for each characteristic.

Characteristic	Snakes	Lizards	Turtles	Crocodiles
13. Guard their nests against predators				
14. Possess shells				
15. Use tongue and Jacobsen's organ for smelling				
16. Kill prey by drowning it				
17. Lack limbs				
18. Have vertebrae and ribs fused to a carapace				
19. Some change color dramatically				
20. Lack teeth				
21. Some inject venom with fangs				
22. Some are aquatic				
23. Are primarily insect eaters				
24. Include marine species that migrate				

Complete each sentence.

25. During the Mesozoic era, _____ were the most abundant land vertebrates.

26. Snakes and lizards are descended from early _____ _____ , which in turn were descended from _____ .

27. _____ are probably the modern, living descendants of some type of dinosaur.

Chapter 31 Reptiles and Birds, *continued*

In your textbook, read about what is a bird.

Answer the following questions.

1. From what type of animal are birds thought to have evolved?

_____

2. List three physical features of birds that link them to reptilian ancestors.

_____

3. Besides making flight possible, what other functions do feathers serve?

_____

4. By what process are old feathers replaced?

_____

In your textbook, read about how birds are adapted for flight.

Determine if the statement is true. If it is not, rewrite the italicized part to make it true.

5. A bird's sternum is *the point of attachment for its flight muscles.*

_____

6. Being endothermic, birds have a body temperature that *fluctuates with environmental temperature.*

_____

7. Because of its energy requirements, you might expect a bird to eat *less* than a reptile of comparable size.

_____

8. Hollow bones, horny beaks, and a lack of teeth are all adaptations that make birds *more efficient predators.*

_____

9. Birds grind up their food in a muscular *gizzard.*

_____

10. The air inside a bird's lungs always has a fairly high *carbon dioxide* content, which makes for efficient gas exchange.

_____

11. For a bird such as a goose or a duck, down feathers are the key to its superior *waterproofing.*

_____

Chapter 31 **Reptiles and Birds,** *continued*

In your textbook, read about the diversity of birds.

For each item in Column A, write the letter of the matching item in Column B.

	Column A	Column B

_____ **12.** long beak that is used for dipping into flowers   **a.** owl
to obtain nectar

_____ **13.** wings and feet modified for swimming; body   **b.** pelican
surrounded with a thick layer of insulating fat

_____ **14.** short, stout beak that is adapted to cracking   **c.** hummingbird
seeds

_____ **15.** feathered legs and feet that make it easier to   **d.** penguin
walk in the snow

_____ **16.** huge beak with a pouch that is used as a net   **e.** ptarmigan
for capturing fish

_____ **17.** large eyes, an acute sense of hearing, and sharp   **f.** goldfinch
claws; adapted for nocturnal predation

In your textbook, read about the origins of birds.

Complete each statement.

18. The fossil record of birds is incomplete because bird skeletons are _____ and

_____ .

19. Unlike modern birds, _____ had _____ , a long _____ ,

and _____ _____ _____ .

20. Scientists hypothesize that _____ used its feathers for _____ ,

_____ , or _____ _____ , rather than for flight.

Chapter 32 Mammals

In your textbook, read about what is a mammal, and mammalian hair.

Answer the following questions.

1. Why are mammals able to live in almost every possible environment on Earth?

   _____

   _____

2. How do sweat glands help regulate body temperature?

   _____

   _____

   _____

Complete the table by checking the column that best fits each example.

	Serves As:		
Example	**Camouflage**	**Defense**	**Warning**
3. The striped fur of a tiger			
4. The sharp quills of a porcupine			
5. A skunk's black-and-white striped fur			
6. The white winter coat of an arctic hare			
7. The white hair patch on a pronghorn			

In your textbook, read about how mammals nurse their young, and about respiration and circulation.

Complete each statement.

8. Female mammals feed their young with milk produced by _____ _____ .

9. In addition to milk and sweat, the glands of mammals produce _____ ,

   _____ _____ , and _____ .

10. The milk of mammals is rich in _____ , sugars, _____ , minerals, and

    _____ .

11. A mammal's muscular _____ expands the _____ _____ bringing air

    into the lungs with each breath.

12. Like birds, mammals have _____ hearts in which _____ _____

    is kept entirely separate from _____ _____ .

Chapter 32   Mammals, *continued*

Section 32.1 Mammal Characteristics,
continued

In your textbook, read about mammalian teeth, limbs, and learning.

Determine if the statement is <u>true</u> or <u>false</u>.

_____ **13.** The size and shape of a mammal's teeth can give valuable clues about its diet.

_____ **14.** Plant-eaters such as horses and cows have well-developed canine teeth for piercing food.

_____ **15.** The teeth of mammals are generally more uniform than the teeth of fishes and reptiles.

_____ **16.** By chewing their cud and then swallowing it, some mammals help bacteria break down the cellulose in their food.

_____ **17.** Mammalian limbs are adapted for a variety of methods of food gathering.

_____ **18.** Moles use their opposable thumbs to grasp objects.

_____ **19.** One reason mammals are successful is that they guard their young and teach them survival skills.

_____ **20.** Complex nervous systems and highly-developed brains make it possible for many kinds of mammals to learn.

Circle the letter of the response that best completes the statement.

21. Premolars and molars are used for
    a. shearing.   **b.** crushing.   **c.** grinding.   **d.** all of these.

22. Cud chewing is an adaptation found in
    a. bears and other omnivores.   **b.** tigers and other carnivores.
    c. many hoofed mammals.   **d.** all of these.

23. The limbs of antelopes are characterized by
    a. greatly elongated finger bones.   **b.** strong, slender bones.
    c. short bones and large claws.   **d.** none of these.

24. Chimpanzees are intelligent enough to
    a. use tools.   **b.** use sign language.
    c. work machines.   **d.** all of these.

Chapter 32 **Mammals,** *continued*

In your textbook, read about placental mammals, mammals with a pouch, and egg-laying mammals.

Answer the following questions.

1. What is a placental mammal?

_____

_____

2. What is the relationship between body size and gestation period in placental mammals?

_____

3. Why are most marsupials found only in and around Australia?

_____

_____

_____

4. What characteristic sets monotremes apart from all other mammals?

_____

_____

_____

Complete the table by checking the correct column(s) for each characteristic.

Characteristic	Type of Mammal		
	Placental	**Marsupial**	**Monotreme**
5. Give birth to young			
6. Young nourished by a placenta during the entire development period			
7. Have a permanent pouch on abdomen			
8. Produce milk in mammary glands			
9. Lay eggs			
10. Include echidnas and duck-billed platypuses			
11. Have hair			
12. Comprise about 95 percent of all mammals			
13. Exhibit parental care			

Chapter 32 **Mammals,** *continued*

In your textbook, read about the origins of mammals.

Use each of the terms below just once to complete the passage.

Cenozoic	climate	dinosaurs	insect-eating
mammals	Pangaea	reptiles	therapsids

Roughly 200 million years ago, the first **(14)** _____ began roaming the earth. Most were small **(15)** _____ descendants of **(16)** _____ , animals that had characteristics in common with both mammals and **(17)** _____ . The breakup of **(18)** _____ , the sudden disappearance of the **(19)** _____ , and a changing **(20)** _____ provided early mammals with new food sources and habitats. During the **(21)** _____ era, mammals diversified greatly into the many species inhabiting Earth today.

Examine the phylogenetic tree below. Then answer the questions that follow.

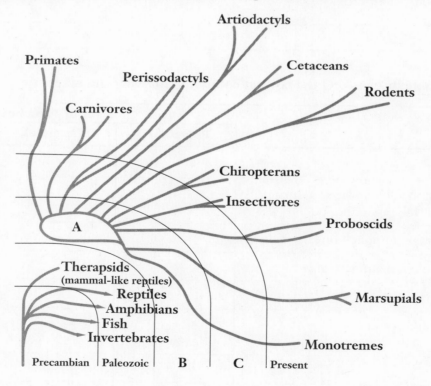

22. What group of animals is represented by the letter A above? _____

23. What era is represented by the letter B? _____

24. What era is represented by the letter C? _____

REINFORCEMENT AND STUDY GUIDE

Chapter
33 Animal Behavior

Section 33.1 Innate Behavior

In your textbook, read about what behavior is, inherited behavior, automatic responses to stimuli, and instinctive behavior.

Answer the following questions.

1. What is meant by animal behavior?

_____

_____

2. How is behavior adaptive?

_____

_____

3. Explain the relationship between innate behaviors and genetics.

_____

_____

_____

4. What is an instinct?

_____

Identify each of the following as being either a reflex or an instinct.

_____ **5.** You leap up after sitting down in shorts on a hot car seat.

_____ **6.** A sea turtle returns to the beach where she was hatched, in order to lay her eggs.

_____ **7.** A giant clam closes its shell when a shadow falls across it.

_____ **8.** A spider spins a complex, circular web.

In your textbook, read about courtship behavior and territoriality.

Determine if the following statements are <u>true</u> or <u>false</u>.

_____ **9.** Courtship behavior is something only male animals can instinctively perform.

_____ **10.** Courtship behavior is adaptive because it ensures that members of the same species can recognize each other and mate.

_____ **11.** A territory is a physical space that one animal defends against all other species of animals.

_____ **12.** Setting up territories reduces conflicts between members of the same species.

Chapter 33 Animal Behavior, *continued*

In your textbook, read about aggressive behavior, submission, and behavior resulting from internal and external cues.

Below are excerpts from the field notebook of a behavorial biologist. Identify the behavioral phenomenon being described in each case.

13.

> **Field Notes**
>
> A large male baboon stares at another male and then suddenly "yawns" to reveal his long, sharp fangs.
>
> **Behavior Exhibited:**
>
> _____

14.

> **Field Notes**
>
> When a herd of elephants arrives at a waterhole, the oldest female drinks first, followed by three females with calves, and finally a young male.
>
> **Behavior Exhibited:**
>
> _____

15.

> **Field Notes**
>
> After fighting briefly with an older pack member, a young wolf stops fighting and rolls onto her back with her tail tucked between her legs and her eyes averted.
>
> **Behavior Exhibited:**
>
> _____

16.

> **Field Notes**
>
> Large numbers of monarch butterflies fly south to roost in the winter.
>
> **Behavior Exhibited:**
>
> _____

Complete the following sentences.

17. The type of dominance hierarchy formed by chickens is called a(n) _____ _____ .

18. A cycle of behavior that occurs roughly every 24 hours is known as a(n) _____

_____ .

19. Some animals use the positions of the _____ _____ _____

to navigate. Others may use _____ clues or Earth's _____

_____ .

20. _____ is similar to hibernation, in that metabolic activity _____

in response to internal and external cues.

Chapter 33 Animal Behavior, continued

In your textbook, read about learned behavior.

Answer the following questions.

1. What is learned behavior?

_____

_____

2. What is a major advantage of being able to learn?

_____

_____

_____

Complete the table by checking the correct column for each example.

Example	Type of Behavior	
	Learned	**Innate**
3. A dog catching a Frisbee		
4. A dog scent-marking a tree with urine		
5. A parrot saying "Polly want a cracker"		
6. A young lioness stalking prey with her mother		
7. A woodchuck going underground to hibernate		

In your textbook, read about habituation, imprinting, and learning by trial and error.

For each item in Column A, write the letter of the matching item in Column B.

Column A	Column B
8. You stay with relatives who have a clock that chimes every hour. The first two nights, the chimes keep you awake, but after that you no longer notice them.	**a.** imprinting
9. A boy receives a day-old duckling as gift. It soon follows the boy wherever he goes.	**b.** trial-and-error learning
10. A young woman takes up archery. At first, her arrows don't hit the target, but after a week of practice, she is hitting the bull's eye fifty percent of the time.	**c.** habituation

_____ **8.**

_____ **9.**

_____ **10.**

In your textbook, read about conditioning and insight.

Determine if the statement is true. If it is not, rewrite the italicized part to make it true.

11. Learning by *repeating something over and over* is known as conditioning. _____

12. In Pavlov's conditioning experiments, the *innate reflex of salivating* was the stimulus that the dogs

learned to associate with food. _____

13. Once conditioned, Pavlov's dogs would salivate at the sound of the bell *even when no food was present.*

_____

14. A child figuring out how to use a chair to reach a cookie jar is an example of *trial and error.*

_____

15. Insight is learning in which an animal uses *previous experience* to respond to a new situation.

_____

In your textbook, read about the role of communication.

Use each of the terms below just once to complete the passage.

behavior	communication	information	innate	language
meanings	odors	pheromones	sounds	symbols

Through various forms of **(16)** _____ , animals exchange **(17)** _____

that affects their **(18)** _____ . Animals can communicate with visual signals, by touching

each other, and by producing **(19)** _____ , some of which can be heard over great dis-

tances. Communicating with **(20)** _____ is another strategy; **(21)** _____ are

species-specific odor chemicals that can have a powerful effect on behavior. Some types of communication

involve both **(22)** _____ and learned behavior. Human **(23)** _____ has

evolved as a way of communicating with written and spoken **(24)** _____ that have specific

(25) _____ .

BioDigest 9 Vertebrates

In your textbook, read about fishes, amphibians, reptiles, birds, and mammals.

FISHES

Complete the chart by checking the correct column(s) for each characteristic of fishes.

Adaptation	Jawless	Cartilaginous	Bony
1. Jaws			
2. Gills			
3. Lateral line system			
4. Paired fins			
5. Skeleton made of cartilage			
6. Swim bladder			

AMPHIBIANS

Complete the following sentences.

7. Amphibians are _____ , which means that their body temperature depends upon

the temperature of their surroundings. These vertebrates also carry out gas exchange through

their _____ . Amphibians live on _____ but reproduce in

_____ . Almost all amphibians go through _____ , a radical

change between the form of the young and the form of the adult.

REPTILES

**Complete the table by describing the advantages that reptiles have because of certain adaptations.
List one advantage for each adaptation.**

Adaptation	Advantage
8. Scaly skin	
9. Amniotic egg	

BioDigest
9   **Vertebrates,** continued

BIRDS

Flight affects almost every system in birds. Explain the flight adaptations in each system listed here.

System	Adaptation
10. Bones	
11. Respiration	
12. Body covering	
13. Legs	
14. Wings	

MAMMALS

Various adaptations of mammals serve certain functions. In the space provided, write the letter of the adaptations that perform the function. Any letter may be used more than once.

Function	Adaptation
15. protection from low temperatures	**a.** hair
	b. sweat glands
16. protection from high temperatures	**c.** four-chambered heart
	d. diaphragm
17. feeding young	**e.** canine teeth
	f. mammary glands
18. stabbing or holding food	**g.** small ears
	h. body fat
19. grinding or chewing food	**i.** molars and premolars
	j. hibernation
20. providing large amounts of oxygen	**k.** estivation

Copyright © Glencoe/McGraw-Hill, a division of The McGraw-Hill Companies, Inc.

Chapter 34 Protection, Support, and Locomotion

Section 34.1 Skin: The Body's Protection

In your textbook, read about the structure and function of the skin.

Complete the table by checking the correct column for each description.

Description	Epidermis	Dermis
1. The outermost layer of skin		
2. Contains connective tissue, glands, and muscles		
3. The thicker, inner layer of skin		
4. Partly composed of dead, keratin-containing cells		
5. Contains pigmented cells that protect against the sun's rays		
6. Hair follicles grow out of this layer		
7. Site of continual mitotic cell divisions		
8. Richly supplied with blood vessels and nerves		

Answer the following questions.

9. Describe the change that takes place in your skin when you get a suntan.

_____

_____

_____

_____

10. How does skin help regulate body temperature?

_____

_____

_____

11. List three other functions of skin.

_____

_____

_____

_____

In your textbook, read about the structure of the skeletal system and joints.

Identify the following as being part of the axial or appendicular skeleton.

_____ **1.** the tarsals, metatarsals, and phalanges in your foot

_____ **2.** the seven vertebrae in your neck

_____ **3.** your rib cage

_____ **4.** the bones in your shoulder

_____ **5.** your lower jaw

_____ **6.** the humerus in your arm

For each answer below, write an appropriate question.

7. **Answer:** They are bands of connective tissue that attach muscles to bones.

Question: _____

8. **Answer:** It absorbs shocks and reduces friction between bones in a joint.

Question: _____

9. **Answer:** They connect bones to other bones.

Question: _____

10. **Answer:** One allows the bones to move back and forth; the other allows the bones to rotate.

Question: _____

In your textbook, read about the formation of bone and bone growth.

Complete each sentence.

11. In a human embryo's skeleton, _____ is gradually replaced by _____ except in a few places like the tip of the _____ .

12. Some cells in cartilage are stimulated to become _____ . They secrete a substance in which _____ _____ and other minerals are deposited.

13. Your bones increase in length near their _____ .

14. Even after you reach your full adult height, the bone-forming cells in your body will still be involved in _____ and _____ .

In your textbook, read about compact and spongy bone and skeletal system functions.

Answer the following questions.

15. If you cut through to the center of a large leg bone, what bone components (in order, from the outside in) would you encounter?

_____

_____

16. How do blood vessels and nerves reach individual bone cells in compact bone?

_____

17. What role does bone marrow play in the functioning of your circulatory system?

_____

_____

18. In what way is the skeleton a storehouse?

_____

_____

_____

In your textbook, read about growth, mineral storage, and injury and disease in bone.

Determine if the statement is <u>true</u> or <u>false</u>.

_____ **19.** Once you have finished growing, your bones no longer change.

_____ **20.** Calcium is both deposited in and removed from bones.

_____ **21.** Calcium removed from bone is rapidly excreted in the urine as an unnecessary body waste.

_____ **22.** As a person ages, his or her bone density usually decreases.

_____ **23.** Because bones in an adult's skeleton are harder than children's bones, adults are less likely to break a bone in a fall.

_____ **24.** Osteoporosis is most common in older women because they rarely include milk in their diet.

Chapter 34 Protection, Support, and Locomotion, *continued*

Section 34.3 Muscles for Locomotion

In your textbook, read about three types of muscles and skeletal muscle contraction.

Complete the table by checking the correct column for each description.

Description	Type of Muscle		
	Smooth	Skeletal	Cardiac
1. under voluntary control			
2. striated			
3. slow, prolonged contractions			
4. attached to bones			
5. found only in the heart			
6. not under voluntary control			
7. lines cavities and surrounds organs			

In your textbook, read about muscle strength and exercise.

Determine if the statement is true. If it is not, rewrite the italicized part to make it true.

8. Muscle strength depends on *the number of fibers in a muscle*.

_____

9. When oxygen is limited, *aerobic respiration* becomes a muscle's primary source for ATP.

_____

10. During anaerobic respiration, *oxygen* builds up in muscle cells.

_____

11. A drop in the amount of lactic acid in the bloodstream indicates that muscular activity has *decreased*.

_____

Chapter 35 **The Digestive and Endocrine Systems**

In your textbook, read about the functions of the digestive tract, the mouth, and the stomach.

Complete each statement.

1. The entire process of digestion involves first _____ food, then _____ it into simpler compounds, then _____ nutrients for use by body cells, and, finally, _____ wastes.

2. By chewing your food, you _____ its surface area.

3. Various enzymes play a role in _____ digestion, while the action of teeth, tongue, and muscles are involved in _____ digestion.

4. In your mouth, the enzyme _____ is released from _____ glands to begin the chemical breakdown of _____ .

5. Your _____ are adapted for cutting food, while your _____ are best suited for grinding food.

Determine if the statement is true. If it is not, rewrite the italicized part to make it true.

6. During swallowing, the epiglottis covers the *esophagus* to prevent choking.

   _____

7. Food is moved through the digestive tract by rhythmic waves of *voluntary muscle contractions* called peristalsis.

   _____

8. The churning actions of the stomach help mix the food with *pancreatic juices*.

   _____

9. Pepsin is a *protein-digesting enzyme* that only works in an acidic environment.

   _____

10. The stomach releases its contents into the small intestine *suddenly, all at once*.

    _____

Chapter 35 **The Digestive and Endocrine Systems,** *continued*

In your textbook, read about the small intestine and the large intestine.

Answer the following questions.

11. What role do the enzymes secreted by the pancreas play in the digestive process?

_____

_____

_____

12. Explain the relationship between the liver, the gallbladder, and bile.

_____

_____

_____

13. Once in the small intestine, what happens to

a. digested food?

_____

_____

b. indigestible materials?

_____

_____

_____

Complete the table by checking the correct column(s) for each function.

Function	Small Intestine	Large Intestine
14. Water is absorbed through walls.		
15. Digestion is essentially completed.		
16. Vitamin K is produced.		
17. Nutrients are absorbed by villi.		
18. Contents are moved by peristalsis.		
19. Indigestible material is collected.		
20. Bile and pancreatic juices are added.		

Chapter 35 The Digestive and Endocrine Systems, *continued*

In your textbook, read about carbohydrates, fats, and proteins.

Complete the table by checking the correct column(s) for each description.

Description	Carbohydrates	Fats	Proteins
1. the most energy-rich nutrients			
2. sugars, starches, and cellulose			
3. broken down into amino acids			
4. part of a nutritious, balanced diet			
5. normally used for building muscle, but can be used for energy			
6. broken down into glucose, fructose, and other simple sugars			
7. used to insulate the body from cold			

In your textbook, read about minerals and vitamins, water, and metabolism and calories.

Complete each statement.

8. _____ are inorganic substances that help to build tissue or take part in chemical reactions in the body.

9. Unlike minerals, _____ are organic nutrients that help to regulate body processes.

10. The two major vitamin groups are the _____ and the _____ vitamins.

11. The energy content of food is measured in _____ , each of which is equal to _____ calories.

12. Despite the claims of many fad diets, the only way to lose weight is to _____ more calories than you _____ .

In your textbook, read about control of the body and negative feedback control.

Complete each statement.

1. Internal control of the body is handled by the _____ system and the _____ system.

2. Most endocrine glands are controlled by the action of the _____ , or master gland.

3. A(n) _____ is a chemical released in one part of the body that affects another part.

4. The amount of hormone released by an endocrine gland is determined by the body's _____ for that hormone at a given time.

5. A _____ system is one in which hormones are fed back to inhibit the original signal.

6. When your body is dehydrated, the pituitary releases ADH hormone, which reduces the amount of _____ in your urine.

7. When you have just eaten and your blood glucose levels are high, your pancreas releases the hormone _____ , which signals the liver to take in glucose, thereby lowering blood glucose levels.

In your textbook, read about hormone action, adrenal hormones and stress, and other hormones.

For each item in column A, write the letter of the matching item from Column B.

Column A	Column B
_____ 8. Determines the body's food intake requirements	**a.** steroid hormones
_____ 9. Made from lipids and diffuse freely into cells through the plasma membrane	**b.** glucocorticoids and aldosterone
_____ 10. Bind to receptors embedded in the plasma membrane of the target cell.	**c.** calcitonin and parathyroid hormone
_____ 11. Produce a feeling called "adrenaline rush"	**d.** epinephrine and norepinephrine
_____ 12. Help the body prepare for stressful situations	**e.** amino acid hormones
_____ 13. Regulate calcium levels in blood	**f.** thyroxine

Chapter 36 **The Nervous System**

In your textbook, read about neurons–basic units of the nervous system.

Complete the table by filling in the missing information in each case.

Structure	Function
1.	carry impulses toward the brain and spinal cord
2. dendrites	
3. motor neurons	
4.	transmit impulses within the brain and spinal cord
5.	carry impulses away from neuron cell bodies

Order the steps in impulse transmission from 1 to 7.

_____ **6.** A wave of depolarization moves down the neuron.

_____ **7.** The Na^+/K^+ pump takes over again, pumping sodium ions out across the membrane, and pumping potassium ions in.

_____ **8.** Sodium channels in the neural membrane open.

_____ **9.** A neuron receives a stimulus.

_____ **10.** As the wave of depolarization passes, sodium channels close and potassium channels open.

_____ **11.** The neuron returns to a resting state.

_____ **12.** Sodium ions flow into the neuron, causing the inside of the neuron to become positively charged.

Chapter 36 **The Nervous System,** *continued*

Section 36.1 The Nervous System, continued

In your textbook, read about the central nervous system and the peripheral nervous system.

Label the diagram of the brain to show the cerebrum, cerebellum, and brain stem.

13. _____

14. _____

15. _____

Write the name of the part labeled above that matches each description in the table.

Description	Part
16. Includes the medulla and pons	
17. Controls conscious activities and movement	
18. Important for keeping your balance	
19. If damaged, heart rate might be affected	
20. If damaged, memory might be affected	
21. Ensures that movements are coordinated	

Complete the table by checking the correct column for each description.

	Autonomic Nervous System Division	
Description	**Sympathetic**	**Parasympathetic**
22. Controls internal activities when the body is at rest		
23. Increases breathing rate		
24. Tenses muscles		
25. Slows heart rate down		
26. Activates fight or flight response		

In your textbook, read about sensing chemicals and sensing light.

Determine if each statement is <u>true</u> or <u>false</u>.

_____ **1.** Impulses coming from sensory receptors in your nose and mouth are interpreted as odors and tastes by the cerebrum.

_____ **2.** All of your tongue's tastebuds respond equally well to all taste sensations.

_____ **3.** The lens in the eye controls the amount of light that strikes the retina.

_____ **4.** On a bright sunny day, the cones in your eyes play a greater role in your sense of sight than the rods.

_____ **5.** Only the left hemisphere of the brain is involved in the sense of sight.

_____ **6.** When you are looking at an object, each of your eyes sees the object from the same perspective.

_____ **7.** Much of what you taste depends on your sense of smell.

In your textbook, read about sensing mechanical stimulation.

Circle the letter of the response that best completes each statement.

8. Sound waves are converted into nerve impulses inside the
   a. ear canal.   **b.** cochlea.   **c.** malleus.   **d.** optic nerve.

9. If the semicircular canals in one of your ears were damaged, you might
   a. lose your ability to hear low-frequency sounds.
   b. lose your ability to coordinate your neck muscles.
   c. lose your sense of balance.
   d. lose your sense of rhythm.

10. The malleus, incus, and stapes are found in the
   a. outer ear.   **b.** eardrum.   **c.** middle ear.   **d.** inner ear.

11. Your senses of hearing and touch *both* depend on nerve impulses being generated by
   a. electrical stimulation.   **b.** sound waves.
   c. a change in temperature.   **d.** mechanical stimulation.

12. In the skin of your fingertips, you might expect to find receptors for
   a. touch.   **b.** pressure.   **c.** pain.   **d.** all of these

Chapter 36 **The Nervous System,** *continued*

In your textbook, read about how drugs act on the body, their medicinal uses, and abuse of drugs.

Answer the following questions.

1. Distinguish between a drug and a medicine.

   _____

   _____

   _____

2. What is a narcotic?

   _____

3. Compare the effect of a stimulant on the CNS with the effect of a depressant.

   _____

   _____

4. What is an addiction?

   _____

5. How does a person's body develop a tolerance for a drug?

   _____

   _____

   _____

In your textbook, read about the classes of commonly abused drugs.

Complete the table by checking the correct column for each example.

Example	Stimulant	Depressant
6. Drugs that cause an increase in heart rate		
7. Alcohol		
8. Nicotine		
9. Drugs that increase neurotransmitter levels		
10. Barbiturates		
11. Drugs that cause vasoconstriction		
12. Opiates		
13. Hallucinogens		

Chapter 37 Respiration, Circulation, and Excretion

In your textbook, read about air passageways and lungs.

Circle the letter of the choice that best completes the statement or answers the question.

1. During the process of respiration,
   a. oxygen is delivered to body cells.
   b. carbon dioxide is expelled from the body.
   c. oxygen is used in cells to produce ATP.
   d. all of these.

2. When you swallow, your epiglottis momentarily covers the top of the trachea so that
   a. you can swallow more easily.
   b. you can breathe more easily.
   c. you don't get food in your air passages.
   d. you can cough up foreign matter.

3. The cilia that line your trachea and bronchi
   a. produce dirt-trapping mucus.
   b. help in the exchange of oxygen and CO_2.
   c. move mucus and dirt upward.
   d. only beat when you inhale.

4. The first branches off the trachea are called
   a. bronchioles.
   b. bronchi.
   c. arterioles.
   d. alveoli.

5. Inside the alveoli, carbon dioxide and oxygen
   a. are exchanged between air and blood.
   b. are transported along microscopic tubules.
   c. are produced inside cells.
   d. are exchanged for other gases.

6. Which is the correct sequence for the path of oxygen through the respiratory system?
   a. nasal passages, bronchi, trachea, bronchioles, cells, blood, alveoli
   b. cells, blood, alveoli, bronchioles, bronchi, trachea, nasal passages
   c. nasal passages, blood, alveoli, bronchi, cells, trachea, bronchioles
   d. nasal passages, trachea, bronchi, bronchioles, alveoli, blood, cells

In your textbook, read about the mechanics of breathing and the control of respiration.

For each statement below, write <u>true</u> or <u>false</u>.

_____ 7. Homeostasis in respiration is controlled by the cerebrum.

_____ 8. As you exhale, the bronchioles in the lungs release most of their air.

_____ 9. When you inhale, the muscles between your ribs contract.

_____ 10. Relaxation of the diaphragm causes a slight vacuum in the lungs.

_____ 11. Air rushes into the lungs because the air pressure outside the body is greater than the air pressure inside the lungs.

_____ 12. Relaxation of the diaphragm causes it to flatten.

Chapter 37 **Respiration, Circulation, and Excretion,** *continued*

In your textbook, read about your blood, ABO blood types, and blood vessels.

Answer the following questions.

1. What cells and substances would you expect to find suspended or dissolved in plasma?

_____

_____

2. How is carbon dioxide transported in blood?

_____

_____

Complete the table below by checking the correct column for each description.

Description	Red Blood Cells	White Blood Cells	Platelets
3. Contain hemoglobin			
4. Fight infection			
5. Lack a nucleus			
6. Help clot blood			
7. Transport oxygen			
8. Comparatively large and nucleated			

For each statement below, write <u>true</u> or <u>false</u>.

_____ **9.** Your blood type can be changed with a blood transfusion.

_____ **10.** Different blood types result from different antibodies being present on the membranes of red blood cells.

_____ **11.** If you have type B blood, then you have anti-A antibodies in your plasma.

_____ **12.** Risks involving incompatible Rh factors are greatest for a woman's first child.

Chapter 37 Respiration, Circulation, and Excretion, *continued*

In your textbook, read about your heart, blood's path through the heart, and inside your heart.

Label the parts of the human heart in the diagram below. Use these choices:

aorta	left atrium	left ventricle	pulmonary arteries
pulmonary veins	right atrium	right ventricle	

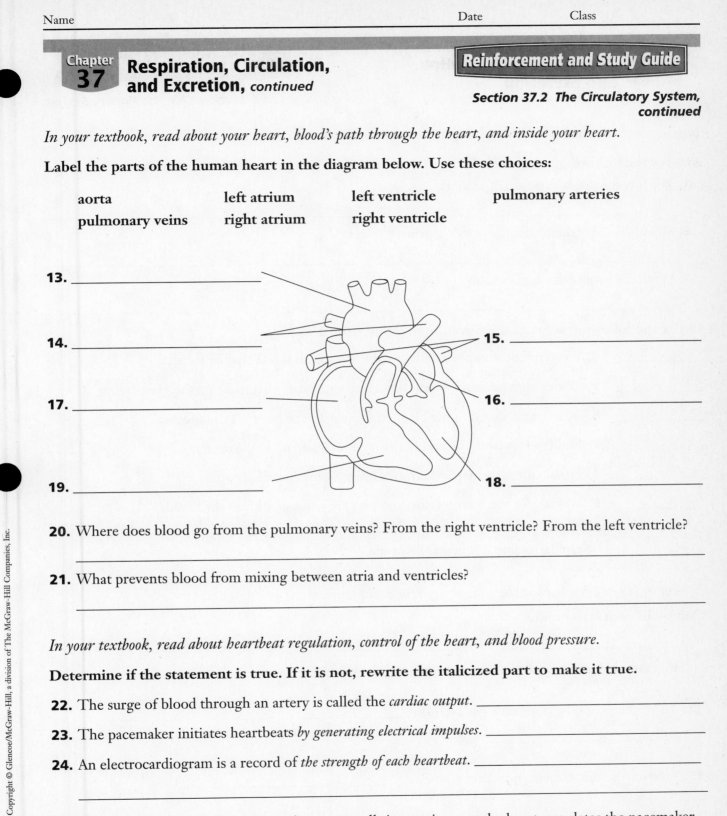

13. _____

14. _____

17. _____

19. _____

15. _____

16. _____

18. _____

20. Where does blood go from the pulmonary veins? From the right ventricle? From the left ventricle?

_____

21. What prevents blood from mixing between atria and ventricles?

_____

In your textbook, read about heartbeat regulation, control of the heart, and blood pressure.

Determine if the statement is true. If it is not, rewrite the italicized part to make it true.

22. The surge of blood through an artery is called the *cardiac output*. _____

23. The pacemaker initiates heartbeats *by generating electrical impulses*. _____

24. An electrocardiogram is a record of *the strength of each heartbeat*. _____

_____

25. The *atrioventricular node*, along with sensory cells in arteries near the heart, regulates the pacemaker.

_____

26. *Diastolic pressure* occurs when the heart's ventricles contract. _____

In your textbook, read about kidneys, nephrons, and the formation of urine.

Answer the following questions.

1. What is the major function of kidneys?

_____

2. What role does the bladder play in the urinary system?

_____

3. What are nephrons?

_____

Order the following steps in the filtration of blood from 1 to 7.

_____ 4. From the Bowman's capsule, fluid flows through a U-shaped tubule.

_____ 5. Under high pressure, blood flows into capillaries that make up the glomerulus.

_____ 6. After being stored in the bladder, urine exits the body via the urethra.

_____ 7. Fluid moves from the end of the nephron's tubule to the ureter.

_____ 8. Blood enters the nephron from a branch of the renal artery.

_____ 9. Water, glucose, amino acids, and ions are reabsorbed into the blood.

_____ 10. Water, glucose, amino acids, wastes, and other substances move from glomerular capillaries into a Bowman's capsule.

In your textbook, read about the urinary system and homeostasis.

Complete each statement.

11. _____ and _____ are two toxic nitrogenous wastes that your kidneys constantly remove from your bloodstream.

12. The kidneys also help regulate the blood's _____ _____ , and _____ .

13. Individuals with diabetes have excess levels of _____ in their blood.

Chapter 38 Reproduction and Development

In your textbook, read about human male anatomy and hormonal control.

Answer the following questions.

1. What are the primary functions of the male reproductive system?

_____

_____

2. How does the location of the scrotum affect sperm?

_____

_____

3. How many sperm can the average mature male produce in one day?

_____

Order the steps in the formation and transportation of sperm from 1 to 6.

_____ **4.** Mature sperm enter the vas deferens.

_____ **5.** Newly formed haploid sperm cells pass through a series of coiled ducts to the epididymis.

_____ **6.** Sperm leave the body via the urethra.

_____ **7.** Sperm mature in the epididymis.

_____ **8.** Cells lining tubules in the testes undergo meiosis.

_____ **9.** Sperm travel along the ejaculatory ducts and into the urethra.

Complete each sentence.

10. When a young man's voice "changes," he is probably entering _____ , a time when he will develop other secondary _____ _____ .

11. A hormone released by the _____ stimulates the _____ gland to release _____ - _____ and _____ hormones.

12. FSH regulates _____ production, while LH controls the production of the steroid hormone _____ by the testes.

Chapter 38 Reproduction and Development, *continued*

In your textbook, read about human female anatomy and puberty in females.

Determine if each statement is true. If it is not, rewrite the italicized part to make it true.

13. When an egg cell is released from an ovary, it moves down the oviduct by *gravity*.

_____

14. As is the case in human males, a woman's *hypothalamus* produces FSH and LH.

_____

15. *FSH* stimulates follicle development and the release of estrogen from the ovary.

_____

16. In females, *luteinizing hormone (LH)* is responsible for the development of the secondary sex characteristics.

_____

17. Long before a woman is born, cells in her ovaries that are destined to become future eggs undergo several *mitotic divisions*.

_____

In your textbook, read about the menstrual cycle.

Complete the table by checking the correct column for each event.

Event	Phase of Menstrual Cycle		
	Flow	**Follicular**	**Luteal**
18. LH stimulates the corpus luteum to develop from a ruptured follicle.			
19. Estrogen levels are at their peak.			
20. A cell inside a follicle resumes meiotic divisions.			
21. Progesterone levels are at their peak.			
22. The uterine lining is shed.			
23. LH levels rise abruptly.			
24. Ovulation occurs.			
25. The uterine lining becomes engorged with blood, fat, and tissue fluid.			
26. FSH begins to rise.			

Copyright © Glencoe/McGraw-Hill, a division of The McGraw-Hill Companies, Inc.

In your textbook, read about fertilization and implantation, and embryonic membranes.

Use each of the terms below just once to complete the passage.

amnion	blastocyst	chorion	chorionic villi	embryo
implants	oviduct	placenta	umbilical cord	zygote

Usually in the upper part of a(n) **(1)** _____ , an egg and one sperm unite

to form a(n) **(2)** _____ . This single cell divides repeatedly to form a(n)

(3) _____ , which **(4)** _____ in the uterine wall. Part

of the blastocyst becomes the **(5)** _____ , which is surrounded by a fluid-filled,

membranous sac called the **(6)** _____ . The embryo is connected to the wall

of the uterus by its **(7)** _____ . The amniotic sac is enclosed by the

(8) _____ , which later forms the **(9)** _____ .

Nutrients and oxygen from the mother and wastes from the embryo are exchanged in the

(10) _____ .

In your textbook, read about fetal development and genetic counseling.

Complete the table by checking the correct column for each event or example.

	Trimester		
Event/Example	**First**	**Second**	**Third**
11. Fetus can survive outside the uterus with medical assistance.			
12. Fetus weighs more than 3000 grams.			
13. Embryo is most vulnerable to outside influences.			
14. Embryo becomes a fetus.			
15. Fetus can use its muscles to move spontaneously.			
16. Fetus becomes oriented head-down.			
17. Sex of fetus can be determined.			

Chapter **38**	**Reproduction and Development,** *continued*	**Reinforcement and Study Guide**

Section 38.3 Birth, Growth, and Aging

In your textbook, read about birth.

Answer the following questions.

1. What are the three stages of birth? _____

2. Describe the action of oxytocin. _____

_____

3. After the placenta is expelled from a woman's body, what effect do continued uterine contractions

have? _____

_____

In your textbook, read about growth and aging.

Complete each sentence.

4. Your growth rate, as well as the type of growth you undergo, varies with both your

_____ and your _____ .

5. _____ _____ _____ ,

abbreviated _____ , regulates growth.

6. hGH exerts its effects primarily on _____ and on _____

_____ .

7. LGH works by increasing _____ and _____ .

Complete the table by checking the correct column for each description.

Example	Childhood	Adolescence	Adulthood
8. Your growth rate continues at a steady rate.			
9. Lines develop on your face, especially around your eyes and mouth.			
10. You reach maximum physical stature.			
11. You begin to reason.			
12. You may have a sudden growth spurt.			

Chapter 39 **Immunity From Disease**

In your textbook, read about what an infectious disease is, determining what causes a disease, and the spread of infectious diseases.

Answer the following questions.

1. Why is a disease like osteoarthritis not considered an infectious disease?

_____

2. What is meant by Koch's postulates?

_____

_____

3. In terms of disease, what is a reservoir?

_____

Complete the table by writing in the method of transmission for each example.

Example	Method of Transmission
4. While exploring a cave, a person breathes in fungal spores that cause a lung infection.	
5. A person contracts Rocky Mountain spotted fever after being bitten by a tick.	
6. After having unprotected sex, a person contracts syphilis.	

In your textbook, read about what causes the symptoms of a disease, patterns of disease, and treating diseases.

For each statement below, write <u>true</u> or <u>false</u>.

_____ **7.** The toxin produced by a particular microorganism might be far more destructive than the direct damage the microbe does to its host cells.

_____ **8.** Endemic diseases often disappear in a population, only to resurface unexpectedly many years later.

_____ **9.** If you catch the flu during an influenza epidemic, your best hope of recovery is to take antibiotics.

_____ **10.** It is important for researchers to try to discover new antibiotics because many types of bacteria are becoming resistant to the ones now being used.

Chapter 39 **Immunity From Disease,** *continued*

Section 39.2 Defense Against Infectious Diseases

In your textbook, read about the innate immune system.

Determine if the statement is true. If it is not, rewrite the italicized part to make it true.

1. Healthy skin is a good defense against the invasion of pathogens because it is *free of bacteria*.

_____

_____

2. In your trachea, *saliva* traps microbes and prevents them from entering your lungs.

_____

3. Macrophages migrate *into the bloodstream* when the body is challenged by a pathogen.

_____

4. Phagocytes at the site of an infection or inflammation destroy pathogens by surrounding and engulfing them. _____

5. The third line of defense against infection is the consumption of pathogens by *neutrophils*.

_____

6. Interferon is produced by cells infected by *pathogenic bacteria*.

_____

In your textbook, read about acquired immunity.

Circle the letter of the choice that best completes the statement.

7. The human lymphatic system is important in
   a. filtering pathogens from lymph.
   b. keeping body fluids constant.
   c. resistance to disease.
   d. all of the above.

8. Tissue fluid is found
   a. in lymph vessels.
   b. in the bloodstream.
   c. around body cells.
   d. in lymph ducts.

9. The main function of lymph nodes is to
   a. store red blood cells.
   b. filter lymph.
   c. filter excess fluid.
   d. trigger an immune response.

10. A reservoir for lymphocytes that can be transformed into specific disease-fighting cells is the
   a. thymus gland.
   b. thyroid gland.
   c. pituitary gland.
   d. pancreas.

Chapter 39 **Immunity From Disease,** *continued*

Section 39.2 Defense Against Infectious Diseases, continued

In your textbook, read about antibody immunity and cellular immunity.

Complete each sentence.

11. _____ is the building up of a _____ to a specific pathogen.

12. Two types of immunity that involve different kinds of cells and cellular actions are _____ immunity and _____ immunity.

13. The presence of foreign _____ in the body triggers the production of _____ by plasma cells.

14. A _____ is a lymphocyte that, when activated by a _____, becomes a plasma cell and produces _____ .

15. Cellular immunity involves several different types of _____ cells.

16. A _____ releases enzymes directly into the _____ .

Complete the table by checking the correct columns for each example.

	Type of Immunity	
Example	**Cellular**	**Antibody**
17. Involves the protection of antibodies		
18. Simulated by antigens in the body		
19. Clones of killer T cells produced		
20. Memory cells produced so the body can respond quickly to a second attack		
21. Key role played by antigen-antibody complex		
22. T cells destroyed by pathogens directly		

Reinforcement and Study Guide

Section 39.2 Defense Against Infectious
Diseases, continued

In your textbook, read about passive and active immunity to infectious diseases.

Answer the following questions.

23. Distinguish between active and passive immunity.

_____

_____

_____

24. In what two ways can passive immunity develop?

_____

_____

25. What is a vaccine?

_____

_____

In your textbook, read about AIDS and the immune system.

For each statement below, write <u>true</u> or <u>false</u>.

_____   **26.** The virus that causes AIDS—Human Immunodeficiency Virus—is well-
named because it attacks the immune system.

_____   **27.** HIV can be transmitted by air.

_____   **28.** A child born to a woman who is infected with HIV is at high risk for being
infected, too.

_____   **29.** HIV destroys a person's resistance to disease by attacking and destroying
memory T cells.

_____   **30.** In a blood sample from an HIV-positive person, you would expect to find
most of the viruses existing free in the blood, rather than being hidden
inside cells.

_____   **31.** If a person is infected with HIV, he or she will usually develop AIDS within
about a year.

_____   **32.** The cause of death for a person with AIDS usually is some type of infection
that the body's weakened immune system can no longer fight off.

_____   **33.** The majority of persons infected with HIV will develop AIDS.

BioDigest
10 The Human Body

In your textbook, read about skin, bones, and muscles.

Skin has four functions: **(1)** _____ , **(2)** _____

_____ , **(3)** _____ , and **(4)** _____

_____ . These functions help maintain homeostasis in the body.

Complete the table to describe the role of bones.

Support for	**5.**
Place for	**6.**
Protects	**7.**
Manufacture of	**8.**
Storehouse of	**9.**

This diagram shows the various steps involved in the respiratory process. In the space provided, describe the steps as indicated.

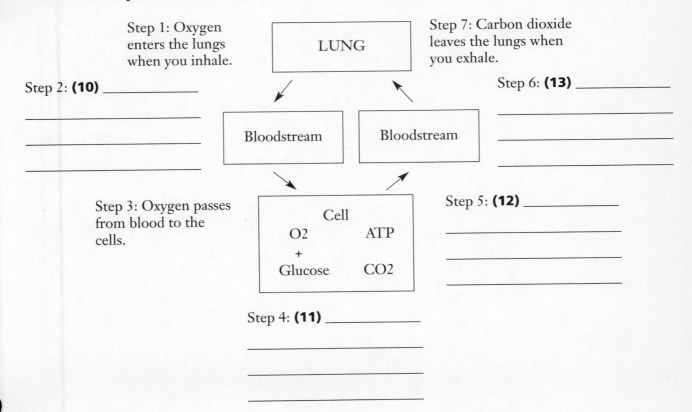

Step 1: Oxygen enters the lungs when you inhale.

LUNG

Step 7: Carbon dioxide leaves the lungs when you exhale.

Step 2: **(10)** _____

_____

_____

Bloodstream

Bloodstream

Step 6: **(13)** _____

_____

_____

Step 3: Oxygen passes from blood to the cells.

Cell

O2 + Glucose

ATP

CO2

Step 5: **(12)** _____

_____

_____

Step 4: **(11)** _____

_____

_____

In your textbook, read about reproductive, endocrine, and lymphatic systems.

14. The endocrine system is a communication system; its messages are hormones. They are produced by

_____ and travel in the _____ to _____

_____ . There they _____ .

15. The structures of the male reproductive system—the scrotum, _____ ,

epididymis, seminal vesicles, _____ , bulbourethral gland, urethra, and

_____ —are involved in _____ and maintaining

sperm cells and _____ into the female reproductive tract.

16. The structures of the female reproductive system—the _____ , oviduct,

_____ , and vagina—produce and maintain _____ ,

receive and transport _____ , and support the development of the

_____ .

Explain how these systems of the body interact with each other.

17. Skeletal system ⟶ Circulatory system ⟶ Muscular system

_____

_____

18. Digestive system ⟶ Circulatory system ⟶ Urinary system

_____

_____

19. Endocrine system ⟶ Reproductive system

_____

_____

20. Respiratory System ⟶ Circulatory system ⟶ Cell ⟶ Circulatory
system ⟶ Urinary and Respiratory systems

_____

_____

_____

21. Circulatory system ⟶ Lymphatic system

_____

_____

ANSWER PAGES

Reinforcement and Study Guide

Chapter 1 — The Study of Life

In your textbook, read about the science of biology.

Answer the following questions.

1. What is the primary focus of all biological studies?

   understanding the world of living things and how they interact

2. What is meant by the statement, "Living things do not exist in isolation"?

   All living things depend on other living things for their existence; all living things
   play a part in the delicate balance of nature.

In your textbook, read about why biologist study the diversity of life.

For each of the statements below, write true or false.

false   3. People study biology only if they are planning to become biologists.

true   4. By studying biology, you can better appreciate the great diversity of species on Earth and the way each species fits into the dynamic pattern of life on the planet.

true   5. The study of biology includes the investigation of interactions among species.

In your textbook, read about the characteristics of living things.

Complete each statement.

6. To be considered **alive**, something must exhibit all of the **characteristics** of life.

7. **Organism** is another word for "living thing."

8. Every living thing, from simple, single-celled organisms to complex, multicellular plants and animals, is made up of parts that function together in an orderly living **system**.

Read each of the following statements. If it describes the process of reproduction, write yes. If not, write no.

no   9. New leaves appear on a tree in spring.

yes   10. An amoeba divides in half.

yes   11. A bean plant produces seeds in long pods.

yes   12. Pollen grains are released from a flower.

no   13. A starfish produces a new arm after losing one to a predator.

Chapter 1 — The Study of Life, continued

Circle the letter of the choice that best completes the statement.

14. A species is defined as a group of similar-looking organisms that
   a. undergo similar developmental changes.   b. can interbreed.
   c. can interbreed and produce fertile offspring.   d. reproduce in the same way. *(c circled)*

15. Every organism begins life as a(n)
   a. embryo.   **b.** single cell.   c. nucleus.   d. fertilized egg. *(b circled)*

16. A corn plant producing ears of corn is an example of
   a. growth.   b. reproduction.   c. development.   **d.** all of these. *(d circled)*

17. If members of a species fail to reproduce successfully, the species
   a. will eventually become extinct.   b. will not develop normally.
   c. will evolve into a new species.   d. will remain unchanged. *(a circled)*

Complete the table below by checking the correct column for each example.

Example	Stimulus	Response
18. The recess bell ringing at an elementary school	✓	
19. Your mouth watering at the sight of food on a plate		✓
20. A sudden drop in air temperature	✓	
21. A flu virus entering your body	✓	
22. Getting butterflies in your stomach before giving a speech		✓

Answer the following questions.

23. Explain the concept of homeostasis.

   Homeostasis refers to the regulation of an organism's internal environment to
   maintain stable, steady conditions suitable for life.

24. What is an adaptation?

   any structure, behavior, or internal process that enables an organism to respond
   to stimuli and better survive in an environment

25. What is evolution?

   Evolution is the gradual accumulation of adaptations over time.

Name _____ Date _____ Class _____

Reinforcement and Study Guide

Chapter 1 **The Study of Life,** *continued*

Section 1.2 The Methods of Biology

In your textbook, read about observing and hypothesizing.

Answer the following questions.

1. What is meant by *scientific methods?* **the common steps that scientists use to gather information to solve problems**

2. What is a hypothesis? **a testable explanation for a question or problem**

3. How is a hypothesis tested? **A hypothesis is tested by conducting an experiment.**

In your textbook, read about experimenting.

For each item in Column A, write the letter of the matching item in Column B.

	Column A	Column B
d	4. A procedure that tests a hypothesis by collecting information under controlled conditions	a. dependent variable
e	5. In an experiment, the group in which all conditions are kept the same	b. experimental group
b	6. In an experiment, the group in which all conditions are kept the same except for the one being tested	c. independent variable
c	7. The condition that is changed by the experimenter	d. experiment
a	8. The condition being observed or measured in an experiment	e. control group

Use each of the terms below just once to complete the passage.

experimental results   experiment(s)   hypothesis   laws
scientific journals   theory   valid   verify

When (9) **experimental results** are reported in (10) **scientific journals**, other scientists may try to (11) **verify** the results by repeating the (12) **experiment(s)**. Usually when a(n) (13) **hypothesis** is supported by data from several scientists, it is considered (14) **valid**. Over time, a hypothesis that is supported by many observations and experiments becomes a (15) **theory**. Some well-established facts of nature, such as gravity, are recognized as (16) **laws**.

REINFORCEMENT AND STUDY GUIDE   CHAPTER 1 BIOLOGY: The Dynamics of Life   **3**

Name _____ Date _____ Class _____

Reinforcement and Study Guide

Chapter 1 **The Study of Life,** *continued*

Section 1.3 The Nature of Biology

In your textbook, read about kinds of research.

Complete the chart by checking the correct column for each example.

Example	Quantitative Research	Descriptive Research
1. Numerical data	✓	
2. Field study of hunting behavior		✓
3. Thermometer, balance scale, stopwatch	✓	
4. Testable hypothesis	✓	
5. Measurements from controlled laboratory experiments	✓	
6. Purely observational data		✓
7. Binoculars, tape recorder, camera		✓

Complete each statement.

8. In order for scientific research to be universally understood, scientists report measurements in the **International System of Measurement**, a modern form of the metric system.

9. This system of measurement is abbreviated **SI**.

10. This system is a **decimal** system in which measurements are expressed in **tens** or **tenths** of a basic unit.

In your textbook, read about science and society.

Determine if the following statement is true. If it is not, rewrite the italicized part to make it true.

11. Ideas about the value of knowledge gained through scientific research come from a society's *social, ethical, and moral concerns.* **true**

12. Pure science is scientific research carried out *primarily to solve a specific environmental problem.* **for the sake of knowledge**

13. *Technology* is the practical application of scientific research to improve human life and the world in which we live. **true**

14. A technological solution to a human problem can benefit humans but may also *cause a different, possibly serious, problem.* **true**

15. *Scientists* have the final say about how the results of scientific discoveries are applied. **People in a society**

4 CHAPTER 1 BIOLOGY: The Dynamics of Life   REINFORCEMENT AND STUDY GUIDE

Name _____ Date _____ Class _____

BioDigest
Reinforcement and Study Guide

What Is Biology?

In your textbook, read about characteristics of life.

Complete the following statements.

Biology is the study of **(1)** __living organisms__ and the **(2)** __interactions__ among them. Biologists use a variety of **(3)** __scientific__ methods to study the details of life.

For each item in Column A, write the letter of the matching item in Column B.

Column A		Column B
d	**4.** The basic unit is the cell.	**a.** development
c	**5.** Maintenance of a stable internal environment	**b.** growth
f	**6.** Reaction to a change in the environment	**c.** homeostasis
b	**7.** Cell enlargement and division	**d.** organization
a	**8.** Changes in an organism that take place over time	**e.** reproduction
e	**9.** Transmission of heredity information from one generation to the next	**f.** response to stimulus

Using what you know about characteristics of life, determine if each of the following describes a living or nonliving thing.

nonliving	**10.** rust on a bucket	nonliving	**13.** lightning
living	**11.** an apple on a tree	nonliving	**14.** a dinosaur fossil
living	**12.** bacteria	nonliving	**15.** a wasp

Name _____ Date _____ Class _____

BioDigest
Reinforcement and Study Guide

What Is Biology, *continued*

In your textbook, read about scientific methods.

Decide if each of the following statements is true. If it is not, rewrite the italicized part to make it true.

16. Scientific methods include observation, hypothesis, experiment, and *theory*.   __true__

17. A statement that can be tested and presents a possible solution to a question is a *law*.
__hypothesis__

18. In a controlled experiment, two groups are tested and all conditions except *two* are kept the same for both groups.   __one__

19. A condition that remains the same for both groups is called the *independent variable*.
__control__

20. A condition that is changed by the experimenter in one group and not the other is called the *dependent variable*.   __independent variable__

21. A scientific experiment can be conducted *only in a laboratory*.   __in a laboratory or in the field__

22. A theory is a *law* that has been confirmed by many experiments.   __hypothesis__

Read each of the following statements. If it is a testable hypothesis, write yes. If it is not a testable hypothesis, write no.

__yes__   **23.** If a person exercises, his or her pulse rate will increase.

__no__   **24.** Cats make better pets than dogs.

__yes__   **25.** When fertilizer is added to soil, plants grow taller.

Identify each of the two italicized items as either an independent or a dependent variable.

26. The *number of red blood cells* in a mouse's blood at *different levels of* iron in its diet
__dependent variable; independent variable__

27. The *amount of starch formed* in a plant leaf for *different times* of exposure to light
__dependent variable; independent variable__

Name _____ Date _____ Class _____

Chapter 2 Principles of Ecology

Section 2.1 Organisms and Their Environment

In your textbook, read about what ecology is and about aspects of ecological study.

Use each of the terms below just once to complete the passage.

ecology	biotic factors	nonliving	environments	atmosphere
humans	organisms	soil	biosphere	abiotic factors

Living organisms in our world are connected to other **(1)** organisms in a variety of ways. The branch of biology called **(2)** ecology is the scientific study of interactions among organisms and their **(3)** environments, including relationships between living and **(4)** nonliving things.

All living things on Earth can be found in the **(5)** biosphere, the portion of Earth that supports life. It extends from high in the **(6)** atmosphere to the bottom of the oceans. Many different environments can be found in the biosphere. All living organisms found in an environment are called **(7)** biotic factors. Nonliving parts of an environment are called **(8)** abiotic factors. For example, whales, trees, and **(9)** humans are biotic factors. Ocean currents, temperature, and **(10)** soil are abiotic factors.

In your textbook, read about levels of organization in ecology.

For each item in Column A, write the letter of the matching item in Column B.

	Column A	Column B
d	11. A group of organisms of one species that interbreed and live in the same place at the same time	a. community
a	12. A collection of interacting populations	b. competition
e	13. Interactions among the populations and abiotic factors in a community	c. forest
b	14. Occurs between organisms when resources are scarce	d. population
c	15. A terrestrial ecosystem	e. ecosystem

Name _____ Date _____ Class _____

Chapter 2 Principles of Ecology, *continued*

Section 2.1 Organisms and Their Environment, continued

In your textbook, read about organisms in ecosystems.

For each statement below, write true or false.

false	16.	A habitat is the role a species plays in a community.
true	17.	Habitats may change.
false	18.	A niche is the place where an organism lives its life.
false	19.	A habitat can include only one niche.
true	20.	A species' niche includes how the species meets its needs for food and shelter.
true	21.	The centipedes and worms that live under a certain log occupy the same habitat but have different niches.
false	22.	It is an advantage for two species to share the same niche.
true	23.	Competition between two species is reduced when the species have different niches.

Complete the table below by writing the kind of relationship described on the left.

Relationships Among Organisms	
Description of Relationship	**Kind of Relationship**
24. Organisms of different species live together in a close, permanent relationship.	symbiosis
25. One species benefits and the other species is neither benefited nor harmed by the relationship.	commensalism
26. One species benefits from the relationship at the expense of the other species.	parasitism
27. Both species benefit from the relationship.	mutualism

Chapter 2 Principles of Ecology, *continued*

Section 2.2 Nutrition and Energy Flow

In your textbook, read about how organisms obtain energy and about matter and energy flow in ecosystems.

Answer the questions below. Use the diagram of a food web to answer questions 1–7.

Snake → Frog
Bird → Insect
Plant

1. How many food chains make up the food web?
   three

2. Which organism is an herbivore?
   insect

3. Which organism is an autotroph?
   plant

4. Which organism is a third-order heterotroph? To what trophic level does that organism belong?
   snake; fourth

5. Which organism is an omnivore?
   bird

6. Which organisms belong to more than one food chain?
   plant, bird, insect, snake

7. Which organism belongs to more than one trophic level?
   bird

8. What are decomposers? From which trophic levels are the organisms that decomposers feed on?
   Decomposers are organisms that break down dead organisms from all trophic levels into simpler molecules that can be absorbed by the decomposers.

9. What does a pyramid of energy show about the amount of energy available at different trophic levels of a food chain?
   The amount of energy decreases as the trophic level increases.

10. Why do different trophic levels have different amounts of energy?
    At each successive trophic level, some available energy is lost as the organisms use energy for metabolism. This energy is given off as heat into the environment.

Chapter 2 Principles of Ecology, *continued*

Section 2.2 Nutrition and Energy Flow, *continued*

In your textbook, read about cycles in nature.

Circle the letter of the choice that best completes the statement or answers the question.

11. Energy that is lost at each trophic level of an ecosystem is replenished by
    a. heat.   b. nutrients.   **c.** sunlight.   d. organisms.

12. Besides energy, what moves through the organisms at each trophic level of an ecosystem?
    a. organisms   **b.** nutrients   c. sunlight   d. cycles

13. Evaporation and condensation a part of the
    a. carbon cycle.   b. nitrogen cycle.   c. phosphorus cycle.   **d.** water cycle.

14. Plants lose water to the air through
    a. condensation.   b. photosynthesis.   c. their roots.   **d.** evaporation.

15. Animals lose water when they
    a. breathe in.   b. urinate.   c. breathe out.   **d.** both b and c.

16. The water in the atmosphere is returned to the earth by
    a. precipitation.   b. evaporation.   c. photosynthesis.   d. decomposition.

17. Autotrophs and heterotrophs use carbon molecules for energy and
    a. photosynthesis.   **b.** growth.   c. decomposition.   d. both a and b.

18. What do plants use in photosynthesis to make carbon molecules?
    a. carbon dioxide   b. carbohydrates   c. fertilizer   d. oxygen

19. Heterotrophs get carbon molecules by
    a. making the molecules themselves.   **b.** feeding on other organisms.
    c. decaying.   d. growing.

20. When decomposers break down the carbon molecules in dead organisms,
    a. the dead organisms are converted to coal.   b. oxygen is released.
    c. carbon dioxide is converted to energy-rich carbon molecules.
    d. carbon dioxide is released.

21. Fertilizers provide plants with
    a. nitrogen.   b. carbon.   c. water.   d. oxygen.

22. Which of the following convert(s) nitrogen in the air into a form plants can use?
    a. bacteria   b. lightning   c. sunlight   **d.** both a and b

23. Plants use nitrogen to make
    a. carbohydrates.   b. nitrogen gas.   **c.** proteins.   d. both b and c.

24. An animal returns nitrogen to the environment when it
    a. breathes.   b. decomposes.   c. urinates.   **d.** both b and c.

25. Animals get phosphorus from
    a. the air.   **b.** eating plants.   c. water.   d. the soil.

26. Phosphorus in the soil comes from
    a. rocks.   b. decaying organisms.   c. the air.   **d.** both a and b.

Reinforcement and Study Guide

Chapter 3

Communities and Biomes

Section 3.1 Communities

In your textbook, read about living in a community.

Determine if the statement is true. If it is not, rewrite the italicized part to make it true.

1. The *interactions* of abiotic and biotic factors result in conditions that are suitable for some organisms but not for others. **true**

2. Food availability and temperature can be *biotic factors* for a particular organism. **limiting factors**

3. A limiting factor is any biotic or abiotic factor that *promotes* the existence, numbers, reproduction, or distribution of organisms. **restricts**

4. At high elevations where the soil is thin, vegetation is limited to *large, deep-rooted* trees. **small, shallow-rooted mosses, ferns, and lichens**

5. Factors that limit one population in a community may also have *an indirect* effect on another population. **true**

6. *Tolerance* is the ability of an organism to withstand fluctuations in biotic and abiotic environmental factors. **true**

7. A population of deer would become *larger* as conditions move away from optimal toward either extreme of the deer's range of tolerance. **smaller**

8. Different species may have different ranges of tolerance. **true**

In your textbook, read about succession: changes over time.

Use each of the terms below just once to complete the passage.

| climax | primary | decades | succeed |
| pioneer | succession | species | slows down |

The natural changes and **(9)** _species_ replacements that take place in the communities of ecosystems are know as **(10)** _succession_ . It can take **(11)** _decades_ or even centuries for one community to **(12)** _succeed_ , or replace, another. When new sites of land are formed, as in a lava flow, the first organisms to colonize the new area are **(13)** _pioneer_ species. This colonization is called **(14)** _primary_ succession. The species inhabiting the area gradually change. Eventually, succession **(15)** _slows down_ and the community becomes more stable. Finally, a mature community that undergoes little or no change, called a **(16)** _climax_ community, develops.

Reinforcement and Study Guide

Chapter 3

Communities and Biomes, continued

Section 3.1 Communities, continued

For each item in Column A, write the letter of the matching item in Column B.

Column A	Column B
b 17. Sequence of community changes where soil is formed, allowing small, weedy plants to inhabit the area	**a.** a severe drought
d 18. Sequence of community changes occurring as a result of a natural disaster, such as a forest fire	**b.** primary succession
e 19. A stable, mature community with little or no succession occurring	**c.** amount of plant growth
c 20. An example of a biotic limiting factor affecting a community of organisms	**d.** secondary succession
a 21. An example of an abiotic limiting factor affecting a community of organisms	**e.** climax community

The statements below describe the secondary succession that occurred within an area of Yellowstone National Park. Number the events in the order in which they occurred.

4 22. Grasses, ferns, and pine seedlings inhabited the area.

3 23. Annual wildflowers grew from the bare soil.

1 24. A fire burned thousands of acres of land.

5 25. A climax community of lodgepole pines developed.

2 26. Bare soil covered the area.

Chapter 3 — Communities and Biomes, *continued*

Reinforcement and Study Guide

Section 3.2 Biomes

In your textbook, read about aquatic biomes: life in the water.

Complete each statement.

1. A large group of ecosystems sharing the same type of **climax community** is called a __**biome**__ .

2. Biomes located in bodies of __**water**__ , such as oceans, lakes, and rivers, are called __**aquatic biomes**__ .

3. The water in marine biomes is __**salty**__ .

4. Oceans contain the largest amount of __**biomass**__ , or living material, of any biome on Earth. Yet, most of the organisms are so __**small**__ that they cannot be seen without magnification.

5. The __**photic zone**__ is that part of marine biomes shallow enough to be penetrated by sunlight.

6. Deep-water regions of marine biomes receiving no sunlight make up the __**aphotic zone**__ .

Circle the letter of the response that best completes the statement.

7. If you followed the course of a river, it would eventually flow into
   a. a lake. **b.** a stream. **c.** an ocean or a sea. **d.** a swamp.

8. The body of water where fresh water from a river mixes with salt water is called
   (a.) an estuary. **b.** a shoreline. **c.** a sandbar. **d.** a sea.

9. Organisms living in intertidal zones have structures that protect them from
   a. the dark. **b.** sunlight. **(c.)** wave action. **d.** temperature.

10. Life is abundant in photic zones because
    a. there are no waves. **b.** the water is warm. **c.** the water is clean. **(d.)** there are many nutrients.

11. The greatest number of organisms living in the photic zone of a marine biome are
    a. dolphins. **(b.)** plankton. **c.** plants. **d.** sharks.

12. Few organisms live at the bottom of a deep lake because of the lack of
    (a.) sunlight. **b.** space. **c.** plankton. **d.** bacteria.

Chapter 3 — Communities and Biomes, *continued*

Reinforcement and Study Guide

Section 3.2 Biomes,
continued

In your textbook, read about terrestrial biomes.

Answer the following questions.

13. Which two abiotic factors generally determine the type of climax community that will develop in a particular part of the world?
    temperature and precipitation

14. In which terrestrial biome is the ground permanently frozen?
    tundra

15. What are some adaptations that desert plants have developed?
    Answers include narrow leaves and waxy coatings to reduce water loss; ability to germinate from seed and quickly mature after sporadic rainfall; spines, thorns, or poisons to discourage desert herbivores; branches and roots that store water.

16. Describe the three layers of a tropical rain forest, including organisms that live in each layer.
    Answers will vary. Canopy: treetops, monkeys, birds; understory: ferns, shrubs, palms, insects, amphibians, reptiles, birds, bats; ground: leaves, decaying materials, ants, worms, rodents, decomposers

Write the name of each major terrestrial biome next to its description.

__**desert**__ 17. Arid land with sparse, drought-resistant plants

__**grassland**__ 18. Largest terrestrial biome that supports small plants and grasses, but few trees

__**tundra**__ 19. Treeless land where only small plants and grasses grow during the long summer days

__**tropical rain forest**__ 20. Warm, wet land that supports many species of organisms

__**taiga**__ 21. Land with coniferous forests, peat swamps, and long, harsh winters

__**temperate forest**__ 22. Land populated with broad-leaved hardwood trees that lose their leaves annually

Name _____ Date _____ Class _____

Reinforcement and Study Guide

Chapter 4 Population Biology

Section 4.1 *Population Dynamics*

In your textbook, read about the principles of population growth.

Refer to Graphs A and B below. Answer the following questions.

Graph A

Graph B

Size of Population — Time

Size of Population — Time

1. What type of population growth is shown in Graph A? Explain this type of growth.
**Graph A shows exponential growth. In exponential growth, the rate of growth
increases rapidly, due to an increase in the number of reproducing organisms.**

2. Which graph shows the most likely growth of a squirrel population living in a forest? **Graph B**

3. Which graph shows a population's growth under ideal conditions? **Graph A**

4. Why don't populations of organisms grow indefinitely?
**All populations of organisms have limiting factors in their environment.
These factors eventually cause populations to level off.**

Use each of the terms below just once to complete the passage.

| grows | carrying capacity | below | births |
| above | under | deaths | exceed |

The number of organisms of one species that an environment can support is called its
(5) carrying capacity . If the number of organisms in a population is **(6)** _____ **under** the
environment's carrying capacity, births **(7)** _____ **exceed** deaths and the population
(8) _____ **grows** . If the number of organisms rises **(9)** _____ **above** the carrying capacity
of the environment, **(10)** _____ **deaths** will exceed **(11)** _____ **births** . This pattern will
continue until the population is once again at or **(12)** _____ **below** the carrying capacity.

Name _____ Date _____ Class _____

Reinforcement and Study Guide

Chapter 4 Population Biology, *continued*

Section 4.1 *Population Dynamics,*
continued

Circle the letter of the choice that best completes the statement.

13. The most important factor that determines population growth is the organism's
    a. social pattern.
    b. carrying capacity.
    (c.) reproductive pattern.
    d. feeding pattern.

14. Organisms that follow a rapid life-history pattern
    a. have short life spans.
    b. have small bodies.
    c. reproduce early.
    (d.) all of the above

15. Organisms that follow a slow life-history pattern
    a. have small bodies.
    b. mature rapidly.
    (c.) reproduce slowly.
    d. all of the above

16. A limiting factor that has an increasing effect as population size increases is
    a. temperature.
    b. habitat disruption.
    c. drought.
    (d.) competition.

In your textbook, read about how organism interactions limit population size.

Answer the following.

17. The snowshoe hare is a primary source of food for the Canadian lynx. Explain how the lynx
    population size changes when the hare population increases.
    The lynx population increases because it has more food—the hares.

18. Explain how the change in the lynx population size affects the hare population.
    Because more hares are being eaten, the hare population decreases.

19. What is the relationship between the lynx and the hare called?
    predator-prey relationship

20. When does competition decrease the size of a population?
    **Competition decreases the size of a population when the demand for resources
    exceeds the supply.**

21. What can cause an organism to exhibit stress, and what symptoms of stress can lead to a decrease
    in population size?
    **overcrowding; aggression, decrease in parental care, decreased fertility, and
    decreased resistance to disease**

Name _____ Date _____ Class _____

Chapter 4   Population Biology, *continued*

Section 4.2   *Human Population Growth*

In your textbook, read about demographic trends.

Determine if the statement is true. If it is not, rewrite the italicized part to make it true.

1. Looking at *past* population trends is a good way to predict the future of human populations.

   true

2. Demography is the study of population *health* characteristics.

   growth

3. Worldwide human populations have *decreased* exponentially over the past few centuries.

   increased

4. Humans are able to *increase* environmental effects on the human population through controlling disease, eliminating competing organisms, and increasing food production.

   decrease

5. To tell whether a population is *growing*, you must know the difference between the birthrate and the death rate.

   true

6. The death rate is *decreasing* in the United States.

   true

7. The birthrate is *increasing* in the United States.

   decreasing

8. *Birthrate* is the number of offspring a female produces during her reproductive years.

   Fertility rate

9. In the United States, families are now *smaller* than in previous decades.

   true

10. Birthrates and death rates of countries around the world *are basically the same.*

    vary greatly

11. If a country has a high death rate, it *may also* have a high birthrate.

    true

12. If a country has a low death rate and a *high* birthrate, it will grow slowly, if at all.

    low

Name _____ Date _____ Class _____

Chapter 4   Population Biology, *continued*

Section 4.2   *Human Population Growth,* continued

For each statement in Column A, write the letter of the item in Column B that completes the statement correctly.

Column A		Column B
c 13. Population growth will change if the largest of a population is in its post-reproductive years.		**a.** age structure
f 14. The proportions of a population that are at different ____ make up its age structure.		**b.** stable
e 15. If you know a population has a large group of individuals in their pre-reproductive years, you would predict that the population's growth will be ____.		**c.** proportion
b 16. If the proportions of a population at different age levels are fairly equal, the population will be ____.		**d.** fertility
d 17. The population growth of a country depends on its birthrate, death rate, and ____ rate.		**e.** rapid
a 18. To make predictions about the growth of a population, demographers must know its ____.		**f.** age levels

Complete each statement.

19. **Migration** ____ is the movement into and out of populations.

20. **Immigration** ____ is the movement of humans into a population.

21. **Emigration** ____ is the movement of humans from a population.

22. Immigration and emigration of people have no effect on total **world** ____ population.

23. Immigration and emigration of people affect **national** ____ population growth rates.

24. Suburban growth due to **immigration** ____ has placed stress on schools and various public services.

Name _____ Date _____ Class _____

Reinforcement and Study Guide

Chapter 5 Biological Diversity and Conservation

Section 5.1 *Vanishing Species*

In your textbook, read about biological diversity.

Use the terms below just once to complete the passage. You will not use all the terms.

| environments | variety | greater | space | species |
| biological diversity | equator | less | decrease | increase |

(1) __Biological diversity__ refers to the (2) __variety__ of life in an area. Another word for biological diversity is biodiversity. The simplest measure of biodiversity is the number of (3) __species__ that live in a certain area. The more species there are, the (4) __greater__ is the biodiversity of the area. Biodiversity on land tends to (5) __increase__ as you move toward the (6) __equator__.

Biodiversity is greater on large islands than on small islands because large islands have more (7) __space__ and a greater variety of (8) __environments__.

In your textbook, read about the importance of biodiversity.

For each statement below, write *true* or *false.*

__true__ 9. Biodiversity provides our world with beauty.

__false__ 10. The loss of a species from an ecosystem usually has no effect because of the presence of other species in the ecosystem.

__false__ 11. Biodiversity decreases the stability of ecosystems because more species are competing with each other.

__true__ 12. Increasing the biodiversity of an ecosystem may result in more niches.

__false__ 13. Diseases are more likely to spread in an ecosystem with high biodiversity than in an ecosystem with low biodiversity.

__true__ 14. A decrease in Earth's biodiversity may affect people's diets.

__true__ 15. Preserving diverse plant species may lead to the discovery of new drugs in the future.

Name _____ Date _____ Class _____

Reinforcement and Study Guide

Chapter 5 Biological Diversity and Conservation, *continued*

Section 5.1 *Vanishing Species,* **continued**

In your textbook, read about the loss of biodiversity.

For each item in Column A, write the letter of the matching item in Column B.

Column A

__f__ 16. The number of members of a species is so low that there is a possibility of extinction.

__c__ 17. This animal is an example of an endangered species.

__b__ 18. The population of a species begins declining rapidly.

__a__ 19. This animal is an example of an extinct species.

__e__ 20. All members of a species have died, so the species no longer exists.

__d__ 21. This animal is an example of a threatened species.

Column B

a. passenger pigeon

b. threatened species

c. black rhinoceros

d. African elephant

e. extinct species

f. endangered species

In your textbook, read about threats to biodiversity.

Complete the table by checking the correct column for each statement.

Statement	Habitat Loss	Habitat Fragmentation	Habitat Degradation
22. Animals have no migratory route.		✓	
23. A rain forest is burned.	✓		
24. A highway divides a forest.		✓	
25. Acid precipitation leaches nutrients from the soil.			✓
26. Detergents and other chemicals pollute bodies of water.			✓
27. Coral is mined for building materials.	✓		
28. The reduction of the ozone layer causes more ultraviolet radiation to reach Earth's surface.			✓

Chapter 5 — Biological Diversity and Conservation, *continued*

Section 5.2 Conservation of Biodiversity

In your textbook, read about strategies of conservation biology.

Answer the following questions.

1. What is conservation biology?
   Conservation biology is a field of biology that studies methods and implements plans to protect biodiversity.

2. How does the U.S. Endangered Species Act protect biodiversity?
   The law prohibits people from harming any species on the endangered or threatened species lists. It also prohibits federal agencies from funding projects that harm organisms on those lists.

3. How do nature preserves help protect biodiversity?
   Nature preserves help protect biodiversity by preserving the habitats of organisms.

4. Why is it usually better to preserve one large area of land instead of a few smaller areas of land?
   There usually is greater biodiversity within large areas than within small areas.

5. Why are habitat corridors used to connect different protected areas?
   The habitat corridors allow organisms to migrate from one area to another.

6. What caused the steady decline of the black-footed ferret population in Wyoming?
   Their decline was due to canine distemper, which spread to the ferrets, and the poisoning of prairie dogs, which were the ferrets' main source of food.

7. What efforts were made to increase the size of the black-footed ferret population?
   The remaining ferrets were captured, bred in captivity, and then returned to their original habitat.

8. How are seed banks useful in protecting biodiversity?
   Seeds from endangered or threatened plant species can be stored in seed banks for long periods of time. If the plant species become extinct, the seeds can be used to reintroduce the species to their original habitats.

9. What are some problems of keeping endangered animals in captivity in their original habitats?
   Keeping animals in captivity is expensive. While in captivity, animals may lose the behaviors they need to survive in their original habitats.

Chapter 5 — Biological Diversity and Conservation, *continued*

Section 5.1 Vanishing Species, continued

Circle the letter of the choice that best completes the statement.

29. When species lose their habitats, they may
    a. lack food.
    b. lack shelter.
    c. be in danger of becoming extinct.
    d. all of the above.

30. Habitat fragmentation often leads to
    a. increased species diversity within an area.
    b. larger habitats for species.
    c. decreased species diversity within an area.
    d. an increased food supply for species.

31. Different conditions along the boundaries of an ecosystem are called
    a. habitat fragmentation.
    b. edge effect.
    c. habitat loss.
    d. canopy effect.

32. The greatest source of air pollution is
    a. volcanic eruptions.
    b. forest fires.
    c. burning fossil fuels.
    d. CFCs.

33. Acid precipitation
    a. may decrease biodiversity on land.
    b. has no effect on biodiversity.
    c. may increase biodiversity in water.
    d. both a and c.

34. The reduction of the ozone layer is caused by
    a. burning fossil fuels.
    b. acid precipitation.
    c. heavy metals.
    d. CFCs.

35. Algal blooms in lakes
    a. are caused by acid precipitation.
    b. decrease the amount of oxygen in the lake when they decay.
    c. clog the gills of fish.
    d. both a and b.

36. When exotic species are introduced into an area, their populations may grow exponentially because the species
    a. are large.
    b. are predators.
    c. lack competitors and predators.
    d. are small.

37. The African elephant population was greatly reduced between 1970 and 1990 due to
    a. habitat degradation.
    b. excessive hunting.
    c. habitat loss.
    d. pollution.

Name _____ Date _____ Class _____

Reinforcement and Study Guide

BioDigest 2

Ecology

In your textbook, read about ecosystems.

For each statement below, write true or false.

true 1. Organisms interact with the nonliving parts of their environments.

false 2. Relationships between organisms are abiotic factors in ecosystems.

false 3. In the carbon cycle, animals produce nutrients from carbon dioxide in the atmosphere.

true 4. Commensalism is a relationship in which one species benefits while the other species is neither helped nor harmed.

true 5. The temperature and precipitation in a certain land area influence the type of biome that is found there.

In your textbook, read about food for life.

Use the diagram on the right to answer questions 6–10.

6. Describe a food chain using organisms in the pyramid.
   Answers will vary but may include plants eaten by the chipmunk and the chipmunk eaten by the snake.
   _____
   _____

7. Which organisms are carnivores?
   eagle, snake, raccoon
   _____

8. How many trophic levels are included in the pyramid?
   three
   _____

9. Which trophic level has the smallest biomass?
   carnivores
   _____

10. How does the biomass of the autotrophs compare with the biomass of the herbivores?
    The biomass of the autotrophs is about ten times the biomass of the herbivores.
    _____

Name _____ Date _____ Class _____

Reinforcement and Study Guide

BioDigest 2

Ecology, *continued*

In your textbook, read about population size.

Use the terms below to complete the passage. You will not use all the terms.

carrying capacity	species	maximum	limit	competition
linear growth	minimum	exceeds	food	exponential growth

A population is the number of organisms of one (11) **species** that live in a certain area. Under ideal conditions in which there are no factors that (12) **limit** the size of a population, a population shows (13) **exponential growth** . However, in the environment, the sizes of populations are influenced by various limiting factors, such as the availability of (14) **food** , water, space, and other resources. As population size increases, (15) **competition** for the resources increases. The (16) **maximum** size of a population that an environment can support is the environment's (17) **carrying capacity** for that population. When a population (18) **exceeds** the carrying capacity, individuals are unable to meet all their needs and die.

In your textbook, read about succession and biodiversity.

Number the steps of succession below in the order in which they occur.

4 19. Shade from grasses and shrubs provides protection for tree saplings.

6 20. Pioneer species and other small plants are unable to grow in the shade and die.

3 21. Grasses and bushes appear.

1 22. A plot of farmland is abandoned.

5 23. Tree saplings grow and increase the amount of shade in the area.

2 24. Pioneer species, such as dandelions, take root in the soil.

Answer the following questions.

25. What effect does succession have on the biodiversity of ecosystems?
    Succession increases the biodiversity of ecosystems.
    _____

26. What human actions decrease the biodiversity of ecosystems?
    Answers will vary. The use of land for housing and roads destroys the habitats of organisms. Pollution kills organisms and may threaten the existence of species.
    _____

REINFORCEMENT AND STUDY GUIDE   ANSWER KEY   BIOLOGY: The Dynamics of Life   **T189**

Chapter 6 — The Chemistry of Life

In your textbook, read about elements, atoms, and isotopes.

Determine if the statement is true. If it is not, rewrite the italicized part to make it true.

1. An element is a substance that *can be* broken down into simpler substances. **cannot be**

2. On Earth, *90* elements occur naturally. **true**

3. Only four elements—*carbon, hydrogen, oxygen, and nitrogen*—make up more than 96 percent of the mass of a human. **true**

4. Each element is abbreviated by a one- or two-letter *formula*. **symbol**

5. Trace elements, such as iron and magnesium, are present in living things in *very large* amounts. **very small**

6. The properties of elements are determined by *the structures of their atoms*. **true**

Label the parts of the atom. Use these choices:

energy level   electron   neutron   proton   nucleus

7. **proton**
8. **neutron**
9. **energy level**
10. **nucleus**
11. **electron**

Answer the following questions.

12. What is the maximum number of electrons in each of the following energy levels: first, second, third? **two in the first, eight in the second, 18 in the third**

13. Boron has two isotopes, boron-10 and boron-11. Boron-10 has five protons and five neutrons. How many protons and neutrons does boron-11 have? Explain. **Isotopes are atoms of the same element that have different numbers of neutrons. Boron-11 has the same number of protons as boron-10, that is, five. Since the isotope number refers to the total number of protons and neutrons, boron-11 has six neutrons.**

Chapter 6 — The Chemistry of Life, *continued*

In your textbook, read about compounds and bonding, chemical reactions, and mixtures and solutions.

Write the type of substance described. Use these choices: compound, element.

compound 14. H_2O, a liquid that no longer resembles either hydrogen or oxygen gas

compound 15. A substance that can be broken down in a chemical reaction

element 16. Carbon, the substance represented by the symbol C

Complete the table by checking the correct column for each description.

Statement	Ionic Bond(s)	Covalent Bond(s)
17. Found in the compound NaCl	✓	
18. Increases the stability of atoms	✓	
19. Results in the formation of a molecule		✓
20. Is formed when atoms share electrons		✓

Fill in the blanks with the correct number of molecules to balance the chemical equation. Then answer the questions.

$$C_6H_{12}O_6 + \mathbf{6}\,O_2 \longrightarrow \mathbf{6}\,CO_2 + \mathbf{6}\,H_2O$$

21. Why must chemical equations always balance? **Chemical equations must balance because atoms are neither created nor destroyed during a chemical reaction.**

22. Which number indicates the number of atoms of each element in a molecule of a substance. **the subscript number to the right of each element**

23. When is a mixture not a solution? **A mixture is not a solution when the substances that make up the mixture are not distributed evenly.**

24. What is the difference between an acid and a base? **An acid forms hydrogen ions in water. A base forms hydroxide ions in water.**

Name _____ Date _____ Class _____

Reinforcement and Study Guide

Chapter **6** **The Chemistry of Life,** continued

Section 6.2 *Water and Diffusion*

In your textbook, read about water and its importance.

For each statement below, write true or false.

false **1.** In a water molecule, electrons are shared equally between the hydrogen atoms and oxygen atom.

false **2.** The attraction of opposite charges between hydrogen and oxygen forms a weak oxygen bond.

true **3.** Because of its polarity, water can move from the roots of a plant up to its leaves.

false **4.** Water changes temperature easily.

true **5.** Unlike most substances, water expands when it freezes.

Circle the letter of the choice that best completes the statement.

6. All objects in motion have
a. potential energy.   b. heat energy.   (c.) kinetic energy.   d. random energy.

7. The first scientist to observe evidence of the random motion of molecules was
(a.) Brown.   b. Darwin.   c. Mendel.   d. Hooke.

8. The net movement of particles from an area of higher concentration to an area of lower concentration is called
a. dynamic equilibrium.   b. nonrandom movement.
c. concentration gradient.   (d.) diffusion.

9. Diffusion occurs because of
a. nonrandom movement of particles.   (b.) random movement of particles.
c. a chemical reaction between particles.   d. chemical energy.

10. When a few drops of colored corn syrup are added to a beaker of pure corn syrup, the color will
a. move from low concentration to high concentration.
b. form a polar bond.
(c.) start to diffuse.
d. remain on the bottom of the beaker.

11. Diffusion can be accelerated by
a. decreasing the pressure.   (b.) increasing the temperature.
c. decreasing the movement of particles.   d. increasing the dynamic equilibrium.

12. When materials pass into and out of a cell at equal rates, there is no net change in concentration inside the cell. The cell is in a state of
(a.) dynamic equilibrium.   b. metabolism.   c. imbalance.   d. inertia.

13. The difference in concentration of a substance across space is called
a. dynamic equilibrium.   (b.) concentration gradient.
c. diffusion.   d. Brownian movement.

Name _____ Date _____ Class _____

Reinforcement and Study Guide

Chapter **6** **The Chemistry of Life,** continued

Section 6.3 *Life Substances*

In your textbook, read about the role of carbon in organisms.

For each of the following statements about carbon, write true or false.

true **1.** Carbon atoms can bond together in straight chains, branched chains, or rings.

false **2.** Large molecules containing carbon atoms are called micromolecules.

false **3.** Polymers are formed by hydrolysis.

true **4.** Cells use carbohydrates for energy.

Write each item below under the correct heading.

sucrose   glucose   starch $C_6H_{12}O_6$
cellulose   glycogen   fructose $C_{12}H_{22}O_{11}$

Monosaccharide
5. $C_6H_{12}O_6$
6. glucose
7. fructose

Disaccharide
8. $C_{12}H_{22}O_{11}$
9. sucrose

Polysaccharide
10. starch
11. cellulose
12. glycogen

Complete the table by checking the correct column for each description.

Description	Lipids	Proteins	Nucleic Acids
13. Made up of nucleotides			✓
14. Most consist of three fatty acids bonded to a glycerol molecule	✓		
15. DNA and RNA			✓
16. Contain peptide bonds		✓	
17. Produce proteins			✓
18. Commonly called fats and oils	✓		
19. Made up of amino acids		✓	
20. Used for long-term energy storage, insulation, and protective coatings	✓		
21. Contain carbon, hydrogen, oxygen, and nitrogen		✓	

Chapter 7 — A View of the Cell

Section 7.1 The Discovery of Cells

In your textbook, read about the history of the cell theory.

For each statement in Column A, write the letter of the matching item in Column B.

	Column A	Column B
f	**1.** The first scientist to describe living cells as seen through a simple microscope	**a.** Schleiden
b	**2.** Uses two or more glass lenses to magnify either living cells or prepared slides	**b.** compound light microscope
e	**3.** A scientist who observed that cork was composed of tiny, hollow boxes that he called cells	**c.** electron microscope
a	**4.** A scientist who concluded that all plants are composed of cells	**d.** Schwann
d	**5.** A scientist who concluded that all animals are composed of cells	**e.** Hooke
c	**6.** The microscope that allowed scientists to view molecules	**f.** Leeuwenhoek

In your textbook, read about the two basic cell types.

Complete the table by checking the correct column for each statement.

Statement	Prokaryotes	Eukaryotes
7. Organisms that have cells lacking internal membrane-bound structures	✓	
8. Do not have a nucleus	✓	
9. Are either single-celled or made up of many cells		✓
10. Generally are single-celled organisms	✓	
11. Organisms that have cells containing organelles		✓

Chapter 7 — A View of the Cell, *continued*

Section 7.2 The Plasma Membrane

In your textbook, read about maintaining a balance.

Use each of the terms below just once to complete the passage.

glucose   plasma membrane   homeostasis
organism   balance   selective permeability

Living cells maintain a **(1)** _balance_ by controlling materials that enter and leave. Without this ability, the cell cannot maintain **(2)** _homeostasis_ and will die. The cell must regulate internal concentrations of water, **(3)** _glucose_ , and other nutrients and must eliminate waste products.

Homeostasis in a cell is maintained by the **(4)** _plasma membrane_ , which allows only certain particles to pass through and keeps other particles out. This property of a membrane is known as **(5)** _selective permeability_ . It allows different cells to carry on different activities within the same **(6)** _organism_ .

In your textbook, read about the structure of the plasma membrane.

For each statement below, write *true* or *false*.

false	**7.** The structure and properties of the cell wall allow it to be selective and maintain homeostasis.
true	**8.** The plasma membrane is a bilayer of lipid molecules with protein molecules embedded in it.
false	**9.** A phospholipid molecule has a nonpolar, water-insoluble head attached to a long polar, soluble tail.
false	**10.** The fluid mosaic model describes the plasma membrane as a structure that is liquid and very rigid.
true	**11.** Eukaryotic plasma membranes can contain cholesterol, which tends to make the membrane more stable.
true	**12.** Transport proteins span the cell membrane, creating the selectively permeable membrane that regulates which molecules enter and leave a cell.
false	**13.** Proteins at the inner surface of the plasma membrane attach the membrane to the cell's support structure, making the cell rigid.

Name _____ Date _____ Class _____

Chapter 7 A View of the Cell, continued

Section 7.3 Eukaryotic Cell Structure

In your textbook, read about cellular boundaries; nucleus and cell control; assembly, transport, and storage in the cell; and energy transformers.

Complete the table by writing the name of the cell part beside its structure/function. A cell part may be used more than once.

Structure/Function	Cell Part
1. A membrane-bound, fluid-filled sac	vacuole
2. Closely stacked, flattened membrane sacs	Golgi apparatus
3. The sites of protein synthesis	ribosomes
4. A folded membrane that forms a network of interconnected compartments in the cytoplasm	endoplasmic reticulum
5. The clear fluid inside the cell	cytoplasm
6. Organelle that manages cell functions in eukaryotic cell	nucleus
7. Contains chlorophyll, a green pigment that traps energy from sunlight and gives plants their green color	chloroplast
8. Digest excess or worn-out cell part, food particles, and invading viruses or bacteria	lysosomes
9. Small bumps located on the endoplasmic reticulum	ribosomes
10. Provides temporary storage of food, enzymes, and waste products	vacuole
11. Firm, protective structure that gives the cell its shape in plants, fungi, most bacteria, and some protists	cell wall
12. Produce a usable form of energy for the cell	mitochondria
13. Modifies proteins chemically, then repackages them	Golgi apparatus
14. Contains inner membranes arranged in stacks of membranous sacs called grana	chloroplast
15. Plant organelles that store starches or lipids or that contain pigments	plastids

---

Name _____ Date _____ Class _____

Chapter 7 A View of the Cell, continued

Section 7.3 Eukaryotic Cell Structure, continued

In your textbook, read about structures for support and locomotion.

Determine if the statement is true. If it is not, rewrite the italicized part to make it true.

16. Cells have a support structure within the *cytoplasm* called the cytoskeleton.
true

17. The *exoskeleton* is composed of thin, fibrous elements that form a framework for the cell.
cytoskeleton

18. *Microtubules* of the cytoskeleton are thin, hollow cylinders made of protein.
true

19. Cilia and flagella are cell surface structures that are adapted for *respiration*.
locomotion

20. *Flagella* are short, numerous, hairlike projections from the plasma membrane.
Cilia

21. Flagella are longer and *more* numerous than cilia.
less

22. In *multicellular* organisms, cilia and flagella are the major means of locomotion.
unicellular

23. In *prokaryotic* cells, both cilia and flagella are composed of microtubules.
eukaryotic

Write titles for each of the generalized diagrams and then label the parts. Use these choices: plant cell, animal cell, plasma membrane, chloroplast, small vacuole, large vacuole, cell wall.

24. __animal cell__

25. __plant cell__

26. __plasma membrane__

27. __small vacuole__

28. __cell wall__

29. __chloroplast__

30. __large vacuole__

Chapter 8 — Cellular Transport and the Cell Cycle, continued

In your textbook, read about cell size limitations.

Determine if the statement is true. If it is not, rewrite the italicized part to make it true.

1. Most *living cells* are between 2 and 200 μm in diameter. **true**

2. Diffusion of materials over long distance is *fast*. **slow**

3. If a cell doesn't have enough *DNA* to make all the proteins it needs, the cell cannot live. **true**

4. As a cell's size increases, its volume increases much *slower* than its surface area. **faster**

5. If a cell's diameter doubled, the cell would require *two* times more nutrients and would have *two* times more wastes to excrete. **eight, eight**

In your textbook, read about cell reproduction.

Use each of the terms below just once to complete the passage.

nucleus   genetic material   chromosomes   packed
identical   chromatin   vanish   cell division

The process by which two cells are produced from one cell is called (6) **cell division** .

The two cells are (7) **identical** to the original cell. Early biologists observed that just

before cell division, several short, stringy structures appeared in the (8) **nucleus** .

These structures seemed to (9) **vanish** soon after cell division. These structures,

which contain DNA and became darkly colored when stained, are now called (10) **chromosomes** .

Scientists eventually learned that chromosomes carry (11) **genetic material** , which

is copied and passed on from generation to generation. Chromosomes normally exist as

(12) **chromatin** , long strands of DNA wrapped around proteins. However, before

a cell divides, the chromatin becomes tightly (13) **packed** .

Chapter 8 — Cellular Transport and the Cell Cycle

In your textbook, read about osmosis: diffusion of water.

Complete the table by checking the correct column for each statement.

Statement	Isotonic Solution	Hypotonic Solution	Hypertonic Solution
1. Causes a cell to swell		✓	
2. Doesn't change the shape of a cell	✓		
3. Causes osmosis		✓	✓
4. Causes a cell to shrink			✓

In your textbook, read about passive transport and active transport.

For each item in Column A, write the letter of the matching item in Column B.

	Column A	Column B
h	5. Transport protein that provides a tubelike opening in the plasma membrane through which particles can diffuse	a. energy
a	6. Is used during active transport but not passive transport	b. facilitated diffusion
c	7. Process by which a cell takes in material by forming a vacuole around it	c. endocytosis
d	8. Particle movement from an area of higher concentration to an area of lower concentration	d. passive transport
f	9. Process by which a cell expels wastes from a vacuole	e. active transport
b	10. A form of passive transport that uses transport proteins	f. exocytosis
e	11. Particle movement from an area of lower concentration to an area of higher concentration	g. carrier protein
g	12. Transport protein that changes shape when a particle binds with it	h. channel protein

Name _____ Date _____ Class _____

Chapter 8 Cellular Transport and the Cell Cycle, *continued*

Section 8.2 Cellular Growth and Reproduction, *continued*

In your textbook, read about the cell cycle and interphase.

Complete the table by checking the correct column for each statement.

Statement	Interphase	Mitosis
14. Cell growth occurs.	✓	
15. Nuclear division occurs.		✓
16. Chromosomes are distributed equally to daughter cells.		✓
17. Protein production is high.	✓	
18. Chromosomes are duplicated.	✓	
19. DNA synthesis occurs.	✓	
20. Cytoplasm divides immediately after this period.		✓
21. Mitochondria and other organelles are manufactured.	✓	

In your textbook, read about the phases of mitosis.

Identify the following phases of mitosis. Use these choices: telophase, metaphase, anaphase, prophase. Then label the diagrams. Use these choices: sister chromatids, centromere, spindle fibers, centrioles.

22. __prophase__   23. __metaphase__   24. __anaphase__   25. __telophase__

26. __centrioles__   27. __sister chromatids__   28. __centromere__   29. __spindle fibers__

Answer the question.

30. How does mitosis result in tissues and organs?

In multicellular organisms, mitosis produces groups of cells that work together to perform a function. These groups are tissues. The tissues are organized in different combinations to form organs that have different functions.

Name _____ Date _____ Class _____

Chapter 8 Cellular Transport and the Cell Cycle, *continued*

Section 8.3 Control of the Cell Cycle

In your textbook, read about normal control of the cell cycle and cancer.

Answer the following questions.

1. In what ways do enzymes control the cell cycle?
Enzymes are needed to begin and drive the cell cycle. They also direct the phases of the cell cycle.

2. What directs the production of these enzymes?
Genes, segments of DNA located on the chromosomes, direct the production of these enzymes.

3. What can cause the cell cycle to become uncontrolled?
Lack of the enzymes needed to control the cell cycle, overproduction of those enzymes, or production of other enzymes at the wrong time all can cause the cell cycle to become uncontrolled.

4. What can result when the cell cycle becomes uncontrolled?
Uncontrolled cell division and possibly cancer can result.

5. What is the relationship between environmental factors and cancer?
Certain environmental factors, such as cigarette smoke, pollution, and UV rays, can damage the genes that control the production of enzymes involved in the cell cycle. Uncontrolled cell division that leads to cancer may result.

6. What is a tumor? Describe the final stages of cancer.
A tumor is a mass of tissue that deprives normal cells of nutrients. In the final stages of cancer, cancer cells metastasize to other parts of the body, forming new tumors that disrupt organ functions.

7. Cancer is the second leading cause of death in the United States. What four types of cancer are the most prevalent?
Lung, colon, breast, and prostate cancers are the most prevalent.

Reinforcement and Study Guide

Chapter 9 Energy in a Cell

Section 9.1 *ATP in a Molecule*

In your textbook, read about cell energy.

Use each of the terms below just once to complete the passage.

energy	phosphate	adenosine	charged
ATP	chemical bonds	work	ribose

To do biological **(1)** _work_ , cells require energy. A quick source
of energy that cells use is the molecule **(2)** _ATP_ . The **(3)** _energy_
in this molecule is stored in its **(4)** _chemical bonds_ . ATP is composed of a(n)
(5) _adenosine_ molecule bonded to a(n) **(6)** _ribose_ sugar.
Three **(7)** _charged_ molecules called **(8)** _phosphate_ groups
are attached to the sugar.

In your textbook, read about forming and breaking down ATP and the uses of cell energy.

Examine the diagram below. Then answer the questions.

ATP

ADP + P$_i$

Energy

Energy from food

9. How is energy stored and released by ATP?
   **Energy that is used to add a phosphate group to ADP becomes stored as a
   chemical bond in the resulting ATP molecule. The stored energy is released
   when ATP is broken down to ADP and a phosphate group.**

10. How do cells use the energy released from ATP?
    **Answers may vary. Cells use energy to make new molecules, maintain
    homeostasis, transmit nerve impulses, move, and produce light.**

Reinforcement and Study Guide

Chapter 9 Energy in a Cell, *continued*

Section 9.2 *Photosynthesis: Trapping
the Sun's Energy*

In your textbook, read about trapping the sun's energy.

Determine if the statement is true. If it is not, rewrite the italicized part to make it true.

1. Photosynthesis is the process plants use to trap the sun's energy to make *glucose*.
   true

2. ATP molecules are made during the *light-independent* reactions of photosynthesis.
   light-dependent

3. *Carbon dioxide* gas is produced during photosynthesis.
   oxygen

4. The light-dependent reactions of photosynthesis take place in the membranes of the
   thylakoid discs in *mitochondria*.
   chloroplasts

5. The thylakoid membranes contain chlorophyll and other pigments that *absorb* sunlight.
   true

In your textbook, read about the light-dependent reactions of photosynthesis.

Number the following steps of the light-dependent reactions in the order in which they occur.

_4_ 6. The energy lost by electrons as they pass through the electron transport chain is used
        to make ATP.

_3_ 7. The electrons pass from the chlorophyll to an electron transport chain.

_1_ 8. Sunlight strikes the chlorophyll molecules in the thylakoid membranes.

_6_ 9. NADP$^+$ molecules change to NADPH as they carry the electrons to the stroma of the
        chloroplast.

_2_ 10. The sunlight's energy is transferred to the chlorophyll's electrons.

_5_ 11. The electrons are passed down a second electron transport chain.

Answer the following questions.

12. How are the electrons that are lost by the chlorophyll molecules replaced?
    **The electrons are replaced by the splitting of water molecules during
    photosynthesis.**

13. How do plants produce oxygen during photosynthesis?
    **Oxygen, as well as hydrogen ions, is produced when water molecules are split
    during photosynthesis.**

Name _____ Date _____ Class _____

Reinforcement and Study Guide

Chapter 9 Energy in a Cell, *continued*

Section 9.2 Photosynthesis: Trapping the Sun's Energy, *continued*

In your textbook, read about the light-independent reactions.

Circle the letter of the choice that best completes the statement or answers the question.

14. The Calvin cycle includes
   a. the light-dependent reactions.   b. an electron transport chain.
   (c.) the light-independent reactions.   d. photolysis.

15. The Calvin cycle takes place in the
   a. mitochondria.   (b.) stroma.
   c. nucleus.   d. thylakoid membrane.

16. What product of the light-dependent reactions is used in the Calvin cycle?
   a. oxygen   b. carbon dioxide   (c.) NADPH   d. chlorophyll

17. What gas is used in the first step of the Calvin cycle?
   a. oxygen   (b.) carbon dioxide   c. hydrogen   d. water

18. A carbon atom from carbon dioxide is used to change the five-carbon sugar RuBP into
   a. ATP.   b. two molecules.   c. PGA.   (d.) a six-carbon sugar.

19. How many molecules of the three-carbon sugar PGA are formed?
   (a.) two   b. one   c. six   d. three

20. ATP, NADPH, and hydrogen ions are used to convert PGA into
   (a.) PGAL.   b. glucose.   c. RuBP.   d. carbon dioxide.

21. How many rounds of the Calvin cycle are needed to form one glucose molecule?
   a. one   (b.) six   c. two   d. three

22. What two molecules leave the Calvin cycle and are combined to form glucose?
   a. RuBP   b. PGA   (c.) PGAL   d. CO_2

23. Which molecule from the Calvin cycle is used to replenish the five-carbon sugar, RuBP, which is used at the beginning of the cycle?
   a. NADP   b. CO_2 c. PGA   (d.) PGAL

Name _____ Date _____ Class _____

Reinforcement and Study Guide

Chapter 9 Energy in a Cell, *continued*

Section 9.3 Getting Energy to Make ATP

In your textbook, read about the cellular respiration and fermentation.

Fill in the names of the molecules to complete the glycolysis reaction. Use these choices:
2PGAL, 4ATP, glucose, 2ADP, 2 pyruvic acid, 2NADH + 2H⁺. Then answer the questions.

1. glucose
2. 2ADP   — 2ATP   — Glycolysis — 4ADP + 4P$_i$ 4. 4ATP
3. 2PGAL
5. 2 pyruvic acid
6. 2NADH + 2H⁺   (2NAD⁺)

7. What happens to pyruvic acid before entering the citric acid cycle?
   Pyruvic acid combines with coenzyme A to form acetyl-CoA.

8. What happens to the electrons carried by the NADH and FADH₂ molecules produced during the citric acid cycle?
   The electrons are passed through an electron transport chain, releasing energy at each step.

9. During which stages of cellular respiration are ATP molecules formed?
   citric acid cycle and electron transport chain

10. Why is oxygen necessary for cellular respiration?
   Oxygen is the final electron acceptor in the electron transport chain.

11. How is fermentation different from cellular respiration?
   Fermentation occurs when no oxygen is available. Fermentation produces fewer ATP molecules.

In your textbook, read about comparing photosynthesis and cellular respiration.

Answer the following question.

12. Describe two ways in which cellular respiration is the opposite of photosynthesis.
   In cellular respiration, chemical energy is released, whereas in photosynthesis, chemical energy is stored. Products of cellular respiration, CO_2 and H_2O, are used in photosynthesis. Products of photosynthesis, glucose and O_2, are used in cellular respiration.

BioDigest 3 — The Life of a Cell

In your textbook, read about the chemistry of life.

Label the diagram below, using these choices:

atom   electron   molecule   neutron   nucleus   proton

1. **proton**

2. **atom**

3. **molecule**

4. **electron**

5. **nucleus**

6. **neutron**

In your textbook, read about eukaryotes, prokaryotes, and organelles.

Complete each statement.

7. Every cell is surrounded by a plasma ___**membrane**___.

8. ___**Eukaryotes**___ are organisms with cells that contain membrane-bound structures called organelles within the cell.

9. Organisms having cells without internal membrane-bound structures are called ___**prokaryotes**___.

10. The plasma membrane is composed of a ___**lipid bilayer**___ with embedded proteins.

11. The ___**nucleus**___ controls cell functions.

12. Ribosomes are organelles found in the cytoplasm that produce ___**proteins**___.

13. The ___**endoplasmic reticulum**___ and Golgi apparatus transport and modify proteins.

14. Plant cells contain ___**chloroplasts**___ that capture the sun's light energy so that it can be transformed into usable chemical energy.

15. A network of microfilaments and microtubules attached to the cell membrane give the cell ___**structure**___.

16. ___**Flagella**___ are long projections from the surface of the plasma membrane and move in a whiplike fashion to propel a cell.

BioDigest 3 — The Life of a Cell, *continued*

In your textbook, read about diffusion and osmosis.

Answer the following questions.

17. What is diffusion? **Diffusion is the movement of a substance from an area of higher concentration to an area of lower concentration.**

18. What is osmosis? **Osmosis is the diffusion of water across a selectively permeable membrane.**

19. What is active transport? **Active transport is the movement of molecules against a concentration gradient.**

In your textbook, read about mitosis.

For each item in Column A, write the letter of the matching item in Column B.

Column A

___d___ 20. Duplicated chromosomes condense and mitotic spindles form on the two opposite ends of the cell.

___a___ 21. Chromosomes slowly separate to opposite ends of cells.

___e___ 22. Chromosomes uncoil, spindle breaks down, and nuclear envelope forms around each set of chromosomes.

___b___ 23. Cells experience a period of intense metabolic activity prior to mitosis.

___c___ 24. Chromosomes line up in center of cell.

Column B

a. anaphase

b. interphase

c. metaphase

d. prophase

e. telophase

In your textbook, read about energy in a cell.

Decide if each of the following statements is true. If it is not, rewrite the italicized part to make it true.

___**energy**___ 25. Adenosine triphosphate (ATP) is the most commonly used source of *protein* in a cell.

___**Light-independent**___ 26. *Light-dependent* reactions convert energy into starch through the Calvin cycle.

___**true**___ 27. *Mitochondria* convert food energy to ATP through a series of chemical reactions.

___**each molecule**___ 28. Glycolysis produces a net gain of two ATP for *every two molecules* of glucose.

REINFORCEMENT AND STUDY GUIDE

Name _____ Date _____ Class _____

Chapter 10 Mendel and Meiosis

Section 10.1 Mendel's Laws of Heredity

In your textbook, read why Mendel succeeded.

Complete each statement.

1. Mendel was the first person to succeed in predicting how traits are __transferred__ from generation to generation.

2. Mendel used __garden pea__ plants in his experiments.

3. In peas, both male and female sex cells—__gametes__—are in the same flower.

4. __Fertilization__ occurs when the male gamete fuses with the female gamete.

5. Mendel used the process called __cross-pollination__ when he wanted to breed one plant with another.

6. Mendel carefully __controlled__ his experiments and the peas he used.

7. Mendel studied only one __trait__ at a time and analyzed his data mathematically.

In your textbook, read about Mendel's monohybrid crosses.

Refer to the table of pea-plant traits on the left. Then complete the table on the right. The missing information for each cross. The first one is done for you.

Parent Plants	F₁ generation Offspring	Appearance
8. round × wrinkled RR × rr	Rr	round
9. yellow × green YY × yy	Yy	yellow
10. axial × terminal AA × aa	Aa	axial
11. tall × short __TT__ × __tt__	Tt	tall
12. inflated × constricted __II__ × ii	Ii	inflated

	Pea-Plant Traits	
Trait	Dominant	Recessive
seed shape	round (R)	wrinkled (r)
seed color	yellow (Y)	green (y)
flower position	axial (A)	terminal (a)
plant height	tall (T)	short (t)
pod shape	inflated (I)	constricted (i)

Name _____ Date _____ Class _____

Chapter 10 Mendel and Meiosis, *continued*

Section 10.1 Mendel's Laws of Heredity, *continued*

In your textbook, read about phenotypes and genotypes and Mendel's dihybrid crosses.

Determine if the statement is true. If it is not, rewrite the underlined part to make it true.

13. A pea plant with the genotype *TT* has the same phenotype as a pea plant with genotype __tt__.   __Tt__

14. When Mendel crossed true-breeding pea plants that had round yellow seeds with true-breeding pea plants that had wrinkled green seeds, __some__ of the offspring had round yellow seeds because round and yellow were the dominant forms of the traits.   __all__

15. When Mendel allowed heterozygous F₁ plants that had round yellow seed to self-pollinate, he found that __some__ of the F₂ plants had wrinkled green seeds.   __true__

16. The law of independent assortment states that __genes__ for different traits are inherited independently of each other.   __true__

In your textbook, read about Punnett squares and probability.

The Punnett square below is for a dihybrid cross between pea plants that are heterozygous for seed shape (Rr) and seed color (Yy). Complete the Punnett square by recording the expected genotypes of the offspring. Then answer the questions.

	RY	Ry	rY	ry
RY	*RRYY* round, yellow	*RRYy* round, yellow	*RrYY* round, yellow	*RrYy* round, yellow
Ry	*RRYy* round, yellow	*RRyy* round, green	*RrYy* round, yellow	*Rryy* round, green
rY	*RrYY* round, yellow	*RrYy* round, yellow	*rrYY* wrinkled, yellow	*rrYy* wrinkled, yellow
ry	*RrYy* round, yellow	*Rryy* round, green	*rrYy* wrinkled, yellow	*rryy* wrinkled, green

17. Use the chart on the previous page to determine the phenotypes of the offspring. Record the phenotypes below the genotypes in the Punnett square. Is an offspring produced by the cross more likely to have wrinkled seeds or round seeds?   __round seeds__

18. What is the probability that an offspring will have wrinkled yellow seeds?   __3/16__

Reinforcement and Study Guide

Chapter 10 Mendel and Meiosis, *continued*

Section 10.2 Meiosis, *continued*

The following statements describe interphase and meiosis I. Identify each phase. Then place them in sequential order using the numbers 1 through 5. Use 1 for the phase that occurs first and 5 for the phase that occurs last.

Statement	Name of Phase	Sequence
15. Homologous chromosomes line up at the equator in pairs.	Metaphase I	3
16. The cell replicates its chromosomes.	Interphase	1
17. Homologous chromosomes separate and move to opposite ends of the cell.	Anaphase I	4
18. The spindle forms, and chromosomes coil up and come together in a tetrad; crossing over may occur.	Prophase I	2
19. Events occur in the reverse order from the events of prophase I. Each cell has only half the genetic information; however, another cell division is needed because each chromosome is still doubled.	Telophase I	5

In your textbook, read about how meiosis provides for genetic variation and about mistakes in meiosis.

For each statement below, write true or false.

true 20. Reassortment of chromosomes can occur during meiosis by crossing over or by independent segregation of homologous chromosomes.

true 21. Genetic recombination is a major source of variation among organisms.

true 22. The random segregation of chromosomes during meiosis explains Mendel's observation that genes for different traits are inherited independently of each other.

false 23. Nondisjunction always results in a zygote with an extra chromosome.

false 24. Down syndrome is a result of polyploidy.

true 25. Mistakes in meiosis can occasionally be beneficial.

Reinforcement and Study Guide

Chapter 10 Mendel and Meiosis, *continued*

Section 10.2 Meiosis

In your textbook, read about genes, chromosomes, and numbers.

Examine the table. Then answer the questions.

Chromosome Numbers of Some Common Organisms

Organism	Body Cell (2n)	Gamete (n)
Human	46	23
Garden pea	14	7
Fruit fly	8	4
Tomato	24	12
Dog	78	39
Chimpanzee	48	24
Leopard frog	26	13
Corn	20	10

1. What is the diploid number of chromosomes in corn?
   20

2. What is the haploid number of chromosomes in corn?
   10

3. Is the chromosome number related to the complexity of the organism?
   no

4. How many pairs of chromosomes do humans have?
   23

5. What process maintains a constant number of chromosomes within a species?
   meiosis

In your textbook, read about the phases of meiosis.

Label the diagrams below. Use these choices: Metaphase I, Metaphase II, Interphase, Telophase I, Telophase II, Anaphase I, Anaphase II, Prophase I, Prophase II.

6. **Interphase** 7. **Prophase I** 8. **Metaphase I** 9. **Anaphase I** 10. **Telophase I**

11. **Prophase II** 12. **Metaphase II** 13. **Anaphase II** 14. **Telophase II**

REINFORCEMENT AND STUDY GUIDE

Name _____ Date _____ Class _____

Reinforcement and Study Guide

Section 11.1 DNA: The Molecule of Heredity

In your textbook, read about what DNA is and the replication of DNA.

Label the diagram. Use these choices: nucleotide, deoxyribose, phosphate group, nitrogen base, hydrogen bonds, base pair.

1. **deoxyribose**

2. **nitrogen base**

3. **nucleotide**

4. **base pair**

5. **hydrogen bonds**

6. **phosphate group**

Complete each statement.

7. Adenine (A), **Adenine (A)**, guanine (G), cytosine (C), and thymine (T) are the four **nitrogen bases** in DNA.

8. In DNA, **cytosine (C)** always forms hydrogen bonds with guanine (G).

9. The sequence of **nucleotides** carries the genetic information of an organism.

10. The process of **replication** produces a new copy of an organism's genetic information, which is passed on to a new cell.

11. The double-coiled shape of DNA is called a **double helix**.

Name _____ Date _____ Class _____

Reinforcement and Study Guide

Section 11.2 From DNA to Protein

In your textbook, read about genes and proteins and RNA.

Complete the chart on the three chemical differences between DNA and RNA.

Structure	DNA	RNA
1. strand of nucleotides	double	single
2. sugar	deoxyribose	ribose
3. nitrogen base	thymine	uracil

In your textbook, read about the genetic code.

Complete each statement.

4. Proteins are made up of **amino acids**.

5. There are twenty different types of **amino acids**.

6. The message of the DNA code is information for building **proteins**.

7. Each set of three nitrogen bases that codes for an amino acid is known as a **codon**.

8. The amino acid **threonine** is represented by the mRNA codon ACA.

9. **UUU** and **UUC** are mRNA codons for phenylalanine.

10. There can be more than one **codon** for the same amino acid.

11. For any one codon, there can be only one **amino acid**.

12. The genetic code is said to be universal because a codon represents the same **amino acid** in almost all organisms.

13. **UAA**, **UAG**, and **UGA** are stop codons.

14. **Tryptophan** and **methionine** are amino acids that are each represented by only one codon.

Chapter 11 | DNA and Genes, *continued*

Reinforcement and Study Guide

Section 11.3 Genetic Changes

In your textbook, read about mutation: a change in DNA.

Circle the letter of the choice that best completes the statement.

1. A mutation is any mistake or change in the
   a. cell. (b.) DNA sequence. c. ribosomes. d. nucleus.

2. A point mutation is a change in
   a. several bases in mRNA. b. several bases in tRNA.
   (c.) a single base pair in DNA. d. several base pairs in DNA.

3. A mutation in which a single base is added or deleted from DNA is called
   (a.) a frame shift mutation. b. a point mutation. c. translocation. d. nondisjunction.

4. Chromosomal mutations are especially common in
   a. humans. b. animals. c. bacteria. (d.) plants.

5. Few chromosome mutations are passed on to the next generation because
   a. the zygote usually dies.
   b. the mature organism is sterile.
   c. the mature organism is often incapable of producing offspring.
   (d.) all of the above.

6. When part of one chromosome breaks off and is added to a different chromosome, the result is a(n)
   (a.) translocation. b. insertion. c. inversion. d. deletion.

7. Many chromosome mutations result when chromosomes fail to separate properly during
   a. mitosis. (b.) meiosis. c. crossing over. d. linkage.

8. The failure of homologous chromosomes to separate properly is called
   a. translocation. b. disjunction. (c.) nondisjunction. d. deletion.

9. Mutations that occur at random are called
   (a.) spontaneous mutations. b. nonspontaneous mutations.
   c. nonrandom mutations. d. environmental mutations.

10. An agent that can cause a change in DNA is called a(n)
    a. zygote. b. inversion.
    (c.) mutagen. d. mutation.

11. Mutations in body cells can sometimes result in
    a. new species. (b.) cancer.
    c. sterile offspring. d. hybrids.

Chapter 11 | DNA and Genes, *continued*

Reinforcement and Study Guide

Section 11.2 From DNA to Protein, *continued*

In your textbook, read about transcription from DNA to mRNA.

Complete each statement.

15. Proteins are made in the cytoplasm of a cell, whereas DNA is found only in the **nucleus**.

16. The process of making RNA from DNA is called **transcription**.

17. The process of transcription is similar to the process of DNA **replication**.

18. **Messenger RNA** carries information from the DNA in the nucleus out into the cytoplasm of the cell.

19. mRNA carries the information for making proteins to the **ribosomes**.

In your textbook, read about translation from mRNA to protein.

Label the diagram. Use these choices: transfer RNA (tRNA), amino acid, amino acid chain, codon, anticodon, messenger RNA (mRNA), ribosome.

20. **amino acid**
21. **transfer RNA (tRNA)**
22. **messenger RNA (mRNA)**
23. **amino acid chain**
24. **ribosome**
25. **anticodon**
26. **codon**

Name _____ Date _____ Class _____

Chapter 12 Patterns of Heredity and Human Genetics

Section 12.1 Mendelian Inheritance of Human Traits

In your textbook, read about making a pedigree.

Examine the pedigree to the right. Then answer the following questions.

1. Is the trait being studied in the pedigree recessive or dominant? How do you know?

Recessive. If the trait were dominant, every individual with the trait would have a parent showing the trait. A recessive trait can be produced by two parents who do not show the trait, as with III-1.

2. Are II-1 and II-2 carriers of the trait? How do you know?
Yes, they are carriers because they produced III-1, who is afflicted with the trait.

3. What is the probability that II-1 and II-2 will produce an individual with the trait being studied? Draw a Punnett square to show your work.
The probability is 1:4. The Punnett square should show the cross of two heterozygotes.

4. What is the likely genotype of II-4 for the trait being studied in the pedigree?
Accept any genotype that includes at least one uppercase letter.

In your textbook, read about simple recessive heredity and simple dominant heredity.

For each item in Column A, write the letter of the matching item from Column B.

	Column A	Column B
c	**5.** Recessive disorder that results from the absence of an enzyme required to break lipids down	**a.** cystic fibrosis
d	**6.** Lethal genetic disorder caused by a dominant allele	**b.** simple dominant traits
a	**7.** Most common genetic disorder among white Americans	**c.** Tay-Sachs disease
e	**8.** Recessive disorder that results from the absence of an enzyme that converts one amino acid into another one	**d.** Huntington's disease
b	**9.** Tongue curling and Hapsburg lip	**e.** phenylketonuria

---

Name _____ Date _____ Class _____

Chapter 12 Patterns of Heredity and Human Genetics, *continued*

Section 12.2 When Heredity Follows Different Rules

In your textbook, read about complex patterns of inheritance.

Answer the following questions.

1. Complete the Punnett square for a cross between a homozygous red-flowered snapdragon (RR) and a homozygous white-flowered snapdragon ($R'R'$). Give the genotype and phenotype of the offspring in the F_1 generation.

Key
RR - red
$R'R'$ - white
RR' - pink

F_1	R	R
R'	RR'	RR'
R'	RR'	RR'

genotype: RR'

phenotype: **100% pink**

2. When traits are inherited in an incomplete dominance pattern, what is true of the phenotype of the heterozygotes?
It is intermediate between those of the two homozygotes.

3. Complete the Punnett square for a cross between two pink-flowered (RR') F_1 plants. Give the phenotype ratio of the offspring in the F_2 generation.

F_2	R	R'
R	RR	RR'
R'	RR'	$R'R'$

phenotype ratio: **1 red; 2 pink; 1 white**

4. In what type of inheritance are both alleles expressed equally?
codominance

5. Complete the Punnett square for a cross between a black chicken (BB) and a white chicken (WW). Give the phenotype of the offspring in the F_1 generation.

Key
BB - black
WW - white
BW - checkered

F_1	B	B
W	BW	BW
W	BW	BW

phenotype: **100% checkered**

Chapter 12 Patterns of Heredity and Human Genetics, continued

Reinforcement and Study Guide

Section 12.3 Complex Inheritance of Human Traits

In your textbook, read about multiple alleles in humans.

Complete the table by filling in the missing information.

Genotypes	Human Blood Groups Surface Molecules	Phenotypes
1. $I^A I^A$ or $I^A i$	A	A
2. $I^B I^B$ or $I^B i$	B	B
3. $I^A I^B$	A and B	AB
4. ii	none	O

Complete each statement.

5. Blood groups are a classic example of __**multiple allelic**__ inheritance in humans.

6. The alleles __I^A and I^B__ are always both expressed.

7. The alleles I^A and I^B are __**codominant**__, meaning they are always both expressed.

8. I^A and I^B are dominant to __i__.

9. Blood typing is necessary before a person can receive a __**blood transfusion**__.

10. A child who inherits I^A from his mother and I^B from his father will have type __AB__ blood.

11. A child whose parents both have type O blood will have type __O__ blood.

12. If a woman with blood type A has a baby with blood type AB, a man with blood type O __**could not**__ be the father.

13. Blood tests __**cannot**__ be used to prove that a certain man is the father of a child.

Chapter 12 Patterns of Heredity and Human Genetics, continued

Reinforcement and Study Guide

Section 12.2 When Heredity Follows Different Rules, continued

For each statement below, write **true** or **false.**

__true__ 6. Traits controlled by more than two alleles are said to have multiple alleles.

__false__ 7. Multiple alleles can be studied only in individuals.

__false__ 8. In humans, there are 23 pairs of matching homologous chromosomes called autosomes.

__true__ 9. Two chromosomes called the sex chromosomes determine the sex of an individual.

__false__ 10. The sex chromosomes of a human male are XX, and the sex chromosomes of a human female are XY.

__true__ 11. Traits controlled by genes located on sex chromosomes are called sex-linked traits.

__false__ 12. The first known example of sex-linked inheritance was discovered in pea plants.

In your textbook, read about environmental influences.

Answer the following questions.

13. What characteristics of an organism can affect gene function?
Age and gender can affect gene function.

14. Do the internal environments of males and females differ? Explain.
yes, because of hormones and structural differences

15. What are some environmental factors that can influence gene expression?
Temperature, nutrition, light, chemicals, and infectious agents all influence gene expression.

16. Give two examples of how an environmental factor can affect the expression of a phenotype.
Temperature affects the production of pigments in certain bacteria. Light affects the size and shape of some leaves.

Copyright © Glencoe/McGraw-Hill, a division of The McGraw-Hill Companies, Inc.

Chapter 13 Genetic Technology

Section 13.1 Applied Genetics

In your textbook, read about selective breeding and determining genotypes.

Complete each statement.

1. Organisms that are homozygous dominant and those that are __heterozygous__ for a trait controlled by Mendelian inheritance have the same phenotype.

2. A __testcross__ determines whether an organism is heterozygous or homozygous dominant for a trait.

3. Usually the parent with the known genotype is __homozygous recessive__ for the trait in question.

4. When two cultivars are crossed, their offspring will be __hybrids__ .

Answer the following.

5. A breeder performs a testcross to determine whether an Alaskan malamute is homozygous dominant (*DD*) or heterozygous (*Dd*) for a recessive dwarf allele. Half the offspring appear dwarf. What is the genotype of the unknown dog? Complete the Punnett square to verify your answer.

__heterozygous (Dd)__

	D	d
d	Dd	dd
d	Dd	dd

6. What results would be expected if the unknown dog was homozygous dominant (*DD*)? Complete the Punnett square to verify your answer.

__All the offspring will be phenotypically__ __dominant.__

	D	D
d	Dd	Dd
d	Dd	Dd

REINFORCEMENT AND STUDY GUIDE

CHAPTER 13   BIOLOGY: The Dynamics of Life   55

Chapter 13 Genetic Technology, *continued*

In your textbook, read about gene engineering.

For each item in Column A, write the letter of the matching item in Column B.

Column A		Column B
c	1. Bacterial proteins that have the ability to cut both strands of the DNA molecule at certain points	a. recombinant DNA
e	2. Contain foreign DNA	b. vector
a	3. Is made by connecting segments of DNA from different sources	c. restriction enzymes
b	4. General term for a vehicle used to transfer a foreign DNA fragment into a host cell	d. plasmid
d	5. A small ring of DNA found in a bacterial cell	e. transgenic organisms
f	6. The procedure for cleaving DNA from an organism into small segments, and inserting the segments into another organism	f. genetic engineering or recombinant DNA technology

Complete the table by checking the correct column for each vector.

Vectors	Mechanical	Biological
7. Viruses		✓
8. Micropipette	✓	
9. Metal bullets	✓	
10. Plasmids		✓

56   CHAPTER 13   BIOLOGY: The Dynamics of Life

REINFORCEMENT AND STUDY GUIDE

Chapter 13 — Genetic Technology, continued

Reinforcement and Study Guide

Section 13.3 The Human Genome

In your textbook, read about mapping and sequencing the human genome and applications of the Human Genome Project.

Determine if the statement is true. If it is not, rewrite the italicized part to make it true.

1. The human genome consists of approximately *1000* genes located on 46 chromosomes.
   80,000

2. Scientists *have* determined the exact chromosomal location of all genes.
   have not

3. The genetic map that shows the location of genes on a chromosome is called a *pedigree map*.
   linkage map

4. Instead of examining actual offspring, scientists examine *egg* cells to create linkage maps.
   sperm

5. Gene therapy is being performed on patients suffering from *sickle-cell anemia*.
   cystic fibrosis

6. *Electrolysis* can be used to separate DNA fragments.
   Electrophoresis

Answer the following questions.

7. What is the Human Genome Project?
   It is an international effort to completely map and sequence the human genome.

8. Why is mapping by linkage data extremely inefficient in humans?
   because humans have only a few children compared to other species and the
   generation time is so long

9. What are the three areas of current research that utilize chromosome maps?
   prenatal diagnosis of human disorders, gene therapy, and DNA fingerprinting

10. Why is DNA fingerprinting reliable?
    because no two individuals with the exception of identical twins have the same
    DNA sequence, and all cells of an individual have the same DNA

Chapter 13 — Genetic Technology, continued

Reinforcement and Study Guide

Section 13.2 Recombinant DNA Technology, continued

In your textbook, read about applications of DNA technology.

Complete the table by checking the correct column for each statement.

Statement	Bacteria	Transgenic Plant(s)	Animal(s)
11. Employed in the production of growth hormone to treat dwarfism and insulin to treat diabetes	✓		
12. Difficult to produce because of thick cell walls and few biological vectors		✓	
13. Some can be made using a bacterium that normally causes tumor-like galls.		✓	
14. Contain many genes common to humans			✓
15. Have been engineered to break down pollutants into harmless products	✓		
16. The first patented organism	✓		
17. Produced using mechanical vectors such as the gene gun		✓	
18. Produce phenylalanine, an amino acid needed to make artificial sweeteners	✓		
19. In the future, they will be more nutritious and be able to grow in unfavorable conditions.		✓	
20. Helps scientists to learn about human diseases			✓
21. Produce insulin, a hormone used in treating diabetes	✓		
22. Produced by using a micropipette to inject DNA into unfertilized eggs			✓
23. Contain foreign genes that slow down the process of spoilage		✓	

Name _____ Date _____ Class _____

BioDigest 4 Genetics

In your textbook, read about simple Mendelian inheritance and meiosis.

Complete each statement.

1. A trait is **dominant** if only one allele is needed for that trait to be expressed.
   If both alleles are needed for the trait to be expressed, the trait is **recessive** .

2. When a *TT* tall pea plant is crossed with a *tt* short pea plant, there is a 100% probability that all offspring will be **tall** and have the genotype **Tt** .

3. Unlike mitosis, **meiosis** produces cells that contain only one copy of each
   chromosome .

4. **Crossing over** and the rearrangement of alleles during **meiosis**
   provide mechanisms for genetic variability.

In your textbook, read about producing physical traits and complex inheritance patterns.

Predict the outcome of the following crosses. Use Punnett squares to support your answers.

5. Homozygous short × Homozygous short
   All offspring should be homozygous short.

	t	t
t	tt	tt
t	tt	tt

6. Heterozygous for purple flowers × Heterozygous for purple flowers
   About 3/4 of the offspring should produce
   purple flowers. About 1/4 should produce
   white flowers.

	P	p
P	PP	Pp
p	Pp	pp

7. Heterozygous pink snapdragon × Heterozygous pink snapdragon
   About 1/2 of the offspring should produce
   pink flowers. About 1/4 should produce red
   flowers. About 1/4 should produce white
   flowers.

	R	R'
R	RR	RR'
R'	RR'	R'R'

Sequence the steps in protein synthesis from 1 to 4.

4 __ 8. Amino acids bond together to form a protein.

1 __ 9. Sequence of bases in DNA is copied into mRNA.

3 __ 10. tRNA molecules bring appropriate amino acids to the mRNA on the ribosome.

2 __ 11. mRNA leaves the cell nucleus.

Name _____ Date _____ Class _____

BioDigest 4 Genetics, *continued*

For each item in Column A, write the letter of the matching item in Column B.

Column A		Column B
d	12. Results in an mRNA copy of DNA	a. incomplete dominance
f	13. Sequence of three bases in mRNA	b. X-linked trait
c	14. Site of translation	c. ribosome
g	15. Governed by several genes	d. transcription
a	16. Heterozygote has an intermediate phenotype.	e. translation
h	17. Double-stranded molecule that stores and transmits genetic information	f. codon
b	18. More likely to appear in males than in females	g. polygenic inheritance
e	19. Results in a sequence of amino acids	h. DNA

In your textbook, read about recombinant DNA technology and gene therapy.

Sequence the steps to making recombinant DNA from 1 to 5.

3 __ 20. The plasmid becomes part of a host cell's chromosome.

1 __ 21. A DNA fragment is inserted into a plasmid.

4 __ 22. The DNA fragment replicates during cell division.

2 __ 23. The plasmid enters a host bacterial cell.

5 __ 24. A host cell produces a protein that it would not have produced naturally.

Answer the following questions.

25. What is gene therapy?
    Gene therapy involves replacing defective genes with normal genes in order to
    correct a genetic disorder.

26. What are clones?
    Clones are identical copies. Identical copies of DNA fragments are DNA clones.

27. What is a vector? Give two examples of vectors.
    A vector is a vehicle for transferring a DNA fragment from one organism to
    another. Viruses and bacterial plasmids can be used as vectors.

Reinforcement and Study Guide

Section 14.1 The Record of Life

Chapter 14 The History of Life

In your textbook, read about the early history of Earth.

For each statement below, write **true** or **false**.

true	1. Earth is thought to have formed about 4.6 billion years ago.
false	2. The conditions on primitive Earth were very suitable for life.
true	3. Geological events on Earth set up conditions that would play a major role in the evolution of life on Earth.
true	4. Violent rainstorms beginning 3.9 million years ago formed Earth's oceans.
false	5. The first organisms appeared on land between 3.9 and 3.5 billion years ago.

In your textbook, read about a history in the rocks.

For each statement in Column A, write the letter of the matching item in Column B.

Column A

c	6. A footprint, trail, or burrow, providing evidence of animal activity
e	7. A fossil embedded in tree sap, valuable because the organism is preserved intact
a	8. An exact stone copy of an original organism, the hard parts of which have been penetrated and replaced by minerals
f	9. Any evidence of an organism that lived long ago
b	10. The fossil of a thin object, such as a leaf or feather, that falls into sediments and leaves an outline when the sediments hardened
g	11. An empty space left in rock, showing the exact shape of the organism that was buried and decayed there
d	12. An object formed when a mold is filled in by minerals from the surrounding rock

Column B

a. petrified fossil

b. imprint

c. trace fossil

d. cast

e. amber-preserved

f. fossil

g. mold

Reinforcement and Study Guide

Section 14.1 The Record of Life, continued

Chapter 14 The History of Life, continued

In your textbook, read about the age of a fossil.

Answer the following questions.

13. Explain how relative dating works.

If rock layers, and the fossils they contain, have been left undisturbed, layers closer to the surface should be younger than those that are lower because they formed after and on top of the lower ones.

14. What is the limitation of relative dating?

Relative dating will reveal only whether one fossil is older than another one.

15. What dating technique is often used by paleontologists to determine the specific age of a fossil?

radiometric dating

16. How do scientists use this dating technique to determine the ages of rocks or fossils?

Age is determined by comparing the amount of the original radioactive element to the amount of the new element formed from decay.

In your textbook, read about a trip through geologic time.

Complete the table by checking the correct column for each statement.

Statement	Pre-Cambrian	Era Paleozoic	Mesozoic	Cenozoic
17. The first photosynthetic bacteria form dome-shaped structures called stromatolites.	✓			
18. Primates evolve and diversify.				✓
19. Divided into three periods: Triassic, Jurassic, and Cretaceous			✓	
20. An explosion of life, characterized by the appearance of many types of invertebrates and plant phyla		✓		
21. Mammals appear.			✓	
22. Dinosaurs roam Earth, and the ancestors of modern birds evolve.			✓	
23. Flowering plants appear.			✓	
24. Amphibians and reptiles appear.		✓		

REINFORCEMENT AND STUDY GUIDE

Name _____ Date _____ Class _____

Reinforcement and Study Guide

Section 14.2 *The Origin of Life*

Chapter 14 — **The History of Life**, *continued*

In your textbook, read about origins: the early ideas.

Use each of the terms below just once to complete the passage.

microorganisms	vital force	biogenesis
nonliving matter	Louis Pasteur	Francesco Redi
organisms	disproved	spontaneous generation
spontaneously	broth	microscope
	air	

Early scientists believed that life arose from **(1)** __nonliving matter__ through a process they called

(2) __spontaneous generation__ . In 1668, the Italian physician **(3)** __Francesco Redi__ conducted

an experiment with flies that **(4)** __disproved__ this idea. At about the same time, biologists

began to use an important new research tool, the **(5)** __microscope__ . They soon discovered the

vast world of **(6)** __microorganisms__ . The number and diversity of these organisms was so great that

scientists were led to believe once again that these organisms must have arisen **(7)** __spontaneously__ .

By the mid-1800s, however, **(8)** __Louis Pasteur__ was able to disprove this hypothesis once and for

all. He set up an experiment, using flasks with unique **(9)** __S-shaped__ necks. These flasks

allowed **(10)** __air__ , but no organisms, to come into contact with a broth containing

nutrients. If some **(11)** __vital force__ existed, as had been suggested, it would be able to get into

the **(12)** __broth__ through the open neck of the flask. His experiment proved that organ-

isms arise only from other **(13)** __organisms__ . This idea, called **(14)** __biogenesis__ ,

is one of the cornerstones of biology today.

Determine if the statement is true. If it is not, rewrite the italicized part to make it true.

15. Biogenesis *explains* how life began on Earth. __does not explain__

16. For life to begin, simple *inorganic* molecules had to be formed and then organized into complex molecules. __organic__

17. Several billion years ago, Earth's atmosphere had no free *methane*. __oxygen__

Name _____ Date _____ Class _____

Reinforcement and Study Guide

Section 14.2 *The Origin of Life*, *continued*

Chapter 14 — **The History of Life**, *continued*

18. Primitive Earth's atmosphere may have been composed of water vapor, hydrogen, methane, and
ammonia. __true__

19. In the early 1900s, Alexander Oparin proposed a widely accepted hypothesis that life began *on land.*
__in the oceans__

20. *Pasteur* hypothesized that many chemical reactions occurring in the atmosphere resulted in the formation of a primordial soup. __Oparin__

21. In 1953, Miller and Urey tested Oparin's hypothesis by simulating the conditions of *modern* Earth in
the laboratory. __early__

22. Miller and Urey showed that organic compounds, including *nucleic acids* and sugars, could be formed
in the laboratory, just as had been predicted. __amino acids__

23. This "life-in-a-test-tube" experiment of Miller and Urey provides support for some modern hypothe-
ses of *biogenesis.* __the origin of life__

24. Sidney Fox took Miller and Urey's experiment further and showed how amino acids could cluster to
form *protocells.* __true__

In your textbook, read about the evolution of cells.

Answer the following questions.

25. Describe the likely characteristics of the first organisms on Earth.
__The first forms of life were probably anaerobic prokaryotes that were__
__heterotrophs.__

26. What is an autotroph? What factors helped them thrive on Earth?
__An autotroph is an organism that can make its own food. Competition for__
__nutrients by heterotrophic prokaryotes probably led to natural selection__
__for autotrophy.__

27. What present-day organisms may be similar to the first autotrophs? Why?
__Archaebacteria; many live in harsh environments and are chemosynthetic.__

28. What change occurred in Earth's atmosphere after the evolution of photosynthesizing prokaryotes?
Why?
__Because photosynthesis released oxygen, the concentration of that gas increased in__
__the atmosphere.__

REINFORCEMENT AND STUDY GUIDE

Page 65

The Theory of Evolution

In your textbook, read about Charles Darwin and natural selection.

For each statement, write true or false.

true 1. H.M.S. *Beagle*, upon which Charles Darwin served as naturalist, set sail on a collecting and mapping expedition in 1831.

false 2. The environments that Darwin studied exhibited little biological diversity.

false 3. By careful anatomical study, Darwin found that the many species of plants and animals on the Galapagos Islands were unique and bore no relation to species seen in other parts of the world.

true 4. The tortoises of the Galapagos Islands are among the largest on Earth.

false 5. After returning to England, Darwin studied his collections for 10 years.

false 6. Darwin named the process by which evolution proceeds *artificial selection*.

You are a naturalist who traveled to the Galapagos Islands. Below are excerpts from field notes. Next to each set of notes, write a heading. Use these choices: Overproduction of Offspring, Natural Selection, Struggle for Existence, Variation.

7.

Field Notes
Female finches found on the Galapagos Islands lay enormous numbers of eggs.

Overproduction of Offspring

8.

Field Notes
These finches compete for a particular species of insect that inhabits the small holes found in tree bark.

Struggle for Existence

9.

Field Notes
Some finches' beaks are long, some are short. The finches with long beaks are better adapted to remove the insects from the bark.

Variation

10.

Field Notes
The finches with the long beaks survive and produce greater numbers of offspring with long beaks.

Natural Selection

Page 66

The Theory of Evolution, *continued*

In your textbook, read about natural selection and adaptations.

Identify the type of structural adaptation that the statement describes. If the statement applies to both, write both. Use these choices: mimicry, camouflage, both.

camouflage 11. Enable(s) an organism to blend in with its surroundings

mimicry 12. Provide(s) protection for an organism by copying the appearance of another species

camouflage 13. The coloration of a flounder that allows the fish to avoid predators

both 14. Involve(s) changes to the external appearance of an organism

mimicry 15. A flower that looks like a female bee

In your textbook, read about evidence for evolution.

Complete the chart by checking the kind of evidence described.

Evidence	Type of Evidence				
	Homologous Structure	Analogous Structure	Vestigial Structure	Embryological Development	Genetic Comparisons
16. A modified structure seen among different groups of descendants	✓				
17. In the earliest stages of development, a tail and gill slits can be seen in fish, birds, rabbits, and mammals.				✓	
18. Exemplified by forelimbs of bats, penguins, lizards, and monkeys	✓				
19. The forelimbs of flightless birds			✓		
20. DNA and RNA comparisons may lead to evolutionary trees.					✓
21. Bird and butterfly wings have same function but different structures		✓			
22. A body structure reduced in function but may have been used in an ancestor			✓		

REINFORCEMENT AND STUDY GUIDE

Name _____ Date _____ Class _____

Chapter 15

The Theory of Evolution, *continued*

Section 15.2 *Mechanisms of Evolution*

In your textbook, read about population genetics and evolution.

Determine if the statement is true. If it is true, write true. If it is not, rewrite the italicized part to make it true.

1. *Adaptations* of species are determined by the genes contained in the DNA code. ___**true**___

2. When Charles *Mendel* developed the theory of natural selection in the 1800s, he did not include a genetic explanation. ___**Darwin**___

3. Natural selection can act upon an individual's *genotype*, the external expression of genes. ___**phenotype**___

4. Natural selection operates on *an individual* over many generations. ___**populations**___

5. The entire collection of genes among a population is its *gene frequency*. ___**gene pool**___

6. If you know the *phenotypes* of all the organisms in a population, you can calculate the allelic frequency of the population. ___**genotypes**___

7. A population in which frequency of alleles *changes* from generation to generation is said to be in genetic equilibrium. ___**does not change**___

8. A population that is in *genetic equilibrium* is not evolving. ___**true**___

9. Any factor that affects *phenotype* can change allelic frequencies, thereby disrupting the genetic equilibrium of a population. ___**genes**___

10. Many *migrations* are caused by factors in the environment, such as radiation or chemicals, but others happen by chance. ___**mutations**___

11. Mutations are *important* in evolution because they result in genetic changes in the gene pool. ___**true**___

12. Genetic *equilibrium* is the alteration of allelic frequencies by chance processes. ___**drift**___

13. Genetic drift is more likely to occur in *large* populations. ___**small**___

14. The factor that causes the greatest change in gene pools is *mutation*. ___**natural selection**___

15. The type of natural selection by which one of the extreme forms of a trait is favored is called *disruptive selection*. ___**directional selection**___

Name _____ Date _____ Class _____

Chapter 15

The Theory of Evolution, *continued*

Section 15.2 *Mechanisms of Evolution,* *continued*

In your textbook, read about the evolution of species.

Complete each statement.

16. ___**Speciation**___ can occur only when either interbreeding or the production of fertile offspring is prevented among members of a population.

17. ___**Reproductive isolation**___ occurs when formerly interbreeding organisms are prevented from producing fertile offspring.

18. Polyploid speciation is perhaps the fastest form of speciation because it results in immediate ___**reproductive isolation**___.

19. The hypothesis that species originate through a slow buildup of new adaptations is known as ___**gradualism**___.

20. This hypothesis is supported by evidence from the ___**fossil**___ record.

21. The hypothesis of ___**punctuated equilibrium**___ states that speciation may occur rapidly.

In your textbook, read about patterns of evolution.

Answer the following questions.

22. What happened to the ancestor of the honey creeper when it left the mainland and encountered the diverse niches of Hawaii? **Speciation occurred, with each species adapting to a different food source.**

23. What is adaptive radiation? **the process of evolution of an ancestral species into an array of species that occupy different niches**

24. Adaptive radiation is one example of divergent evolution. When does divergent evolution occur? **It occurs when species begin to adapt to different environments and change according to the pressures of natural selection.**

25. When will convergent evolution occur? **when unrelated organisms occupy similar environments and face similar selection pressures**

Name _____   Date _____   Class _____

Chapter 16 Primate Evolution

Section 16.1 Primate Adaptation and Evolution

In your textbook, read about the characteristics of a primate.

Complete the chart by checking those structures or functions that are characteristic of primates.

Structure/Function	Primate
1. Round head	✓
2. Flattened face	✓
3. Small head	
4. Large relative brain size	✓
5. Highly developed vision	✓
6. Poor vision	
7. Binocular vision	✓
8. Color vision	✓
9. Color-blind	
10. Vision the dominant sense	✓
11. Smell the dominant sense	
12. Immobile joints	
13. Flexible shoulder joints	✓
14. Skeleton adapted for movement among trees	✓
15. Skeleton adapted for swimming	
16. Hands and feet equipped with claws	
17. Hands and feet equipped with nails	✓
18. Eyes face to the side	
19. Feet constructed for grasping	✓
20. Opposable thumbs	✓

In your textbook, read about primate origins.

For each statement below, write true or false.

false   21. Scientists believe that primates evolved about 66,000 years ago.

true   22. The earliest primate may have been a prosimianlike animal called *Purgatorius*.

false   23. Anthropoids are a group of small-bodied primates.

true   24. Prosimians include lemurs and tarsiers.

false   25. Prosimians can be found in the tropical forests of South America.

Name _____   Date _____   Class _____

Chapter 16 Primate Evolution, continued

Section 16.1 Primate Adaptation and Evolution, continued

Identify the following pictures. Use these choices: baboon, tarsier, spider monkey. Then on the second line write the group that is represented by the picture. Use these choices: New World monkey, Old World monkey, prosimian.

26. baboon
Old World monkey

27. spider monkey
New World monkey

28. tarsier
prosimian

Answer the following questions.

29. What do similarities among monkeys, apes, and humans indicate about their evolution?
They may all share a common ancestor.

30. According to the fossil record, what were the first modern anthropoids to evolve and about when did they evolve?
New World monkeys; about 30 to 35 million years ago

31. What is the evolutionary history of primates based on?
the fossil record and comparative study of living primates

32. What may have led to the eventual speciation of baboons and other ground-living monkeys?
During the Miocene period, when Old World monkeys evolved, the fossil record indicates that global temperatures were dropping.

33. What does DNA analysis of modern hominoids suggest about their evolutionary history?
DNA analysis suggest that gibbons were probably the first apes to evolve, followed by the orangutans, African apes, chimpanzees, and gorillas.

Name _____ Date _____ Class _____

Reinforcement and Study Guide

Chapter
16   **Primate Evolution,** *continued*

Section 16.2 *Human Ancestry*

In your textbook, read about hominids.

Answer the following questions.

1. What is an australopithecine?   **an early hominid that lived in Africa**

2. What fossil skull did Raymond Dart discover in Africa in 1924?   *Australopithecus africanus*

3. Why was *A. africanus* unlike any primate fossil skull that Dart had ever seen?   **It had a foramen magnum that was located at the bottom of the skull, as in humans.**

4. What did the position of the foramen magnum indicate to Dart?   **The organism must have walked upright.**

Label the following skulls. Use these choices: chimpanzee, human, *A. afarensis*

5. ___*A. afarensis*___   6. ___chimpanzee___   7. ___human___

For each statement below, write true or false.

___true___   8. Much of what scientists know about australopithecines comes from the "Lucy" skeleton.

___false___   9. "Lucy" is 3.5 billion years old.

___false___   10. "Lucy" is classified as *A. africanus*.

___true___   11. *A. afarensis* is the earliest known hominid species.

___false___   12. *A. afarensis* walked on all four legs and had a humanlike brain.

___false___   13. Australopithecines are alive today and can be found in southern Africa and Asia.

___true___   14. Australopithecines probably played a role in the evolution of modern hominids.

REINFORCEMENT AND STUDY GUIDE   CHAPTER 16   BIOLOGY: The Dynamics of Life   **71**

Name _____ Date _____ Class _____

Reinforcement and Study Guide

Section 16.2 *Human Ancestry,*
continued

Chapter
16   **Primate Evolution,** *continued*

In your textbook, read about the emergence of modern humans.

Circle the letter of the choice that best completes the statement or answers the question.

15. The first skull of *Homo habilis* was discovered by
   a. Raymond Dart.
   b. Louis and Mary Leakey.
   c. Donald Johanson.
   d. Gert Terblance.

16. When compared to an australopithecine skull, the *Homo habilis* skull is
   a. more humanlike.
   b. less humanlike.
   c. more apelike.
   d. exactly the same.

17. Which of the following is *not* true about *Homo habilis*?
   a. They existed between 1.5 and 2 million years ago.
   b. They were the first hominids to make and use tools.
   c. They were probably scavengers of their food.
   d. They gave rise to *A. africanus*.

18. *Homo habilis* means
   a. "handy human."
   b. "tool-using human."
   c. "upright human."
   d. "talking human."

19. Of the primates below, which has the largest brain?
   a. *Homo habilis*
   b. *Homo erectus*
   c. an ape
   d. an australopithecine

20. Which of the following is *not* true about *Homo erectus*?
   a. They probably hunted.
   b. They were the first hominids to use fire.
   c. They may have given rise to hominids that resemble modern humans.
   d. They were found only in Africa.

21. *Homo sapiens* includes
   a. Neanderthals.
   b. australopithecines.
   c. *A. africanus*.
   d. *A. afarensis*.

Determine whether each statement below best describes Neanderthals, Cro-Magnons, or both.

___Neanderthals___   22. They lived in caves during the ice ages.

___Cro-Magnons___   23. They are identical to modern humans in height, skull, and teeth structure.

___Neanderthals___   24. They may have been the first hominids to develop religious views.

___both___   25. They may have used language.

___Cro-Magnons___   26. They were talented toolmakers and artists.

72   CHAPTER 16   BIOLOGY: The Dynamics of Life   REINFORCEMENT AND STUDY GUIDE

Chapter 17 Organizing Life's Diversity

Section 17.1 Classification

In your textbook, read about how classification began and about biological classification.

For each item in Column A, write the letter of the matching item in Column B.

Column A

		Column B
d	1. Grouping objects or information based on similarities	a. Aristotle
f	2. Naming system that gives each organism a two-word name	b. Linnaeus
a	3. Developed the first system of classification	c. genus
e	4. Branch of biology that groups and names organisms	d. classification
b	5. Designed a system of classifying organisms based on their physical and structural similarities	e. taxonomy
c	6. Consists of a group of similar species	f. binomial nomenclature

Determine if the statement is true. If it is not, rewrite the italicized part to make it true.

7. The scientific name of a species consists of a *family* name and a descriptive name. **genus**

8. The scientific name of modern humans is *Homo sapiens*. **true**

9. *Latin* is the language of scientific names. **true**

10. The *scientific* names of organisms can be misleading. **common**

11. Taxonomists try to identify the *evolutionary relationships* among organisms. **true**

12. Besides comparing the structures of organisms, taxonomists also compare the organisms' geographic distribution and *chemical makeup*. **true**

13. Similarities between living species and extinct species *cannot* be used to determine their relationship to each other. **can**

14. Because the bones of some dinosaurs have large internal spaces, some scientists think dinosaurs are more closely related to *amphibians* than to reptiles. **birds**

15. Classification can be useful in identifying the *characteristics* of an unknown organism. **true**

Chapter 17 Organizing Life's Diversity, continued

Section 17.1 Classification, continued

In your textbook, read about how living things are classified.

Examine the table showing the classification of four organisms. Then answer the questions.

Taxon	Green Frog	Mountain Lion	Domestic Dog	Human
Kingdom	Animalia	Animalia	Animalia	Animalia
Phylum	Chordata	Chordata	Chordata	Chordata
Class	Amphibia	Mammalia	Mammalia	Mammalia
Order	Anura	Carnivora	Carnivora	Primates
Family	Ranidae	Felidae	Canidae	Hominidae
Genus	Rana	Felis	Canis	Homo
Species	Rana clamitans	Felis concolor	Canis familiaris	Homo sapiens

16. Which taxon includes the most specific characteristics? **species**

17. Which taxon includes the broadest characteristics? **kingdom**

18. Which taxon includes more species, an order or a family? **order**

19. Which taxon includes only organisms that can successfully interbreed? **species**

20. If two organisms belong to the same family, what other taxonomic groups do the organisms have in common? **order, class, phylum, and kingdom**

21. Which two organisms in the chart are most closely related? Explain. **The mountain lion and the domestic dog are most closely related because they belong to more of the same taxa (four) than the other animals do: Kingdom Animalia; phylum Chordata; class Mammalia; and order Carnivora.**

22. To which taxa do all four organisms belong? **phylum Chordata and Kingdom Animalia**

23. Which class does not include animals that have hair or fur? **Amphibia**

24. What is the order, family, and genus of a human? **order: Primates; family: Hominidae; genus: Homo**

25. Using the information in the chart, what can you conclude about the classification taxa of an organism with the scientific name *Rana temporaria*? **The organism belongs to the genus Rana, family Ranidae, order Anura, class Amphibia, phylum Chordata, and Kingdom Animalia.**

Name _____ Date _____ Class _____

Chapter 17

Organizing Life's Diversity, *continued*

Section 17.2 *The Six Kingdoms*

In your textbook, read about how evolutionary relationships are determined.

Explain how scientists use each item below to determine the evolutionary relationships among organisms.

1. structural similarities: **Structural similarities between groups of organisms suggest that the groups evolved from a common ancestor.**

2. breeding behavior: **Organisms that show different breeding behaviors are of different species.**

3. geographical distribution: **Similar species that are found in the same isolated geographic area probably evolved from the same ancestral species.**

4. chromosome comparisons: **Groups of organisms that are closely related to each other show similarities in the number, structure, and DNA sequence of their chromosomes.**

5. biochemistry: **The more closely two groups of organisms are related, the more their DNA nucleotide sequences and their proteins are similar.**

In your textbook, read about phylogenetic classification: models.

Use the cladogram to answer the questions.

6. What five probable ancestors of the modern bird (robin) are shown on the cladogram? **theropods, Allosaurus, Sinornis, Velociraptor, and Archaeopteryx**

7. Which dinosaur is probably the most recent common ancestor of *Velociraptor* and *Archaeopteryx*? **Sinornis**

8. Which traits shown on the cladogram are shared by *Archaeopteryx* and modern birds? **light bones, three-toed foot, wishbone, down feathers, and feathers with shafts, veins, and barbs**

Name _____ Date _____ Class _____

Chapter 17

Organizing Life's Diversity, *continued*

Section 17.2 *The Six Kingdoms,* *continued*

Use the fanlike phylogenetic diagram to answer the questions.

9. How does the fanlike diagram differ from a cladogram? **Unlike a cladogram, a fanlike diagram shows when groups of organisms evolved and the relative number of species in each group.**

10. Which group of plants evolved most recently? **flowering plants**

11. To which group are starfishes more closely related, arthropods or jellyfishes? **arthropods**

12. Which group of animals includes the fewest species? **starfishes**

13. About how long ago did plants evolve? **more than 544 million years ago**

In your textbook, read about the six kingdoms of organisms.

Circle the letter of the choice that best completes the statement or answers the question.

14. Organisms that do not have a nucleus bounded by a membrane are
   a. multicellular.   b. eukaryotes.   c. protists.   **(d.)** prokaryotes.

15. Fungi obtain food by
   a. photosynthesis.   b. chemosynthesis.
   c. endocytosis.   **(d.)** absorbing nutrients from organic materials.

16. Animals are
   a. autotrophs.   **(b.)** heterotrophs.   c. prokaryotes.   d. stationary.

BioDigest

5   **Change Through Time**   Reinforcement and Study Guide

In your textbook, read about the Geologic Time Scale.

Complete the table.

Era	Time period	Biologic event
1. Precambrian	4.6 billion–600 million years ago	**2.** Prokaryotic cells and first eukaryotic cells evolved.
3. Paleozoic	600 million–245 million years ago	Ferns and conifers appeared; **4.** worms, insects, fishes, and reptiles evolved.
5. Mesozoic	245 million–66 million years ago	**6.** Reptiles diversified; mammals and flowering plants evolved.
7. Cenozoic	66 million years ago–present	**8.** Primates evolved.

In your textbook, read about origin of life theories.

Complete each statement.

9. Spontaneous generation assumes that life arises spontaneously from **nonliving material** .

10. Francesco Redi and Louis Pasteur designed **controlled experiments** to disprove spontaneous generation.

11. The theory of **biogenesis** states that life comes only from pre-existing life.

12. Clusters of organic molecules might have formed **protocells** , which may have evolved into the first true cells.

Order the evolutionary development of the following organisms from 1 to 4.

2   13. chemosynthetic prokaryotes   **1**   15. heterotrophic prokaryotes

4   14. eukaryotes   **3**   16. oxygen-producing photosynthetic prokaryotes

In your textbook, read about the evidence and mechanics of evolution.

Answer the following questions.

17. What assumption is made in the relative dating of fossils? **Relative dating assumes that in undisturbed layers of rock, the deepest layers contain the oldest fossils.**

18. What are homologous structures? **Homologous structures are similar anatomical structures in different organisms that might indicate possible shared ancestry.**

BioDigest

5   **Change Through Time,** *continued*   Reinforcement and Study Guide

For each statement below, write true or false.

false   19. Evolution occurs when a population's genetic equilibrium remains unchanged.

true   20. Mutations, genetic drift, and migration may disrupt the genetic equilibrium of populations.

true   21. Stabilizing selection favors the survival of a population's average individuals for a feature.

false   22. Disruptive selection occurs when an extreme feature is naturally selected.

true   23. Adaptive radiation occurs when species that once were similar to an ancestral species become increasingly distinct due to natural selection pressures.

In your textbook, read about primate evolution.

For each item in Column A, write the letter of the matching item in Column B.

Column A	Column B
d 24. Primate adaptation	**a.** anthropoids
a 25. Primate category that includes humans and apes	**b.** Australopithecines
e 26. Characteristic of New World monkeys	**c.** genus *Homo*
c 27. Appearing in fossil record about 2 million years ago along with stone tools	**d.** opposable thumb
b 28. Possible human ancestors dating from 5 to 8 million years ago	**e.** prehensile tail

In your textbook, read about organizing life's diversity.

Look at the taxonomic classification of a bobcat shown below. Answer the questions.

Taxon	Name
Kingdom	*Animalia*
Phylum	*Chordata*
Class	*Mammalia*
Order	*Carnivora*
Family	*Felidae*
Genus	*Lynx*
Species	*rufus*

29. What is the largest taxon in this classification system? **kingdom**

30. What is the scientific name of a bobcat? **Lynx rufus**

Name _____ Date _____ Class _____

Reinforcement and Study Guide

Chapter 18 Viruses and Bacteria

Section 18.1 Viruses

In your textbook, read about the characteristics of a virus.

For each item in Column A, write the letter of the matching item in Column B.

	Column A	Column B
c	**1.** Genetic material of a virus	**a.** virus
e	**2.** Where a virus attaches to a host cell	**b.** T4 phage
a	**3.** Nonliving particle that replicates inside a living cell	**c.** DNA or RNA
d	**4.** A virus's protein coat	**d.** capsid
h	**5.** Interlocks with a molecular shape in a host cell's plasma membrane	**e.** receptor site
f	**6.** Layer that surrounds the capsid of some viruses	**f.** envelope
b	**7.** A virus that infects *E. coli* bacteria	**g.** host
g	**8.** A cell in which a virus replicates	**h.** attachment protein

In your textbook, read about viral replication cycles.

Complete the table by checking the correct column for each statement.

Statement	Lytic Cycle	Lysogenic Cycle
9. Viral genes are expressed immediately after the virus infects the host cell.	✓	
10. Many new viruses are assembled.	✓	
11. This cycle is preceded by a virus entering a host cell.	✓	✓
12. Viral DNA is integrated into the host cell's chromosome.		✓
13. Viruses are released from the host cell by lysis or exocytosis.	✓	
14. Reverse transcriptase is used to make DNA from the RNA of a retrovirus.		✓
15. A provirus is replicated along with the host cell's chromosome.		✓

REINFORCEMENT AND STUDY GUIDE

CHAPTER 18 BIOLOGY: The Dynamics of Life **79**

Name _____ Date _____ Class _____

Reinforcement and Study Guide

Chapter 18 Viruses and Bacteria, *continued*

Section 18.1 Viruses, *continued*

Use each of the terms below just once to complete the passage.

DNA	white blood cells	lysogenic
lytic	AIDS	proviruses

Many disease-causing viruses have both lytic and **(16)** __lysogenic__ cycles. For example, when HIVs infect **(17)** __white blood cells__, the viruses enter a lysogenic cycle. Their genetic material becomes incorporated into the **(18)** __DNA__ of the white blood cells, forming **(19)** __proviruses__. When this happens, the white blood cells still function normally, and the person may not appear ill. Eventually, the proviruses enter a **(20)** __lytic__ cycle, killing the white blood cells. As a result, the person loses the ability to fight diseases and develops **(21)** __AIDS__.

In your textbook, read about viruses and cancer, plant viruses, and the origin of viruses.

Determine if the statement is true. If it is not, rewrite the italicized part to make it true.

__true__ **22.** Some viruses can change normal cells to *tumor* cells.

__warts__ **23.** Retroviruses and the papilloma virus, which causes *hepatitis B*, are examples of tumor viruses.

__Some__ **24.** *All* plant viruses cause diseases in plants.

__true__ **25.** The first virus ever identified was the plant virus called *tobacco mosaic virus*.

__plant__ **26.** The patterns of color in some flowers are caused by *tumor* viruses.

__true__ **27.** Tumor viruses contain genes that are found in *normal* cells.

__true__ **28.** Scientists think viruses originated from *their host cells*.

80 CHAPTER 18 BIOLOGY: The Dynamics of Life

REINFORCEMENT AND STUDY GUIDE

Reinforcement and Study Guide

Chapter 18 Viruses and Bacteria, *continued*

Section 18.2 Archaebacteria and Eubacteria

In your textbook, read about the diversity of prokaryotes and about the characteristics of bacteria.

Answer the following questions.

1. What are three types of environments in which archaebacteria are found? **oxygen-free environments, concentrated salt water, and hot, acidic water of sulfur springs**

2. In what three ways do eubacteria obtain nutrients? **from dead or living organic material, by photosynthesis, and by chemosynthesis**

3. How does a bacterium's cell wall protect it? **The cell wall prevents water from entering the bacterial cell by osmosis and causing it to burst.**

4. Where is the genetic material of a bacterium found? **on a single circular chromosome and sometimes on small circular chromosome pieces called plasmids**

5. What structure do some bacteria use to move? **flagella**

6. What is the difference between gram-positive bacteria and gram-negative bacteria? **Gram-positive bacteria are purple after gram staining, and gram-negative bacteria are pink because they have different cell walls. The bacteria also are affected by different antibiotics.**

7. What are three different shapes of bacteria? **rod, sphere, and spiral**

8. Describe the three growth patterns of bacteria and state the prefix used to identify each growth pattern. **paired cells: diplo-; cells bunched like grapes: staphylo-; cells arranged in chains: strepto-**

Identify the type of bacterial reproduction described. Use these choices: binary fission, conjugation.

conjugation 9. Bacterium with a new genetic makeup is produced.

binary fission 10. Circular chromosome is copied.

conjugation 11. Genetic material is transferred through a pilus.

binary fission 12. Two identical cells are produced.

conjugation 13. Sexual reproduction occurs.

Reinforcement and Study Guide

Chapter 18 Viruses and Bacteria, *continued*

Section 18.2 Archaebacteria and Eubacteria, *continued*

In your textbook, read about adaptations in bacteria and the importance of bacteria.

Circle the letter of the choice that best completes the statement.

14. Scientists think the first bacteria on Earth were
   a. aerobic. **b. anaerobic.** c. fatal. d. oxygen-dependent.

15. Bacteria that are obligate anaerobes release energy from food by
   a. cellular respiration. b. using oxygen.
   c. using nitrogen. **d. fermentation.**

16. As an endospore, a bacterium
   a. produces toxins. b. dries out. c. causes diseases. **d. is protected.**

17. Botulism is caused by endospores of *C. botulinum* that have
   a. been killed. b. produced toxins.
   c. germinated. d. reproduced.

18. Nitrogen is important because all organisms need it to make
   a. proteins. b. ATP. c. DNA. **d. all of these.**

19. The process by which bacteria use enzymes to convert nitrogen gas into ammonia is called
   a. nitrogenation. b. atmospheric separation.
   c. nitrogen fixation. d. eutrophication.

20. Bacteria return nutrients to the environment by breaking down
   a. dead organic matter. b. inorganic materials.
   c. enzymes and sugar. d. nitrogen in legumes.

21. Bacteria are *not* used to make
   a. vinegar. **b. jams.** c. cheese. d. yogurt.

22. Bacteria are responsible for the following diseases:
   a. strep throat and tetanus. b. gonorrhea and syphilis.
   c. tuberculosis and diphtheria. **d. all of these.**

23. Due to reduced death rates from bacterial diseases and improved sanitation and living conditions, the average person born in the United States today will live to be about
   a. 25 years old. b. 50 years old.
   c. 75 years old. d. 90 years old.

Name _____ Date _____ Class _____

Reinforcement and Study Guide

Chapter 19 Protists

Section 19.1 **The World of Protists**

In your textbook, read about what a protist is.

Determine if the statement is true. If it is not, rewrite the italicized part to make it true.

1. The kingdom *Protista* is the most diverse of all six kingdoms.   **true**

2. Protists can be grouped into three general types—*animal-like, plantlike, and viruslike.*
   animal-like, plantlike, and funguslike

3. All protists are *eukaryotes* that carry on most of their metabolic processes in membrane-bound organelles.   **true**

In your textbook, read about the characteristics and diversity of protozoans.

Complete each statement.

4. The ___**animal**___-like protists are all unicellular heterotrophs known as protozoans.

5. Amoebas move and change their body shape by forming extensions of their plasma membranes called ___**pseudopodia**___.

6. Amoebas use ___**contractile vacuoles**___ to pump out excess water from their cytoplasm.

7. Most amoebas reproduce by ___**asexual reproduction**___ in which a parent produces one or more identical offspring by dividing into two cells.

8. One group of protozoans are called ___**flagellates**___ because they move by whipping one or more flagella from side to side.

9. A paramecium moves by beating thousands of hairlike ___**cilia**___.

10. When food supplies are low, paramecia may reproduce by undergoing a form of ___**conjugation**___.

11. Parasitic protozoans called ___**sporozoans**___ live inside their hosts and may reproduce by means of a spore.

12. Malaria is caused by protozoans of the genus ___*Plasmodium*___.

13. The insect that is responsible for transmitting malaria-causing protozoans to humans is the ___**mosquito**___.

Name _____ Date _____ Class _____

Reinforcement and Study Guide

Chapter 19 Protists, *continued*

Section 19.2 **Algae: Plantlike Protists**

In your textbook, read about what algae are and about their diversity.

For each item in Column A, write the letter of the item in Column B that completes the statement correctly.

Column A	Column B
e 1. The euglenoids, diatoms, and dinoflagellates are _____.	**a.** algae
d 2. Unicellular protists that are major producers of oxygen in aquatic ecosystems are _____.	**b.** phyla
a 3. Unicellular and multicellular photosynthetic protists are _____.	**c.** pigments
f 4. Most green, red, and brown algae are _____ algae.	**d.** phytoplankton
c 5. Photosynthetic _____ are used to classify algae.	**e.** unicellular
b 6. Algae are classified into six _____.	**f.** multicellular

Identify the phylum of the alga shown below and label its parts. Use these choices: flagellum, mitochondrion, pellicle, chloroplast, nucleus, eyespot, contractile vacuole, Euglenophyta.

7. Phylum ___**Euglenophyta**___

8. ___**contractile vacuole**___

9. ___**nucleus**___

10. ___**chloroplast**___

11. ___**flagellum**___

12. ___**eyespot**___

13. ___**pellicle**___

14. ___**mitochondrion**___

Name _____ Date _____ Class _____

Reinforcement and Study Guide

Chapter 19 Protists, *continued*

Section 19.2 *Algae: Plantlike Protists, continued*

Circle the letter of the choice that best completes the statement.

15. When diatoms that have been reproducing asexually reach about one-fourth of their original size, they
    a. die.   b. triple in size.
    (c.) reproduce sexually.   d. all of these.

16. Dinoflagellates are unicellular algae that
    a. have two flagella.   b. create red tides.
    c. have thick cellulose plates.   **(d.) all of these.**

17. Red algae are a kind of seaweed having pigments that absorb green, violet, and blue light waves, which allows the algae to
    a. live only in fresh water.   **(b.) photosynthesize in limited light.**
    c. live only in salt water.   d. both a and b.

18. The air bladders of brown algae allow the algae to
    a. breathe.   b. reproduce.
    (c.) float near the water's surface.   d. live in salt water.

19. A green alga that forms colonies is
    a. Spirogyra.   b. Ulva.
    c. Chlamydomonas.   **(d.) Volvox.**

In your textbook, read about alternation of generations.

Use each of the terms below just once to complete the passage.

| diploid | gametophyte | alternation of generations | meiosis |
| haploid | sporophyte | spores | zygote |

Some algae have a life cycle that has a pattern called (20) **alternation of generations**.
These algae alternate between a(n) (21) **haploid** form that is called the
(22) **gametophyte** because it produces gametes, and a(n)
(23) **diploid** form called the (24) **sporophyte**. When the
haploid gametes fuse, they form a(n) (25) **zygote** from which the sporophyte
develops. Certain cells in the sporophyte undergo (26) **meiosis** to form haploid
(27) **spores** that develop into gametophytes.

Name _____ Date _____ Class _____

Reinforcement and Study Guide

Chapter 19 Protists, *continued*

Section 19.3 *Slime Molds, Water Molds, and Downy Mildews*

In your textbook, read about the different kinds of funguslike protists.
Use all the terms in the list below at least once to complete the concept map for funguslike protists.

cell division   three phyla   spores   cellular slime molds
plasmodial slime molds   water molds and mildew   flagellated reproductive cells

Concept map:

Funguslike protists
obtain energy by
decomposing organic materials
and can be divided into

1. **three phyla**
which are

2. **plasmodial slime molds** — that reproduce by — 5. **spores**

3. **cellular slime molds** — that reproduce by — 6. **cell division** — **spores**

4. **water molds and mildew** — that reproduce by — 7. **flagellated reproductive cells**

In your textbook, read about the origin of protists.
Answer the following question.

8. What does scientific evidence show is the relationship between protists and other groups of organisms?
   The scientific evidence is inconclusive as to whether ancient protists were the evolutionary ancestors of fungi, plants, and animals or whether the different groups of protists evolved separately.

Name _____ Date _____ Class _____

Reinforcement and Study Guide

Chapter 20 Fungi

Section 20.1 **What Is a Fungus?**

In your textbook, read about the general characteristics of fungi.

Answer the following questions.

1. What are the threadlike filaments in a multicellular fungus called? What do they form?
The threadlike filaments are called hyphae, which branch out to form a mycelium.

2. Some hyphae are divided into individual cells by cross walls with pores in them. What are these cross walls called? What purpose do the pores serve?
The cross walls are called septa. Cytoplasm and organelles flow through the pores. The free-flowing cytoplasm quickly moves nutrients to different parts of the fungus.

3. What is one way that fungi are like plants and one way they are unlike plants?
Like plants, fungi have cell walls, and some fungi anchor themselves in soil. Fungi are unlike plants because their cell walls are made of chitin instead of cellulose, and they are not autotrophs.

In your textbook, read about adaptations in fungi.

Determine if the statement is true. If it is not, rewrite the italicized part to make it true.

4. Many fungi are decomposers, which *break down organic substances* into raw materials that can be used by other organisms. **extracellular digestion**

5. Fungi use *cellular digestion* to obtain nutrients. **true**

6. Hyphae release *digestive enzymes* that break down molecules in their food source. **true**

7. *Mutualistic* fungi are decomposers. **Saprophytic**

8. *Parasitic fungi grow spores* into host cells and absorb the cell's nutrients.
Parasitic fungi grow haustoria

Name _____ Date _____ Class _____

Reinforcement and Study Guide

Chapter 20 Fungi, continued

Section 20.1 **What Is a Fungus?, continued**

In your textbook, read about reproduction in fungi.

Complete each statement.

9. Fungi reproduce **asexually** by fragmentation, budding, or producing spores.

10. In **fragmentation** , pieces of hyphae grow into new mycelia.

11. The process of a parent cell undergoing mitosis and producing a new individual that pinches off, matures, and separates from the parent is called **budding** .

12. When environmental conditions are right, a **spore** may germinate and produce a threadlike **hypha** that will grow into a mycelium.

13. Some hyphae grow away from the mycelium to produce a spore-containing structure called a **sporangium** .

14. In most fungi, the structures that support **sporangia** are the only part of the fungus that can be seen.

15. Fungi may produce spores by **mitosis** or **meiosis** .

16. Many adaptations of fungi for survival involve **spores** .

17. **Sporangia** protect spores and keep them from from drying out until they are released.

18. A single puffball may produce a cloud containing as many as **1 trillion** spores.

19. Producing a large number of spores increases a species' chances of **survival** .

20. Fungal spores can be dispersed by **water** , **wind** , and **animals** .

Reinforcement and Study Guide

Chapter 20   Fungi, continued

Section 20.2 The Diversity of Fungi

In your textbook, read about zygomycotes.

Order the steps of growth and reproduction in zygomycotes from 1 to 5.

2   **1.** Hyphae called rhizoids penetrate the food, anchor the mycelium, and absorb nutrients.

1   **2.** An asexual spore germinates on a food source and hyphae begin to grow.

5   **3.** Spores are released and another asexual cycle begins.

3   **4.** Hyphae called stolons grow across the surface of the food source and form a mycelium.

4   **5.** Special hyphae grow upward to form sporangia that are filled with asexual spores.

Use each of the terms below just once to complete the passage.

yeasts	conidia	multicellular	conidiophores	yeast cells
sac fungi	ascospores	unicellular	vaccine	ascus

Ascomycotes are also called (6) __sac fungi__ because they produce sexual spores, called (7) __ascospores__, in a saclike structure, called a(n) (8) __ascus__.

During asexual reproduction, ascomycotes produce spores called (9) __conidia__.

These asexual spores are produced in chains or clusters at the tips of structures called (10) __conidiophores__, which are elongated hyphae.

Morels and truffles are (11) __multicellular__ ascomycotes that are edible. Yeasts are (12) __unicellular__ ascomycotes. (13) __Yeasts__ are used to make beer, wine, and bread. They are also used in genetic research. A(n) (14) __vaccine__ for the disease hepatitis B is produced from rapidly growing (15) __yeast cells__, which contain spliced human genes.

Reinforcement and Study Guide

Chapter 20   Fungi, continued

Section 20.2 The Diversity of Fungi, continued

In your textbook, read about basidiomycotes.

Answer the following questions about the life of a mushroom.

16. What are basidia and where are they found?
Basidia are spore-producing club-shaped hyphae found on gills, the thin tissues under the mushroom cap.

17. What happens when mycelia of two different mating strains meet?
Their hyphae fuse and form a mycelium with two nuclei in its cells.

18. What does a mycelium with two nuclei in its cells form?
It forms a button, which develops into a mushroom.

19. What does a diploid cell inside a basidium produce as a result of meiosis?
A diploid cell produces four haploid nuclei, each of which becomes a basidiospore.

In your textbook, read about deuteromycotes, the mutualistic relationships of mycorrhizae and lichens, and the origins of fungi.

Write the letter of the item in Column B that best completes each statement in Column A.

	Column A	Column B
d	**20.** _____ is an example of a deuteromycote.	**a.** basidiomycotes
h	**21.** A mycorrhiza is a mutualistic relationship between a fungus and a(n) _____.	**b.** mycorrhizae
g	**22.** _____ is an antibiotic produced by a deuteromycote.	**c.** alga
b	**23.** Plants that have _____ associated with their roots grow larger.	**d.** *Penicillium*
f	**24.** _____ make up a division of fungi that have no known sexual stage.	**e.** pioneer species
c	**25.** A lichen is a mutualistic relationship between a fungus and a(n) _____ or cyanobacterium.	**f.** deuteromycotes
e	**26.** Lichens are _____ in all parts of the world.	**g.** penicillin
a	**27.** Scientists think that ascomycotes and evolved from a common ancestor.	**h.** plant

Name _____ Date _____ Class _____

BioDigest 6

Viruses, Bacteria, Protists, and Fungi

In your textbook, read about viruses.

Label the parts of a virus.

1. nucleic acid

2. envelope

3. capsid

Number the following steps of the lytic cycle in the order in which they occur.

3 **4.** The viral nucleic acid causes the host cell to produce new virus particles.

1 **5.** A virus attaches to the membrane of a host cell.

4 **6.** The new virus particles are released from the host cell, killing the cell.

2 **7.** The viral nucleic acid enters the host cell.

In your textbook, read about bacteria.

Determine if the statement is true. If it is true. If it is not, rewrite the italicized part to make it true.

prokaryote **8.** A bacterium is a unicellular *eukaryote.*

true **9.** Bacteria may be heterotrophs, photosynthetic autotrophs, or *chemosynthetic autotrophs.*

binary fission **10.** Bacteria reproduce asexually by *conjugation.*

obligate anaerobes **11.** Bacteria that are *obligate aerobes* are killed by oxygen.

true **12.** *Archaebacteria* often live in extreme environments.

nitrogen **13.** Some bacteria fix *oxygen.*

Name _____ Date _____ Class _____

BioDigest 6

Viruses, Bacteria, Protists, and Fungi, *continued*

In your textbook, read about protists.

Write the letter of the item in Column B that best matches the item in Column A.

Column A	Column B
a **14.** Can be unicellular, colonial, or multicellular	**a.** green algae
b **15.** Parasitic protozoans	**b.** sporozoans
f **16.** Causes malaria	**c.** amoeba
g **17.** Can be both autotrophic and heterotrophic	**d.** slime mold
d **18.** Funguslike protist	**e.** brown algae
h **19.** Uses cilia to move	**f.** *Plasmodium*
j **20.** Contain carotenoids	**g.** euglenas
i **21.** Have hard, armorlike plates	**h.** *Paramecium*
e **22.** Kelps	**i.** dinoflagellates
c **23.** Uses pseudopodia to move	**j.** diatoms
k **24.** Have red and blue pigments	**k.** red algae

In your textbook, read about fungi.

Answer the following questions.

25. How do fungi obtain nutrients from a food source? **Fungi secrete enzymes into a food source and then absorb the digested nutrients.** _____

26. How do fungi play a role in recycling nutrients on Earth? **Fungi decompose organic material.** _____

27. What are hyphae? **Hyphae are the structural units of fungi.** _____

28. In what structure do club fungi produce sexual spores? **basidium** _____

29. In what structure do sac fungi produce sexual spores? **ascus** _____

30. How do mycorrhizae benefit both the plants and the fungi? **The plants benefit because the fungi that are entwined with their roots provide more surface area, thereby allowing the roots to absorb more water and minerals. The fungi benefit by absorbing nutrients from the plants' root cells.** _____

31. What is a lichen? **A lichen is a symbiotic association of a mutualistic fungus and an alga or cyanobacterium.** _____

Chapter 21 What Is a Plant?

In your textbook, read about the origins and adaptations of plants.

For each answer given below, write an appropriate question.

1. **Answer:** Multicellular eukaryotes having thick cell walls made of cellulose, a protective, waterproof covering, and that can produce its own food in the form of glucose through photosynthesis

   Question: What are plants?

2. **Answer:** The earliest known plant fossils

   Question: What are psilophytes?

3. **Answer:** Protective, waxy layers that cover most fruits, leaves, and stems

   Question: What are cuticles?

4. **Answer:** The organ of a plant that traps light energy for photosynthesis, and is supported by a stem

   Question: What is a leaf?

5. **Answer:** The organ that works like an anchor, transports nutrients, and absorbs water and minerals

   Question: What is a root?

In your textbook, read about alternation of generations.

Use each of the terms below just once to complete the passage.

diploid   generations   meiosis
gametes   haploid   sporophyte

The lives of all plants consist of two alternating stages, or (6) **generations** . The gametophyte generation of a plant is responsible for the development of (7) **gametes** . All seeds of the gametophyte, including the gametes, are (8) **haploid** . The (9) **sporophyte** generation is responsible for the production of spores. All cells of the sporophyte are (10) **diploid** . The spores are produced by the sporophyte plant body by (11) **meiosis** and are, therefore, haploid.

Chapter 21 What Is a Plant?, continued

In your textbook, read about the origin and adaptations of plants.

Circle the letter of the choice that best completes the statement.

12. The lives of _____ plants include two generations that alternate.
    a. non-seed producing   b. seed
    c. all *(circled)*   d. most

13. The generation of a plant responsible for producing gametes is the
    a. alternation of generations.   b. gametophyte generation. *(circled)*
    c. sporophyte generation.   d. seed-producing generation.

14. All gametophyte spores are _____ and all sporophyte tissue cells are _____ .
    a. haploid/diploid. *(circled)*   b. diploid/haploid.
    c. haploid/haploid.   d. diploid/diploid.

15. Non-seed plants _____ that grow into gametophytes.
    a. release spores into the environment *(circled)*   b. retain spores in the parent plant
    c. release seeds into the environment   d. retain seeds in the parent plant

Answer the following questions.

16. What is the difference between vascular and nonvascular plants?
    Vascular plants have long, tubelike cells that form tissues that transport food, water, and other materials. Nonvascular plants have thin tissues that allow nutrients and water to travel from one cell to another by osmosis and diffusion.

17. Some land plants produce seeds. What is their function? How do they differ from spores?
    Seeds and spores protect the embryos and haploid cells and keep them from drying out. Seeds have an embryo with a food supply and are covered with a protective coat. Spores have a single haploid cell with a hard protective covering.

18. How do algae and land plants get nutrients?
    Algae live in water and absorb dissolved nutrients directly into its cells. Most land plants absorb nutrients from the soil, using only the portions of the plant in the soil.

Name _____ Date _____ Class _____

Reinforcement and Study Guide

In your textbook, read about non-seed plants.

For each item in Column A, write the letter of the matching item in Column B.

	Column A	Column B
c	1. Leaves that are found on ferns	a. leafy liverworts
e	2. Scaly structures that support male or female reproductive structures	b. thallose liverworts
b	3. Plants with a broad, flattened body that resembles a lobed leaf	c. fronds
a	4. Plants with three flattened rows of thin leaves	d. hornworts
d	5. Nonvascular plants that grow in damp, shady habitats and whose sporophytes resemble horns	e. cones

Complete the chart below by marking the appropriate columns for each division of plants.

Division	Vascular	Nonvascular	Non-seed Plants	Seeds in Fruits	Seeds in Cones
6. Hepatophyta		✓	✓		
7. Anthocerophyta		✓	✓		
8. Bryophyta		✓	✓		
9. Psilophyta	✓		✓		
10. Lycophyta	✓		✓		
11. Sphenophyta	✓		✓		
12. Pterophyta	✓		✓		
13. Cycadophyta	✓				✓
14. Gnetophyta	✓				✓
15. Ginkgophyta	✓				✓
16. Coniferophyta	✓				✓
17. Anthophyta	✓			✓	

Name _____ Date _____ Class _____

Reinforcement and Study Guide

In your textbook, read about non-seed plants.

For each answer given below, write an appropriate question.

18. **Answer:** Vascular plants that have neither roots nor leaves

    Question: What are plants of the Psilophyta division, or whisk ferns?

19. **Answer:** Vascular plants that have hollow, jointed stems surrounded by whorls of scalelike leaves, whose cells contain large deposits of silica

    Question: What are plants of the Sphenophyta division, or horsetails?

20. **Answer:** Plants that may be the ancestors of all plants

    Question: What are plants of the Hepatophyta division, or liverworts?

21. **Answer:** Hard-walled reproductive cells found in non-seed plants

    Question: What are spores?

22. **Answer:** Nonvascular plants that rely on osmosis and diffusion to transport water and nutrients, although some members have elongated cells that conduct water and sugars

    Question: What are plants of the Bryophyta division, or mosses?

In your textbook, read about seed plants.

Use each of the terms below just once to complete the passage.

Anthophyta	Cycadophyta	Gnetophyta
Coniferophyta	Ginkgophyta	

Seed plants are classified into five divisions. Plants from the (23) __Cycadophyta__ division are palmlike trees with scaly trunks and are often mistaken for ferns or small palm trees. There is only one living species in the (24) __Ginkgophyta__ division. The members of the (25) __Anthophyta__ division are the largest, most diverse group of seed plant on Earth and are commonly known as the flowering plants. Three distinct genera make up the plant division called (26) __Gnetophyta__. Species of the (27) __Coniferophyta__ division can be identified by the characteristics of their needlelike or scaly leaves.

Chapter 22 The Diversity of Plants

Section 22.1 Nonvascular Plants

In your textbook, read about nonvascular plants—bryophyta, hepatophyta, and anthocerophyta.

Complete each statement.

1. Nonvascular plants are successful in habitats with adequate __water__.

2. The __gametophyte__ generation is dominant in nonvascular plants.

3. Sperm are produced in male reproductive structures called __antheridia__, and eggs are produced in female reproductive structures called __archegonia__.

4. Mosses have colorless multicellular structures called __rhizoids__, which help anchor the stem to the soil.

5. Most liverworts have __an oily or a shiny surface__ that helps reduce evaporation of water from the plant's tissues.

6. Liverworts occur in many environments and include two groups: the __thallose__ liverworts and the __leafy__ liverworts.

7. One unique feature of hornworts is the presence of a(n) __single chloroplast__ in each cell.

8. The common names for the nonvascular plants, Bryophyta, Hepatophyta, and Anthocerophyta are __mosses__, __liverworts__, and __hornworts__.

Circle the letter of the response that best completes the statement.

9. Nonvascular plants are not as common or as widespread as vascular plants because
a. nonvascular plants are small.
(b.) the life functions of nonvascular plants require a close association with water.
c. nonvascular plants are limited to dry habitats.
d. none of the above.

10. The life cycle of nonvascular plants includes an alternation of generations between a
a. diploid sporophyte and a diploid gametophyte.
b. haploid sporophyte and a haploid gametophyte.
(c.) diploid sporophyte and a haploid gametophyte.
d. haploid sporophyte and a diploid gametophyte.

11. Fossil and genetic evidence suggests that the first land plants were
a. mosses.
b. sphagnum moss.
(c.) liverworts.
d. hornworts.

Chapter 22 The Diversity of Plants, *continued*

Section 22.2 Non-Seed Vascular Plants

In your textbook, read about the alternation of generations of non-seed vascular plants and lycophyta.

Use each of the terms below just once to complete the passage.

antheridia	leaves	sporophyte
archegonia	prothallus	strobilus
egg	reproductive cells	zygote
fertilization	sperm	

Unlike nonvascular plants, the spore-producing (1) __sporophyte__ is the dominant generation in vascular plants. A major advance in vascular plants was the adaptation of (2) __leaves__ to form structures that protect the developing (3) __reproductive cells__. In some non-seed vascular plants, spore-bearing leaves form a compact cluster called a(n) (4) __strobilus__. Spores are released from this compact cluster. These spores then grow to form the gametophyte, called a(n) (5) __prothallus__. This structure is relatively small and lives in or on soil. The prothallus then forms (6) __antheridia__, male reproductive structures, and (7) __archegonia__, female reproductive structures. (8) __Sperm__ are released from the antheridium and swim through a film of water to the (9) __egg__ in the archegonium. (10) __Fertilization__ occurs and a large, dominant sporophyte plant develops from the fertilized (11) __zygote__.

For each statement below, write true or false.

__false__ 12. The leafy stems of lycophytes resemble clubs, and their reproductive structures are moss shaped.

__true__ 13. The leaves of lycophytes occur as pairs, whorls, or spirals along the stem.

__false__ 14. Lycophytes are simple vascular plants with creeping leaves.

__true__ 15. The club moss is commonly called ground pine because it is evergreen and resembles a miniature pine tree.

Name _____ Date _____ Class _____

Reinforcement and Study Guide

Chapter 22 The Diversity of Plants, continued

Section 22.2 Non-Seed Vascular Plants, continued

In your textbook, read about sphenophyta and pterophyta.

Complete each statement.

16. The hollow-stemmed horsetail appears to be jointed with scalelike **leaves** surrounding each joint.

17. The most recognized generation of ferns is the **sporophyte** generation.

18. The **gametophyte** in most ferns is a thin, flat structure.

19. In most ferns, the main stem, called a **rhizome**, is underground. It contains many starch-filled cells for **storage**.

20. The leaves of a fern are called **fronds**.

21. Fronds are often divided into leaflets called **pinnae**, which are attached to a central stipe.

22. Ferns were the first vascular plants to evolve leaves with branching **veins** of vascular tissue.

23. The common names for the seedless vascular plants, Lycophyta, Sphenophyta, and Pterophyta are **club or spike mosses**, **horsetails**, and **ferns**.

Answer the following questions on the lines provided.

24. Why are sphenophytes, or horsetails, sometimes referred to as scouring rushes?
Sphenophytes are called scouring rushes because they contain silica, an abrasive substance, and were once used to scour cooking utensils.

25. Why might you be more familiar with ferns than with club mosses and horsetails?
Ferns evolved into many more species and are more abundant. Also, ferns can be found in many types of environments.

Name _____ Date _____ Class _____

Reinforcement and Study Guide

Chapter 22 The Diversity of Plants, continued

Section 22.3 Seed Plants

In your textbook, read about the seed plants—cyadophyta, gingkophyta, gnetophyta, coniferophyta, and anthophyta.

Complete each statement.

1. An **embryo**, or young diploid sporophyte, has food-storage organs called **cotyledons**, which develop into leaves.

2. Vascular plants that produce **seeds** in cones are sometimes called **gymnosperms**.

3. Seed plants do not require **water** for **fertilization**.

4. The male gametophyte develops inside a structure called a(n) **pollen grain** that includes sperm cells, nutrients, and a protective outer covering.

5. The female gametophyte, which produces the egg cell, is contained within a sporophyte structure called a(n) **ovule**.

6. Biennials develop large storage roots and live for **two years**.

7. Perennials produce flowers and seeds periodically for **several years**.

8. Annual plants live for **one year or less**.

9. **Monocotyledons** have one seed leaf; **dicotyledons** have two seed leaves.

For each statement below, write true or false.

false 10. Cycads are related to palm trees but their leaves unfurl like fern fronds.

true 11. There is only one species of ginkgo tree alive today.

true 12. Most gnetophytes today are found in the deserts or mountains of Africa, Asia, North America, and Central or South America.

false 13. Most conifers are evergreen plants that lose their needlelike leaves all at once and only grow in nutrient-rich soil.

true 14. Dropping leaves is an adaptation in deciduous plants to reduce water loss when it is less available during winter.

true 15. Anthophytes are unique in that they are the only division of plants that produce fruits.

Chapter 23 Plant Structure and Function

Reinforcement and Study Guide

Section 23.1 Plant Cells and Tissues

In your textbook, read about plant cells and tissues.

Match the definitions in Column 1 with the terms in describes from Column 2. Place the letter from Column 2 in the spaces under Column 1.

Column 1

- h **1.** The most abundant kind of plant cells
- b **2.** Long cells with unevenly thickened cell walls. This type of cell wall allows the cells to grow.
- j **3.** Cells with walls that are very thick and rigid. At maturity, these cells often die, leaving the cell walls to provide support for the plant.
- e **4.** Dermal tissue that is composed of flattened parenchyma cells that cover all parts of the plant
- l **5.** Openings in the cuticle of the leaf that control the exchange of gases
- f **6.** Cells that control the opening and closing of the stomata.
- n **7.** Hairlike projections that extend from the epidermis
- q **8.** Plant tissue composed of tubular cells that transports water and minerals from the roots to the rest of the plant
- m **9.** Tubular cells, with tapered ends, which transport water throughout a plant
- d **10.** Lateral meristem that produces a tough covering for the surface of stems and roots
- i **11.** Vascular tissue that transport sugars from the leaves to all parts of the plant
- k **12.** Long, cylindrical phloem cells through which sugars and organic compounds flow
- c **13.** Nucleated cells that help manage the transport of sugars and other organic compounds through the sieve cells of the phloem
- g **14.** Areas where new cells are produced
- a **15.** Growth tissue found at or near the tips of roots and stems
- p **16.** Tubular cells that transport water throughout the plant. These cells are wider and shorter than tracheids.
- o **17.** Lateral meristem that produces new xylem and phloem cells in the stems and roots

Column 2

- **a.** apical meristem
- **b.** collenchyma
- **c.** companion cell
- **d.** cork cambium
- **e.** epidermis
- **f.** guard cells
- **g.** meristem
- **h.** parenchyma
- **i.** phloem
- **j.** sclerenchyma
- **k.** sieve tube member
- **l.** stomata
- **m.** tracheids
- **n.** trichomes
- **o.** vascular cambium
- **p.** vessel element
- **q.** xylem

Chapter 23 Plant Structure and Function, *continued*

Reinforcement and Study Guide

Section 23.2 Roots, Stems, and Leaves

In your textbook, read about roots and stems.

Label the parts of the dicot root. Use these choices:

cortex   phloem   epidermis   endodermis   xylem

Dicot Root

1. **epidermis**
2. **endodermis**
3. **phloem**
4. **xylem**
5. **cortex**

For each statement below, write true or false.

- true **6.** A root hair is a small extension of an epidermal, or outermost, cell layer of a dicot root.
- true **7.** Layers of parenchyma cells make up the cortex of a dicot root and the central pith of a monocot root.
- false **8.** Outside the endodermis is a tissue called the pericycle that develops vertical roots.
- true **9.** Vascular cambium cells found at the center of a root grow more xylem and phloem cells that increase the size of the root.
- false **10.** Behind the root tip are cell-producing growth tissues called the root cap.
- false **11.** The difference between roots and stems lies in the way they transport water.
- true **12.** Primary growth in a stem occurs in the apical meristem.

Name _____ Date _____ Class _____

Reinforcement and Study Guide

In your textbook, read about plant hormones and plant responses.

Complete each statement.

1. A **hormone** is a chemical that is produced in one part of an organism and transported to another part, where it causes a physiological change.

2. The group of plant hormones called **auxins** promote cell elongation. Indoleacetic acid (IAA) is an example of this group of hormones.

3. The group of growth hormones that cause plants to grow taller because, like auxins, they stimulate cell elongation, are called **gibberellins** .

4. The hormones called **cytokinins** are so named because they stimulate cell division by stimulating the production of proteins needed for mitosis.

5. The plant hormone called **ethylene** is a simple, gaseous compound composed of carbon and hydrogen that speeds the ripening of fruits.

6. A plant's response to an external stimulus that comes from a particular direction is called a **tropism** .

7. A responsive movement of a plant that is not dependent on the direction of the stimulus is called a **nastic movement** .

Determine if the statement is true. If it is true, write true. If it is not, rewrite the italicized part to make it true.

8. A *large* amount of hormone is needed to make physiological changes in a plant. **small**

9. If gibberellins are applied to the tip of a dwarf plant, it will grow *taller*. **true**

10. The growth of a plant towards light is caused by an unequal distribution of *ethylene* in the plant's stem. **auxin**

11. If a tropism is *negative*, the plant grows toward the stimulus. **positive**

12. The growth of a plant toward light is called *phototropism*. **true**

13. *Gravitropism* is the direction of plant growth in response to gravity. **true**

14. A plant's response to touch is called *cytokinin*. **thigmotropism**

Name _____ Date _____ Class _____

Reinforcement and Study Guide

In your textbook, read about stems and leaves.

Circle the letter of the response that best completes the statement.

13. Many wildflowers with soft, green stems are plants that have
   a. woody stems.
   b. herbaceous stems.
   c. woody roots.
   d. all of the above.

14. The functions of a plant's stem include
   a. transporting sugar.
   b. supporting the plant.
   c. transporting water and minerals.
   d. all of the above.

15. Any portion of the plant that stores sugars is called a
   a. petiole.
   b. mesophyll.
   c. root cap.
   d. sink.

16. The movement of sugars from the leaves through the phloem is called
   a. photosynthesis.
   b. transpiration.
   c. translocation.
   d. food storage.

In your textbook, read about the leaves of a plant.

Use each of the terms below just once to complete the passage.

| stomata | extend | cuticle | transpiration | epidermis |
| veins | stem | petiole | photosynthesis | mesophyll |

There are many parts to a leaf. Grass leaves grow right out of the **(17)** **stem** , but other leaves are connected to the stem by a stalk called the **(18)** **petiole** . The petiole is made of vascular tissues that **(19)** **extend** up into the leaf to form **(20)** **veins** .

The outer surface of a leaf has a **(21)** **cuticle** that covers the epidermis. Inside the epidermis are two layers of photosynthetic cells that make up the **(22)** **mesophyll** . Cells in the palisade layer have many chloroplasts and carry out most of the leaf's **(23)** **photosynthesis** . Leaves have a(n) **(24)** **epidermis** with a waxy cuticle and **(25)** **stomata** help prevent water loss. The loss of water through the stomata is called **(26)** **transpiration** .

Chapter 24 — Reproduction in Plants

In your textbook, read about alternation of generations and the life cycles of mosses and ferns.

Use each of the terms below just once to complete the following statements.

diploid   meiosis   sporophyte
dominant   mitosis   vegetative reproduction
egg   protonema
gametophyte   sperm

1. The two phases of the plant life are the **gametophyte** stage and the **sporophyte** stage.

2. The cells of the sporophyte are all **diploid**.

3. The female gamete is the **egg**, and the male gamete is the **sperm**.

4. Some plants reproduce asexually by a process called **vegetative reproduction**, in which a new plant is produced from an existing vegetative structure.

5. Mosses belong to one of the few plant divisions in which the gametophyte plant is the **dominant** generation.

6. A small, green filament of moss cells that develops into either a male or female moss gametophyte is known as a(n) **protonema**.

7. The moss diploid zygote divides by **mitosis** to form a new sporophyte in the form of a stalk and capsule.

8. Spores are produced by **meiosis** in the capsule of the moss sporophyte.

Number each description to order the stages from spore release of the life cycle of a fern, from 1 to 7.

2   9. A spore germinates and grows into a heart-shaped gametophyte called a prothallus.

4   10. After fertilization, the diploid zygote grows into a sporophyte.

5   11. As the sporophyte grows, roots and fronds grow out from the rhizome.

3   12. Sperm swim through a film of water on the prothallus to reach and fertilize an egg in the archegonium.

7   13. In each sporangium, spores are produced by meiosis, and the cycle begins again as the spores are dispersed by the wind.

6   14. Sori, or clusters of sporangia, grow on the pinnae.

1   15. A sporangium bursts, releasing haploid spores.

Chapter 24 — Reproduction in Plants, *continued*

In your textbook, read about the life cycle of conifers.

Answer the following questions.

1. What is the dominant stage in conifers?
The dominant stage in conifers is the sporophyte stage.

2. What does the adult conifer produce on its branches?
Adult conifers produce male and female cones on separate branches of the tree.

3. What is a megaspore?
A megaspore is a female spore that eventually becomes the female gametophyte.

4. What are microspores and how are they produced?
Microspores are male spores. The male cones have sporangia that undergo meiosis to produces microspores.

5. What do the microspores develop into?
Microspores develop into male gametophytes, or pollen grains.

6. What is a micropyle?
A micropyle is the opening of the ovule.

7. How does fertilization take place?
As the pollen grain matures, it produces a pollen tube that grows through the micropyle and into the ovule. A sperm cell from the male gametophyte is transported by the pollen tube to the egg, where fertilization takes place.

8. After fertilization, a zygote develops inside the ovule into an embryo with several cotyledons. What happens to the ovule?
The ovule provides the seed coat as the mature seed is produced.

9. What happens to the seeds when the female cone opens and falls to the ground?
When conditions are favorable, the seed germinates into a new, young sporophyte—a conifer seedling.

10. What will the seedling become?
The seedling will become an adult conifer sporophyte.

Name _____ Date _____ Class _____

Reinforcement and Study Guide

Chapter 24 **Reproduction in Plants,** *continued*

Section 24.2 Flowers and Flowering

In your textbook, read about the structure of a flower.

Determine if the statement is true. If it is not, rewrite the italicized part to make it true.

1. In flowering plants, sexual reproduction takes place in the *seed*, which has several parts.
   flower

2. The structure of a flower includes four kinds of organs: *sepals, petals, stamens, and ovaries.*
   sepals, petals, stamens, and pistils

3. *Petals* are usually colorful, leaflike structures that encircle the flower stem.
   true

4. The male reproductive structure located inside the petals of a flower is a *stamen.* Sperm-containing pollen is produced in the *amber* at the tip of the stamen.
   true/true

5. The female reproductive structure at the center of a flower is the *ovary.* Eggs are formed in the *pistil*, which is located in the bottom portion of the *ovary.*
   pistil/ovary/pistil

Label the parts of the flower. Use these choices:

sepal	petal	stigma	ovule
anther	ovary	filament	

6. stigma

7. anther

8. petal

9. filament

10. ovary

11. ovule

12. sepal

Name _____ Date _____ Class _____

Reinforcement and Study Guide

Chapter 24 **Reproduction in Plants,** *continued*

Section 24.3 The Life Cycle of a Flowering Plant

In your textbook, read about the life cycle of a flowering plant.

For each item in Column A, write the letter of the matching item from Column B.

Column A

f **1.** Two nuclei in one cell at the center of the embryo sac

b **2.** A process in which one sperm fertilizes the egg and the other sperm joins with the central cell

c **3.** Food-storing tissue that develops from the triploid central cell and supports the development of the embryo

a **4.** A period of inactivity in which seeds of some plant species remain until conditions are favorable for growth and development

d **5.** The beginning of the development of the embryo into a new plant

g **6.** This embryonic root is the first part of the embryo to appear from the seed

e **7.** The portion of the stem near the seed

Column B

a. dormancy

b. double fertilization

c. endosperm

d. germination

e. hypocotyl

f. polar nuclei

g. radicle

Answer the following questions.

8. How do anthophytes attract animal pollinators?
   Some plants produce nectar as a food source. Some plants have bright, attractive flowers. Some flowers have a strong scent, and others have structural adaptations to attract animals (for example, some orchids resemble female wasps).

9. How do seeds form after fertilization takes place?
   After fertilization, most flower parts die and seeds begin to develop. The wall of the ovule becomes the hard seed coat and inside the ovule, the zygote divides and grows into the plant embryo. The triploid central cell develops into the endosperm.

10. Name three ways seeds are dispersed.
    Accept any three of the following methods: Animals may eat the fruit containing seeds; they may spit the seeds out or the seeds may pass through their digestive systems. Some seeds have air pockets in their walls that enable them to float away on water. Still other tiny seeds are easily blown about by the wind or become attached to animal fur.

BioDigest
7 Plants

In your textbook, read about plants.

Study the following diagram of alternation of generations in plants. Then answer the questions.

Sporophyte → diploid plant (2*n*) → undergoes meiosis → produces spores (*n*) → which do not require fertilization to produce a ⌐

Gametophyte → haploid plant (*n*) → undergoes mitosis → produces gametes (*n*) → which require fertilization to produce a ⌐

Sporophyte . . . and so on

1. Is the sporophyte generation a haploid or diploid generation? **diploid (2*n*)**

2. Is the gametophyte generation a haploid or diploid generation? **haploid (*n*)**

3. Is a spore haploid or diploid? **haploid (*n*)**

4. Is a gamete haploid or diploid? **haploid (*n*)**

5. Does a spore produce a gametophyte without fertilization? **yes**

6. Does a gamete produce a sporophyte without fertilization? **no**

7. Which generation—sporophyte or gametophyte—produces a generation that is diploid? **gametophyte**

Seed Plants
Explain how these adaptations enable conifers to survive in cold or dry climates.

8. *Needles* **compact shape, thick waxy covering that helps reduce evaporation and conserve water**

9. *Stems* **thick layer of bark that insulates the tissue inside**

10. *Flexible leaves and branches* **bend under weight of snow and ice, allowing buildup to slide off before it becomes heavy enough to break the branch**

BioDigest
7 Plants, *continued*

Flowering Plants
Fill in the following blanks to explain the function of a flower.

11. A flower has two major reproductive structures. The **pistil** is the _____ reproductive organ. At the base of the pistil is the **ovary**, which houses ovules, the female **gametophyte** generation of the plant. In each ovule, female gametes, or **egg cells**, form.

12. The **stamen** and anther form the **male** reproductive organ. The male **gametophyte** generation of the plant is **pollen**. Within it, the male gametes are formed.

13. When pollination occurs, a **pollen tube** extends from the pollen grain to the ovary, and two **sperm** travel down the tube to fertilize the eggs in the ovule.

14. Some flowers are colorful and showy. Others are small and inconspicuous. Explain how these two flower types are adapted to different pollinators.
Flowers that are colorful attract birds, insects, or other animals that are in search of nectar or pollen. Flowers that lack petals such as those in tree catkins and grasses are pollinated by the wind.

15. Discuss three ways that seeds may be spread through the environment.
a. Students can choose from four methods: seeds can be dispersed by the wind,
b. eaten and dropped by animals, floated away on water, or carried by animals
c. because of tiny hooks or barbs that catch upon the animals' fur.

Name _____ Date _____ Class _____

Chapter 25 What Is an Animal?

Section 25.1 Typical Animal Characteristics

In your textbook, read about the characteristics of animals.

Answer the following questions.

1. You have just discovered a new organism that you think is an animal. In order to be classified as an animal, what characteristics must it have?
   It must be multicellular, heterotrophic (feed on other organisms), and its cells must
   lack cell walls.

2. What is one important factor that influences how an animal obtains its food?
   its ability to move

3. How might an animal be free-moving at one stage in its life and sessile at another? Give an example.
   Animals such as sponges, corals, and barnacles are sessile as adults, but they
   develop from free-swimming larvae.

4. How do sessile, aquatic animals get their food?
   They rely on water currents to bring food to them.

If the animal described below is a sessile organism, write yes. If it is not, write no.

yes   5. Barnacles attached to a ship's hull

no   6. A spider lying in wait in the center of its web

no   7. Coral larvae drifting in a tropical ocean

yes   8. Sponges growing on the outside of a crab's shell

Complete each statement.

9. Digestion in a sponge takes place in ____**individual**____ ____**cells**____, while digestion in a more complex animal like a tiger takes place in a(n) ____**internal**____ ____**cavity**____.

10. Some of the food you had for breakfast has been stored as ____**fat**____ or ____**glycogen**____, ready to be used if it's a long time until your next meal.

Name _____ Date _____ Class _____

Chapter 25 What Is an Animal?, continued

Section 25.1 Typical Animal Characteristics, continued

In your textbook, read about the development of animals.

Determine if the statement is true. If it is not, rewrite the italicized part to make it true.

11. Most animals develop from a single, fertilized egg called a *blastula*. ____**zygote**____

12. A zygote divides by a process known as *cleavage*. ____**true**____

13. The blastula is a *solid ball of cells*. ____**a hollow ball formed by a single layer of cells**____
    ____**surrounding a fluid-filled space**____

Label the parts of the gastrula shown here. Use these choices:

ectoderm   endoderm   mesoderm   opening in gastrula

14. ____**endoderm**____

15. ____**mesoderm**____

16. ____**opening in gastrula**____

17. ____**ectoderm**____

Complete the chart by checking the correct column for each description.

Description	Endoderm	Ectoderm	Mesoderm
18. Gives rise to digestive tract	✓		
19. Continues to grow and divide	✓	✓	✓
20. Lines the inner surface of gastrula	✓		
21. Gives rise to muscles			✓
22. Develops into skin and nervous tissue		✓	
23. Forms from cells that break off endoderm			✓

In your textbook, read about kinds of symmetry in animals.

Circle the letter of the choice that best completes the statement or answers the question.

1. Different kinds of symmetry make it possible for animals to
   a. grow very large.
   b. survive when cut into pieces.
   c. move and find food in different ways.
   d. live a long time.

2. The irregularly shaped body of a sponge is an example of
   a. asymmetry.
   b. gastrulation.
   c. symmetry.
   d. balance.

3. A sponge's body has how many layers of cells?
   a. one
   b. two
   c. three
   d. four

4. The embryonic development of a sponge does *not* include which of the following?
   a. formation of endoderm
   b. formation of mesoderm
   c. a gastrula stage
   d. a, b, and c

5. If you divided a radially symmetrical animal along any plane through its central axis, you would end up with
   a. roughly equal halves.
   b. front and back halves.
   c. top and bottom halves.
   d. three pieces.

6. Which of the following animals is *not* radially symmetrical?
   a. a hydra
   b. a sea urchin
   c. a spider
   d. a starfish

7. An organism with bilateral symmetry can be divided lengthwise into right and left halves that are
   a. asymmetrical.
   b. mirror images of each other.
   c. made up of two cell layers.
   d. flattened.

Identify each of the following body parts as being either dorsal or ventral on the animal's body.

ventral ____ 8. the navel of a killer whale

dorsal ____ 9. the sail fin on an iguana

dorsal ____ 10. the back of your neck

ventral ____ 11. the mouth of a shark

ventral ____ 12. the pouch of a kangaroo

In your textbook, read about bilateral symmetry and body plans.

Answer the following questions.

13. In what ways was the development of a body cavity, or coelom, an advantage for bilaterally symmetrical animals?
   provided space for complex internal organs; made it possible for animals to grow larger and to move and feed more efficiently

14. Describe an acoelomate animal's body plan.
   Acoelomate animals have three cell layers with a digestive tract but no body cavity.

15. How do nutrients get to the cells in a flatworm's solid, acoelomate body?
   by diffusion

Use each of the terms below just once to complete the passage.

coelom	completely	double
mesoderm	partly	pseudocoelom

A roundworm has a (16) **mesoderm** ____, a body lined with (17) **partly** ____ internal organs cavity that is (18) **pseudocoelom** ____. Coelomate animals have a (19) **coelom** ____, a body cavity that is (20) **completely** ____ surrounded by mesoderm and in which complex (21) **internal organs** ____ are suspended by (22) **double** ____ layers of mesoderm tissue.

In your textbook, read about animal protection and support.

For each statement below, write true or false.

false ____ 23. During the course of evolution, animal body plans have decreased in complexity.

true ____ 24. An exoskeleton provides protection and support on the outside of an animal's body, as well as a place for muscle attachment.

true ____ 25. An endoskeleton is a support framework housed within the body, a protective enclosure for internal organs, and a brace for muscles to pull against.

false ____ 26. An invertebrate is an animal with a backbone.

Name _____ Date _____ Class _____

Chapter 26

Sponges, Cnidarians, Flatworms, and Roundworms

In your textbook, read about sponges.

Answer the following questions.

1. How does the name *Porifera* relate to the structure of a sponge?
   Porifera means "pore-bearer," which refers to the many pores in a sponge's
   body wall.

2. How do sponges obtain food from their environment?
   Sponges are filter feeders; they filter small particles of food out of the water that
   they draw through their bodies.

3. Describe a sponge's body plan.
   two cell layers between which lies a jellylike layer; no body cavity, tissues,
   or organs

Complete the table by writing a cell type or structure in sponges that fits each description.

Type of Cell or Structure	Description
4. amoebocytes	Aid in reproduction and nutrient transport Help produce spicules
5. epithelial cells	Form the outside surface of body Contract to close pores
6. collar cells	Line interior of sponge's body Use flagella to draw water through pores
7. spicules	Found in jellylike substance between layers Make up sponge's support system

Use each of the terms below just once to complete the passage.

external buds	eggs	hermaphroditic	internal fertilization
larvae	sexual	sperm	

Sponges sometimes reproduce asexually by forming **(8)** external buds . Being
(9) hermaphroditic , a sponge can also produce both **(10)** eggs and sperm. During
(11) sexual reproduction, **(12)** sperm from one sponge fertilize the eggs
of another. Fertilization can be external, but **(13)** internal fertilization is more common.
Free-swimming **(14)** larvae settle and develop into sessile adults.

Name _____ Date _____ Class _____

Chapter 26

Sponges, Cnidarians, Flatworms, and Roundworms, *continued*

In your textbook, read about cnidarians.

Identify each of the following descriptions as either the polyp or medusa form of a cnidarian.

polyp	1. Reef-building corals on the Great Barrier Reef
medusa	2. *Aurelia*, the moon jellyfish
polyp	3. Deep sea anemones with meter-long tentacles
polyp	4. The asexual phase in a jellyfish's life cycle

Answer the following questions.

5. Nematocysts are characteristic of cnidarians. How does a nematocyst work?
   When a nematocyst is triggered, a coiled tube is explosively discharged, which
   stabs, entangles, or injects toxin into prey.

6. Compare and contrast how food is digested in a sponge and in a cnidarian.
   In sponges, food is digested inside individual body cells. In cnidarians, digestion
   takes place inside a space called a gastrovascular cavity.

7. How does a nerve net function?
   It conducts nerve impulses from all over the body and stimulates contractions of
   muscle-like cells.

Order the following steps in the life cycle of a jellyfish from A to F, beginning with the release of eggs and sperm.

E	8. A polyp grows and buds repeatedly.
B	9. External fertilization takes place in the sea.
C	10. A zygote develops into a blastula, which develops into a larva.
A	11. Male and female medusae release sperm and eggs, respectively.
D	12. A cilia-covered larva settles onto a surface.
F	13. A tiny medusa breaks free from its sessile parent and drifts away.

Chapter 26 — Reinforcement and Study Guide

Sponges, Cnidarians, Flatworms, and Roundworms, *continued*

Section 26.4 Roundworms

In your textbook, read about roundworms.

Answer the following questions.

1. What impact do parasitic roundworms have on other organisms?

Virtually all plant and animal species are affected by parasitic roundworms of some type; they cause infection and disease.

2. List three ways in which roundworms differ from flatworms.

(1) rounded, with tapered ends; (2) pseudocoelomate; (3) have both mouth and anus

3. What accounts for the characteristic wriggling movement of roundworms?

Roundworms have pairs of lengthwise muscles that alternately contract and relax, causing the worms to thrash from side to side.

4. What are four of the most common parasitic roundworms that infect humans?

***Ascaris*, hookworm, *Trichinella*, pinworms**

5. Can roundworms cause plant diseases? Explain.

Yes; over 1200 species of roundworms are known to cause diseases in plants.

6. What parts of plants are most commonly susceptible to parasitic roundworms?

plant roots

Below are two medical reports. After reading each report, give a preliminary diagnosis of what you think might be causing the problem.

7.
MEDICAL REPORT

Patient is an active 5-year-old girl. Complains about a constant itching around the anal area, especially at night.

Preliminary Diagnosis:

pinworm infection

8.
MEDICAL REPORT

Patient is a 29-year-old female Peace Corps volunteer. Lived with remote tribe whose primary food is pigs. Complains of muscle pain.

Preliminary Diagnosis:

***Trichinella* infection**

Chapter 26 — Reinforcement and Study Guide

Sponges, Cnidarians, Flatworms, and Roundworms, *continued*

Section 26.3 Flatworms

In your textbook, read about flatworms.

For each statement below, write *true* or *false*.

true   1. Flatworms are bilaterally symmetrical and have a clearly defined head.

false   2. Adult planarians can focus well enough with their eyespots to form images of objects in their environment.

true   3. Flame cells play an important role in maintaining water balance in planaria.

false   4. A planarian uses its pharynx to locate food.

false   5. Planarians reproduce sexually by producing encapsulated zygotes that hatch into free-swimming larvae.

In part C of the illustration below, draw in what you think will happen to the two halves of the cut planarian. Then, answer the question.

6.

A   B   C

7. How is regeneration adaptive for survival in planarians?

Loss of part of the body is not necessarily fatal; two worms can result where there was only one.

Complete the table by checking the correct column for each description.

Description	Planarian	Tapeworm	Fluke
8. Lives parasitically within a host		✓	✓
9. Body made up of proglottids		✓	
10. Body is thin and solid	✓	✓	✓
11. Free-living in aquatic environments	✓		
12. Attaches to host's intestine with scolex		✓	
13. Extends a pharynx to suck up food	✓		
14. May live in host's blood vessels			✓

Chapter 27 — Mollusks and Segmented Worms

Reinforcement and Study Guide
Section 27.1 Mollusks

In your textbook, read about what a mollusk is.

The phylum *Mollusca* is a very diverse group of animals. Complete the correct column for each characteristic.

Characteristic	Exhibited In:	
	All Mollusks	**Some Mollusks**
1. Possess a hard, external shell		✓
2. Bilaterally symmetrical	✓	
3. Have a mantle	✓	
4. Live on land		✓
5. Digestive tract has two openings.	✓	
6. Inhabit aquatic environments		✓
7. Share similar developmental patterns	✓	
8. Are slow-moving		✓
9. Have a coelom	✓	

In your textbook, read about diversity of mollusks.

Identify each mollusk shown below. Write the name of the class to which it belongs and briefly describe where it lives.

10. snail; gastropods; live in water or on land, in generally moist areas

11. clam; bivalves; aquatic, many live attached to some kind of surface

12. octopus; cephalopods; free-swimming in ocean habitats

Chapter 27 — Mollusks and Segmented Worms, continued

Reinforcement and Study Guide
Section 27.1 Mollusks, continued

In your textbook, read about a mollusk's body systems and the diversity of mollusks.

Complete each statement.

13. Gastropods have either a(n) **single** shell or **no** shell.

14. Most mollusks have a(n) **open** circulatory system in which blood flows through **vessels** into open **spaces** around tissues and organs.

15. Most mollusks use **gills** for respiration, while a garden slug uses a primitive **lung** for gas exchange.

16. **Nephridia** are involved in removing wastes from a mollusk's body.

17. Fertilization in most aquatic mollusks takes place **externally** .

For each statement below, write true or false.

false 18. All shelled gastropods are predators.

true 19. When a snail is disturbed, it pulls its body inside its shell for protection.

false 20. Without a shell, terrestrial slugs and sea slugs (nudibranchs) have no protection against predators.

false 21. The two shells of bivalve mollusks are held together by the mantle.

Determine whether each of the statements below best describes bivalves, gastropods, or both.

bivalves 22. Nearly all feed by filtering particles from the water around them.

both 23. Most have a large muscular foot.

gastropods 24. They use a radula for feeding.

bivalves 25. Water flows through their bodies via well-developed incurrent and excurrent siphons.

Chapter 27 — Mollusks and Segmented Worms, continued

Reinforcement and Study Guide

Section 27.2 Segmented Worms

In your textbook, read about segmented worms, including the Inside Story about earthworms.

Use each of the terms below just once to complete the passage:

Annelida   bristleworms   earthworms   muscles
parapodia   segments   setae

Members of the phylum (1) __Annelida__ all have bodies made up of multiple
(2) __segments__. Each segment has its own (3) __muscles__ that function to lengthen
and shorten the worm's body. When present, bristlelike (4) __setae__ act as anchors while the
worm is moving along. In (5) __bristleworms__, each segment has a pair of (6) __parapodia__.
The most familiar annelids are probably (7) __earthworms__.

Determine if the statement is true. If it is not, rewrite the italicized part to make it true.

8. Earthworms have a *mouth with tiny teeth in which food particles are ground up before entering
the digestive tract.* __gizzard__

9. Blood is pumped throughout an earthworm's closed circulatory system by *an elongated,
four-chambered heart.* __enlarged blood vessels that act as hearts__

10. Some body segments in annelids are *specialized for reproduction.* __true__

*Below are the field notes of a biologist studying several newly collected annelid worms. Write the
type of annelid—earthworm, bristleworm, or leech—being described.*

11. Collected in rain forest of Papua, New Guinea;
very active; flattened, with 32 body segments;
has suckers on the ends of its body; no setae   Type of annelid: __leech__

12. Found crawling over corals on a reef;
contains only eggs; no male reproductive
organs; well-developed parapodia   Type of annelid: __bristleworm__

13. Uncovered in top layer of moist soil;
body has minute setae on ventral
surface of each segment;
hermaphroditic   Type of annelid: __earthworm__

REINFORCEMENT AND STUDY GUIDE

Chapter 27 — Mollusks and Segmented Worms, continued

Reinforcement and Study Guide

Section 27.1 Mollusks, continued

In your textbook, read about cephalopods.

Answer the following questions.

26. Describe the "head-foot" region of a cephalopod.
**Instead of having a single muscular foot, cephalopods have multiple arms and
tentacles that are arranged around the head.**

27. What would you expect to find on the interior surfaces of a squid's many arms?
suckers

28. How does the intelligence of an octopus compare to that of a clam?
Cephalopods are intelligent invertebrates that can be trained to distinguish colors.

Using what you know about the three major classes of mollusks, complete the chart below by
checking the correct column(s) for each characteristic.

Characteristics	Type of Mollusk		
	Gastropods	Bivalves	Cephalopods
29. Intelligent, with a well-developed nervous system			✓
30. Have no distinct head		✓	
31. Have an open circulatory system	✓	✓	
32. External shells present in some species	✓	✓	✓
33. All species are carnivorous predators.			✓
34. Use a radula in feeding	✓		✓
35. All use gills for both respiration and food collection.		✓	
36. Bite prey with a beak			✓

Name _____ Date _____ Class _____

Reinforcement and Study Guide

Section 28.1 Characteristics of
Arthropods

Chapter 28 Arthropods

In your textbook, read about what an arthropod is and exoskeletons.

Answer the following questions.

1. What is the most distinguishing arthropod characteristic?
   jointed appendages

2. Explain the advantage of having appendages with joints.
   Joints allow for more powerful movements during locomotion, and they make
   certain types of appendages multifunctional.

3. List three functions of an arthropod exoskeleton.
   (1) protects and supports internal tissues; (2) provides places for muscles to
   attach; (3) helps prevent water loss

In your textbook, read about molting, segmentation, and gas exchange.

Complete each statement.

4. Prior to molting, a new exoskeleton forms _____beneath_____ the old one.

5. Many arthropods have three distinct body sections: a(n) _____head_____ ,
   a(n) _____thorax_____ , and a(n) _____abdomen_____ .

6. In arthropods that have a _____cephalothorax_____ , the head and thorax are fused.

Complete the table by checking the correct column to indicate the respiratory structure you
would expect to find in each example.

Example	Type of Respiratory Structure		
	Book Lungs	Gills	Tracheal Tubes
7. freshwater crayfish		✓	
8. tarantula	✓		
9. hissing cockroach			✓
10. swallowtail butterfly			✓

Name _____ Date _____ Class _____

Reinforcement and Study Guide

Section 28.1 Characteristics of
Arthropods, continued

Chapter 28 Arthropods, *continued*

In your textbook, read about arthropods' senses, body systems, and reproduction.

Identify the following as characteristics of either simple or compound eyes.

_____compound_____ 11. have multiple lenses

_____compound_____ 12. well-adapted for detecting slight movements

_____single_____ 13. have a single, focusing-type lens

_____compound_____ 14. produce an image made up of thousands of parts

Determine if the statement is true. If it is not, rewrite the italicized part to make it true.

15. Animals produce pheromones, or *low frequency sounds*, that affect the behavior of others.
    chemical odor signals

16. In many arthropods, large, fused ganglia act as nervous system control centers *for the entire body.*
    for the body section in which they are located

17. Arthropods have an open circulatory system, in which blood leaves vessels and *comes in direct contact
    with body tissues.*   true

18. *Respiration* occurs in arthropods via the Malpighian tubules.   Excretion

19. During parthenogenesis, *fertilized eggs* develop into offspring.   unfertilized eggs

In your textbook, read about arthropod origins.

Answer the following questions.

20. What are the major reasons for the widespread success of arthropods?
    As a group, they can exploit just about every type of food source available.

21. From what animal group did arthropods probably evolve?
    from ancient annelids

22. List three adaptations that have evolved in arthropods.
    (1) reduced number of body segments; (2) specialization of body segments;
    (3) greater development of nervous tissue in the head

Reinforcement and Study Guide

Section 28.2 Diversity of Arthropods

Chapter 28   Arthropods, continued

In your textbook, read about arachnids.

Circle the letter of the response that best completes the statement.

1. An animal that is *not* a member of the class Arachnida is

   a. a spider.   **b.** a deer tick.   **(c.)** a walking stick.   **d.** a dust mite.

2. In spiders, chelicerae are highly modified appendages that are adapted for

   (a.) holding food and injecting poison.   **b.** spinning silk and weaving webs.

   c. chewing food.   **d.** mating and reproduction.

3. The appendages of a spider that function as sense organs are

   a. its chelicerae.   **(b.)** its pedipalps.   **c.** its legs.   **d.** its spinnerets.

4. After catching their prey and injecting it with poison, spiders

   a. eat the prey whole.

   b. lay their eggs in the prey.

   c. chew the prey into small pieces.

   (d.) suck up the prey's contents, which have been liquified with enzymes.

5. In ticks and mites, the head, thorax, and abdomen

   a. are absent.   **b.** are well-defined.

   (c.) are fused into one section.   **d.** are all the same size.

6. The fact that horseshoe crabs have remained relatively unchanged for 500 million years indicates that

   a. natural selection has not taken place.   **b.** they must reproduce by parthenogenesis.

   c. they have very little genetic diversity.   **(d.)** their environment has changed very little.

In your textbook, read about crustaceans, centipedes, and millipedes.

Determine if each statement is true or false.

  true   7. Having compound eyes on movable stalks is an advantage for aquatic crustaceans whose potential predators could attack from almost any direction.

  false   8. The legs of most crustaceans are unspecialized and used only for walking.

  true   9. You might be more likely to see pill bugs moving around out in the open on a rainy day than on a sunny one.

  false   10. Both centipedes and millipedes have book lungs for gas exchange.

Reinforcement and Study Guide

Section 28.2 Diversity of Arthropods, continued

Chapter 28   Arthropods, continued

In your textbook, read about insects.

Using the choices below, label the diagram of a honeybee.

antennae   compound eye   legs   mandibles   spiracles   wings

11. _____ wings

12. _____ spiracles

13. _____ legs

14. _____ compound eye

15. _____ mandibles

16. _____ antennae

Complete the table by checking the correct column for each statement.

Description	Type of Metamorphosis	
	Complete	Incomplete
17. Insect begins life as a fertilized egg.	✓	✓
18. Larva hatches from an egg.	✓	
19. Nymph repeatedly molts and increases in size.		✓
20. Nymph hatches from an egg.		✓
21. Pupa undergoes changes while encased in cocoon.	✓	
22. Adults and young usually eat the same food.		✓
23. Adults are the only sexually mature form.	✓	✓

Name _____ Date _____ Class _____

Chapter 29 Echinoderms and Invertebrate Chordates

In your textbook, read about echinoderms' internal skeleton, radial symmetry, and the water vascular system.

Answer the following questions.

1. Describe the "spiny skin" that is a characteristic of echinoderms.
a hard, spiny, or bumpy endoskeleton composed primarily of calcium carbonate
and covered by a thin epidermis

2. In what way is being radially symmetrical an advantage for adult echinoderms?
Radial symmetry enables these slow-moving or sessile animals to sense food, predators, and other environmental cues from all directions.

For each item in Column A, write the letter of the matching item in Column B.

	Column A	Column B
c	3. Has a flattened, immovable endoskeleton made up of fused plates	a. brittle star
a	4. Has thin, flexible rays made up of small, overlapping, calcified plates	b. sea star
b	5. Has a flexible endoskeleton divided into rather long, tapering rays	c. sand dollar
e	6. Has tiny, calcified plates embedded in fleshy skin	d. sea lily
d	7. Has feathery, branching rays made up of tiny, calcified plates	e. sea cucumber

Complete the following sentences.

8. Tube feet are part of an echinoderm's __water__ __vascular__ __system__, which is involved not only in locomotion, but also in __gas__ __exchange__, __excretion__, and food collecting.

9. In a sea star, water enters and exits the water vascular system through a structure called the __madreporite__, a sievelike, disc-shaped opening on the __dorsal__ side of the body.

Name _____ Date _____ Class _____

Chapter 29 Echinoderms and Invertebrate Chordates, continued

In your textbook, read about sea star structure, echinoderm larvae, nutrition, nervous systems, and origins.

Label this drawing of a sea star and of a cross section of one of its rays. Use these choices:

ampulla   eyespot   madreporite   pedicellariae   tube foot

10. madreporite
11. pedicellariae
12. eyespot
13. ampulla
14. tube foot

Identify each of the following as describing either larva or an adult echinoderm.

larva 15. free-swimming

larva 16. bilaterally symmetrical

adult 17. radially symmetrical

adult 18. moves with tube feet

Determine if each of the following statements is **true** or **false**.

true 19. If a sea urchin population underwent a population explosion, you might expect to see a rapid decline in the amount of algal life in the area.

false 20. Sea stars and brittle stars both eat suspended organic particles.

false 21. Most echinoderms have highly developed sense organs.

true 22. The fact that echinoderms have bilaterally symmetrical larvae and deuterostome development is strong evidence that they are most closely related to chordates.

Name _____ Date _____ Class _____

Chapter 29

Echinoderms and Invertebrate Chordates, *continued*

In your textbook, read about invertebrate chordates.

Complete the following sentences.

1. At some time in their life, all chordates possess a **notochord**, a dorsal hollow **nerve** **cord**, **gill** **slits**, and muscle blocks.

2. During your early development, your notochord became your **backbone**, and your gill slits disappeared.

3. The **spinal** **cord** is derived from the **brain** portion of the dorsal nerve cord, whereas the **brain** is derived from the anterior portion.

4. At some time during their lives, all chordates have a muscular **tail**.

In your textbook, read about tunicates and lancelets.

Trace the path of water through a tunicate, starting with water entering the animal's body, by numbering the following statements from 1 to 5.

4 5. Water leaves the pharynx region.

3 6. Water passes through the gill slits, which filter food out of the water.

1 7. Water is drawn into the body through the incurrent siphon.

5 8. Water passes out of the body via the excurrent siphon.

2 9. Water enters the pharynx, where the gill slits are located.

Complete the table by checking the correct column(s) for each description.

Description	Tunicates	Lancelets
10. Only larval forms have a tail	✓	
11. Are filter feeders	✓	✓
12. Retain all chordate traits throughout life		✓
13. Blood flow is continually reversed in the adult body	✓	
14. Capable of actively swimming as adults		✓

Name _____ Date _____ Class _____

Chapter 29

Echinoderms and Invertebrate Chordates, *continued*

In your textbook, read about the diversity of echinoderms.

Answer the following questions.

23. List the five classes of living echinoderms and the types of animals in each class.

class Asteroidea, the sea stars; class Ophiuroidea, the brittle stars; class Echinoidea, the sea urchins and sand dollars; class Holothuroidea, the sea cucumbers; class Crinoidea, the sea lilies and feather stars

24. How is the ability to regenerate lost body parts adaptive for most echinoderms?

An echinoderm can survive an attack and escape from a predator with only minimal losses that can gradually be replaced.

Complete the table by checking the column(s) that best fit(s) each description.

Description	Asteroidea	Ophiuroidea	Echinoidea	Holothuroidea	Crinoidea
25. Have multiple rays	✓				✓
26. May rupture and release internal organs when threatened				✓	
27. Some members of the class are sessile					✓
28. Burrow into rock or sand			✓		
29. Use mucus-coated tentacles for feeding				✓	
30. Some members of the class can actively swim from place to place					✓
31. Use rays, not tube feet, for locomotion		✓			✓
32. The most inflexible type of echinoderm			✓		
33. Use long, feathery arms to trap food particles drifting past					✓
34. Eat bivalves and other small animals	✓				

BioDigest 8 Invertebrates

In your textbook, read about invertebrates.

Study the definitions on the next page and write the terms in the appropriate spaces in the crossword puzzle below. All terms are important in the Biodigest.

BioDigest 8 Invertebrates, *continued*

ACROSS

1. In a animal with _____ symmetry, the right and left sides are mirrors of each other.

7. An echinoderm has an inner skeleton; its _____ covering is called the epidermis.

9. Bivalves, gastropods, and cephalopods are _____ .

10. Some echinoderms have long _____ that are used for locomotion.

12. The _____ have radial symmetry and a water vascular system.

16. Because arthropods have _____ , fossil arthropods are frequently found.

19. _____ such as planaria have no body cavity.

21. In earthworms, internal _____ are suspended from the mesoderm.

22. In some invertebrates, an exoskeleton offers _____ and support for internal tissues.

25. A(n) _____ belongs to the phylum Cnidaria.

26. Sponges have a(n) _____ body shape.

27. In earthworms and other segmented worms, each _____ has its own muscles.

28. Some segments in chordates have been modified into stacked layers called (2 words) _____ .

29. In arthropods like grasshoppers, a set of jointed appendages called antennae are adapted to give the insect acute _____ .

DOWN

1. The mouthparts of an arthropod may be adapted for such things as chewing, lapping, or _____ .

2. _____ have bilateral symmetry, which suggests a close relationship to the chordates.

3. _____ go through metamorphosis during their life cycles.

4. A dorsal nerve _____ is a hollow, fluid-filled canal lying above the notochord.

5. Setae, or small bristles, help earthworms with _____ .

6. Mesoderm differentiates into _____ , circulatory vessels, and reproductive organs.

8. Echinoderms have a supporting _____ , which is inside of the body instead of outside.

11. The _____ of a mollusk such as a clam is secreted by the mantle.

13. A(n) _____ functions as a watery skeleton against which muscles can work.

14. Many _____ are parasitic, such as *Trichinella*.

15. Arthropods are characterized by having a wide variety of _____ for feeding.

17. The _____ of a cnidarian is found in a highly specialized stinging cell.

18. _____ are made up of two cell layers and have only one body opening.

20. Special _____ feet enable sea stars to move from place to place.

22. Water enters a sponge through _____ .

23. A jellyfish, a(n) _____ , and an anemone are types of cnidarians.

24. Bivalves acquire food by filtering water through their _____ .

26. A radula is a tonguelike organ used by snails to scrape _____ from surfaces.

Reinforcement and Study Guide

Chapter 30 Fishes and Amphibians

Section 30.1 Fishes

In your textbook, read about what is a fish.

Complete each statement.

1. All vertebrates are in the phylum **Chordata**, and fish, amphibians, reptiles, birds, and mammals are in the subphylum **Vertebrata**.

2. Vertebrates are bilaterally symmetrical, coelomate animals with endoskeletons, closed **circulatory** systems, complex **brains**, and efficient **respiratory** systems.

3. If you compared the number of fish species to the number of all other vertebrate species combined, there would be more species of **fishes**.

Complete the table below to compare the three different kinds of fishes.

Class	Kind of Fish	Jaws?	Skeleton	Fertilization
4. **Agnatha**	Lamprey and Hagfish	5. **No**	6. **Cartilage**	7. **External**
Chondrichthyes	8. **Sharks and Rays**	9. **Yes**	Cartilage	10. **External and Internal**
11. **Osteichthyes**	12. **Bony Fishes**	Yes	13. **Bone**	External and Internal

Answer the following questions.

14. How does a fish breathe through its gills?
A fish takes in water through its mouth and then passes the water over capillary-rich gills and out through slits on the side of its body. Oxygen and carbon dioxide are exchanged through the capillaries.

15. What two adaptations of cartilaginous and bony fishes help them to locate food?
These fishes have an excellent sense of smell and can detect movement and vibrations in the water through their lateral line systems.

Reinforcement and Study Guide

Chapter 30 Fishes and Amphibians, *continued*

Section 30.1 Fishes, continued

In your textbook, read about bony fishes.

Determine if the statement is true. If it is not, rewrite the italicized part to make it true.

16. While spawning, a female bony fish may lay *millions of eggs* to be fertilized externally by the male, but only a few will survive. **true**

17. The development of *bone* was an important event in the evolution of vertebrates because it eventually allowed them to move onto land and support their body weight. **true**

18. The backbone, comprised of separate *gills*, was a major evolutionary event for fishes because it provided support as well as flexibility, which helped to propel them through the water. **vertebrae**

19. The *swim bladder*, an organ found in bony fishes, allows fish to control their depth in water. **true**

In your textbook, read about origins of fishes.

Examine the phylogenetic tree below. Then answer the question that follows.

Frogs and Toads · Salamanders · Early tetrapods · Lungfishes · Coelacanths · Ray-finned fishes · Placoderms · Chondrichthyes · Sharks and Rays · Agnatha · Lampreys · Hagfishes · Ostracoderms

20. Which group of fishes do you think are most closely related to ancestral amphibians? Why?
Lungfishes, because the bone structure of their fins resembles the bone structure of ancestral amphibians; also, lungfishes could survive on land for short periods because they had lungs.

Name _____ Date _____ Class _____

Chapter 30 — Fishes and Amphibians, continued

Section 30.2 Amphibians

In your textbook, read about what is an amphibian.

Answer the following questions.

1. What three orders make up the class Amphibia?
The three orders are Caudata, Anura, and Apoda.

2. Why do amphibian eggs need to be laid in water?
The eggs lack protective membranes and shells. Water is necessary to keep them from drying out and to transport sperm.

3. Where does an amphibian heart pump oxygen-rich blood, and where does it pump oxygen-poor blood?
Oxygen-rich blood is pumped to body tissues, and oxygen-poor blood is pumped to the lungs and skin.

For each item in Column A, write the letter of the matching item in Column B.

	Column A	Column B
b	4. Adult frogs and toads have legs, lungs, and a _____ heart.	a. two-chambered
a	5. Tadpoles have gills, fins, and a _____ heart.	b. three-chambered
e	6. Amphibians are _____, animals whose body temperature changes with the temperature of their surroundings.	c. skin
d	7. Fertilized amphibian eggs hatch into _____ during the aquatic phase of their life.	d. tadpoles
c	8. Some salamanders have no lungs and breathe through their _____.	e. ectotherms

---

Name _____ Date _____ Class _____

Chapter 30 — Fishes and Amphibians, continued

Section 30.2 Amphibians, continued

In your textbook, read about the characteristics and diversity of amphibians.

Circle the letter of the response that best completes the statement.

9. Early amphibians needed large amounts of food and oxygen to
(a.) walk on land.   b. breathe on land.   c. become dormant in cold weather.   d. all of these.

10. In many amphibians, the most important organ for gas exchange is the
a. blood.   **(b.)** skin.   c. lungs.   d. circulatory system.

11. Many frogs and toads use _____ as a defense against predators.
(a.) toxins   b. electricity   c. sharp claws   d. all of these

12. Frogs and toads have sound-producing bands of tissues in their throat called
a. tongues.   **(b.)** vocal cords.   c. vocal tissue.   d. none of these.

13. Salamanders are unlike frogs and toads because they have
a. long, slender bodies.   b. tails.   c. necks.   **(d.)** all of these.

14. Caecilians are amphibians that have no
a. eyes.   b. skin.   **(c.)** limbs.   d. heart.

In your textbook, read about the origins of amphibians.

For each statement below, write true or false.

false 15. Ancestral amphibians appeared on Earth about the same time as ancestral fishes.

true 16. Amphibians probably evolved from tetrapods during the Paleozoic Era.

false 17. Because the climate was hot and dry when amphibians first appeared on Earth, they had to stay near water.

true 18. Like modern-day salamanders, early amphibians probably had legs set at right angles to the body.

false 19. Because amphibians were a transitional group, they never were the dominant vertebrates on land.

Name _____ Date _____ Class _____

Chapter 31 Reptiles and Birds

Reinforcement and Study Guide

Section 31.1 Reptiles

In your textbook, read about what is a reptile and the amniotic egg.

Complete the following table about reptilian adaptations and their advantages by writing in the missing information in each case.

Adaptation	Advantage
1. Four-chambered heart	In crocodilians, oxygenated and deoxygenated blood kept separate; higher level of energy production
2. Thick, scaly skin	**prevents water loss; added protection from predators**
3. Internal fertilization	Water not necessary for fertilization
4. Legs positioned for walking and running on land	**better chance of catching prey and avoiding predators**
5. Amniotic egg	Water not necessary for reproduction; young not overly vulnerable to aquatic predators; prevents injury or dehydration of embryo

Label the diagram below, using these choices:

albumen   allantois   amnion   chorion   embryo   shell   yolk sac

6. **amnion**

9. **yolk sac**

11. **allantois**

7. **shell**

8. **albumen**

10. **embryo**

12. **chorion**

Name _____ Date _____ Class _____

Chapter 31 Reptiles and Birds, continued

Reinforcement and Study Guide

Section 31.1 Reptiles, continued

In your textbook, read about the diversity of reptiles and the origins of reptiles.

Complete the chart by checking the correct column(s) for each characteristic.

Characteristic	Snakes	Lizards	Turtles	Crocodiles
13. Guard their nests against predators				✓
14. Possess shells			✓	
15. Use tongue and Jacobsen's organ for smelling	✓	✓		
16. Kill prey by drowning it				✓
17. Lack limbs	✓			
18. Have vertebrae and ribs fused to a carapace			✓	
19. Some change color dramatically		✓		
20. Lack teeth			✓	
21. Some inject venom with fangs	✓			
22. Some are aquatic	✓	✓	✓	✓
23. Are primarily insect eaters		✓		
24. Include marine species that migrate			✓	

Complete each sentence.

25. During the Mesozoic era, **dinosaurs** were the most abundant land vertebrates.

26. Snakes and lizards are descended from early **scaly** **reptiles**, which in turn were descended from **cotylosaurs**.

27. **Birds** are probably the modern, living descendants of some type of dinosaur.

Name _____ Date _____ Class _____

Reinforcement and Study Guide

Chapter 31

Section 31.2 Birds

Reptiles and Birds, *continued*

In your textbook, read about what is a bird.

Answer the following questions.

1. From what type of animal are birds thought to have evolved?
   from small, two-legged dinosaurs called theropods

2. List three physical features of birds that link them to reptilian ancestors.
   (1) clawed toes and scaly feet; (2) internal fertilization; (3) amniotic eggs

3. Besides making flight possible, what other functions do feathers serve?
   provide insulation; streamline the body for flight; provide a waterproof covering

4. By what process are old feathers replaced?
   periodic molting

In your textbook, read about how birds are adapted for flight.

Determine if the statement is true. If it is not, rewrite the italicized part to make it true.

5. A bird's sternum is *the point of attachment for its flight muscles.*
   true

6. Being endothermic, birds have a body temperature that *fluctuates with environmental temperature.*
   remains constant

7. Because of its energy requirements, you might expect a bird to eat *less* than a reptile of comparable size.
   more

8. Hollow bones, horny beaks, and a lack of teeth are all adaptations that make birds *more efficient predators.*
   lighter in weight

9. Birds grind up their food in a muscular *gizzard.*
   true

10. The air inside a bird's lungs always has a fairly high *carbon dioxide* content, which makes for efficient gas exchange.
    oxygen

11. For a bird such as a goose or a duck, down feathers are the key to its superior *waterproofing.*
    insulation

Name _____ Date _____ Class _____

Reinforcement and Study Guide

Chapter 31

Section 31.2 Birds, *continued*

Reptiles and Birds, *continued*

In your textbook, read about the diversity of birds.

For each item in Column A, write the letter of the matching item in Column B.

Column A	Column B
c 12. long beak that is used for dipping into flowers to obtain nectar	**a.** owl
d 13. wings and feet modified for swimming; body surrounded with a thick layer of insulating fat	**b.** pelican
f 14. short, stout beak that is adapted to cracking seeds	**c.** hummingbird
e 15. feathered legs and feet that make it easier to walk in the snow	**d.** penguin
b 16. huge beak with a pouch that is used as a net for capturing fish	**e.** ptarmigan
a 17. large eyes, an acute sense of hearing, and sharp claws; adapted for nocturnal predation	**f.** goldfinch

In your textbook, read about the origins of birds.

Complete each statement.

18. The fossil record of birds is incomplete because bird skeletons are ___**light**___ and ___**delicate**___.

19. Unlike modern birds, *Archaeopteryx* had ___**teeth**___, a long ___**tail**___, and ___**clawed**___ front ___**toes**___.

20. Scientists hypothesize that *Caudipteryx* used its feathers for ___**insulation**___, ___**camouflage**___, or ___**courtship behavior**___, rather than for flight.

Chapter 32 Mammals

Section 32.1 Mammal Characteristics

In your textbook, read about what is a mammal, and mammalian hair.

Answer the following questions.

1. Why are mammals able to live in almost every possible environment on Earth?
As endotherms, they can maintain a fairly constant body temperature.

2. How do sweat glands help regulate body temperature?
They secrete water onto the skin's surface. As the water evaporates, it removes heat from the body.

Complete the table by checking the column that best fits each example.

Example	Serves As:		
	Camouflage	Defense	Warning
3. The striped fur of a tiger	✓		
4. The sharp quills of a porcupine		✓	
5. A skunk's black-and-white striped fur			✓
6. The white winter coat of an arctic hare	✓		
7. The white hair patch on a pronghorn			✓

In your textbook, read about how mammals nurse their young, and about respiration and circulation.

Complete each statement.

8. Female mammals feed their young with milk produced by **mammary** **glands**.

9. In addition to milk and sweat, the glands of mammals produce **saliva**, **hormones**, and **enzymes**.

10. The milk of mammals is rich in **fats**, sugars, **proteins**, minerals, and **vitamins**.

11. A mammal's muscular **diaphragm** expands the **chest** **cavity** bringing air into the lungs with each breath.

12. Like birds, mammals have **four-chambered** hearts in which **oxygenated** **blood** is kept entirely separate from **deoxygenated** **blood**.

Chapter 32 Mammals, *continued*

Section 32.1 Mammal Characteristics, *continued*

In your textbook, read about mammalian teeth, limbs, and learning.

Determine if the statement is true or false.

true 13. The size and shape of a mammal's teeth can give valuable clues about its diet.

false 14. Plant-eaters such as horses and cows have well-developed canine teeth for piercing food.

false 15. The teeth of mammals are generally more uniform than the teeth of fishes and reptiles.

true 16. By chewing their cud and then swallowing it, some mammals help bacteria break down the cellulose in their food.

true 17. Mammalian limbs are adapted for a variety of methods of food gathering.

false 18. Moles use their opposable thumbs to grasp objects.

true 19. One reason mammals are successful is that they guard their young and teach them survival skills.

true 20. Complex nervous systems and highly-developed brains make it possible for many kinds of mammals to learn.

Circle the letter of the response that best completes the statement.

21. Premolars and molars are used for
a. shearing. b. crushing. c. grinding. **(d.)** all of these.

22. Cud chewing is an adaptation found in
a. bears and other omnivores. b. tigers and other carnivores.
(c.) many hoofed mammals. d. all of these.

23. The limbs of antelopes are characterized by
a. greatly elongated finger bones. **(b.)** strong, slender bones.
c. short bones and large claws. d. none of these.

24. Chimpanzees are intelligent enough to
a. use tools. b. use sign language.
c. work machines. **(d.)** all of these.

Left page (143)

Reinforcement and Study Guide

Chapter 32

Mammals, *continued*

Section 32.2 Diversity of Mammals

In your textbook, read about placental mammals, mammals with a pouch, and egg-laying mammals.

Answer the following questions.

1. What is a placental mammal?
a mammal that carries its young inside its uterus until development is almost complete

2. What is the relationship between body size and gestation period in placental mammals?
In general, the larger the placental mammal is, the longer the gestation period.

3. Why are most marsupials found only in and around Australia?
Ancient marsupials that lived in what is now Australia evolved without competition from placental mammals, which become dominant on all other continents.

4. What characteristic sets monotremes apart from all other mammals?
Monotremes lay eggs instead of giving birth to live young.

Complete the table by checking the correct column(s) for each characteristic.

Characteristic	Placental	Marsupial	Monotreme
5. Give birth to young	✓	✓	
6. Young nourished by a placenta during the entire development period	✓		
7. Have a permanent pouch on abdomen		✓	
8. Produce milk in mammary glands	✓	✓	✓
9. Lay eggs			✓
10. Include echidnas and duck-billed platypuses			✓
11. Have hair	✓	✓	✓
12. Comprise about 95 percent of all mammals	✓		
13. Exhibit parental care	✓	✓	✓

Right page (144)

Reinforcement and Study Guide

Chapter 32

Mammals, *continued*

Section 32.2 Diversity of Mammals, continued

In your textbook, read about the origins of mammals.

Use each of the terms below just once to complete the passage.

Cenozoic	climate	dinosaurs	insect-eating
mammals	Pangaea	reptiles	therapsids

Roughly 200 million years ago, the first **(14)** **mammals** began roaming the earth. Most were small **(15)** **insect-eating** descendants of **(16)** **therapsids**, animals that had characteristics in common with both mammals and **(17)** **reptiles**. The breakup of **(18)** **Pangaea**, the sudden disappearance of the **(19)** **dinosaurs**, and a changing **(20)** **climate** provided early mammals with new food sources and habitats. During the **(21)** **Cenozoic** era, mammals diversified greatly into the many species inhabiting Earth today.

Examine the phylogenetic tree below. Then answer the questions that follow.

22. What group of animals is represented by the letter A above? **placental mammals**

23. What era is represented by the letter B? **Mesozoic**

24. What era is represented by the letter C? **Cenozoic**

Reinforcement and Study Guide

Chapter 33   Animal Behavior

Section 33.1 Innate Behavior

In your textbook, read about what behavior is, inherited behavior, automatic responses to stimuli, and instinctive behavior.

Answer the following questions.

1. What is meant by animal behavior?
   anything an animal does in response to a stimulus in its environment

2. How is behavior adaptive?
   An animal's behavior enables it to carry out activities, such as getting food or reproducing, that enhance its survival.

3. Explain the relationship between innate behaviors and genetics.
   Innate behaviors are genetically programmed responses to certain stimuli.
   Offspring inherit the genetic basis for innate behaviors from their parents.

4. What is an instinct?
   a complex pattern of innate behavior

Identify each of the following as being either a reflex or an instinct.

reflex   5. You leap up after sitting down in shorts on a hot car seat.

instinct   6. A sea turtle returns to the beach where she was hatched, in order to lay her eggs.

reflex   7. A giant clam closes its shell when a shadow falls across it.

instinct   8. A spider spins a complex, circular web.

In your textbook, read about courtship behavior and territoriality.

Determine if the following statements are true or false.

false   9. Courtship behavior is something only male animals can instinctively perform.

true   10. Courtship behavior is adaptive because it ensures that members of the same species can recognize each other and mate.

false   11. A territory is a physical space that one animal defends against all other species of animals.

true   12. Setting up territories reduces conflicts between members of the same species.

Reinforcement and Study Guide

Chapter 33   Animal Behavior, *continued*

Section 33.1 Innate Behavior, continued

In your textbook, read about aggressive behavior, submission, and behavior resulting from internal and external cues.

Below are excerpts from the field notebook of a behaviorial biologist. Identify the behavioral phenomenon being described in each case.

13.
Field Notes
A large male baboon stares at another male and then suddenly "yawns" to reveal his long, sharp fangs.

Behavior Exhibited:
aggressive behavior

14.
Field Notes
When a herd of elephants arrives at a waterhole, the oldest female drinks first, followed by three females with calves, and finally a young male.

Behavior Exhibited:
dominance hierarchy

15.
Field Notes
After fighting briefly with an older pack member, a young wolf stops fighting and rolls onto her back with her tail tucked between her legs and her eyes averted.

Behavior Exhibited:
submission

16.
Field Notes
Large numbers of monarch butterflies fly south to roost in the winter.

Behavior Exhibited:
migration

Complete the following sentences.

17. The type of dominance hierarchy formed by chickens is called a(n) **pecking** **order**.

18. A cycle of behavior that occurs roughly every 24 hours is known as a(n) **circadian** **rhythm**.

19. Some animals use the positions of the **sun** and **stars** to navigate. Others may use **geographic** clues or Earth's **magnetic** **field**.

20. **Estivation** is similar to hibernation, in that metabolic activity **decreases** in response to internal and external cues.

Name _____ Date _____ Class _____

Reinforcement and Study Guide

Chapter 33

Animal Behavior, *continued*

Section 33.2 Learned Behavior

In your textbook, read about learned behavior.

Answer the following questions.

1. What is learned behavior?
behavior that can be changed through practice or experience

2. What is a major advantage of being able to learn?
Learning makes it possible for behavior to change, or adapt, in response to a changing environment.

Complete the table by checking the correct column for each example.

Example	Type of Behavior	
	Learned	Innate
3. A dog catching a Frisbee	✓	
4. A dog scent-marking a tree with urine		✓
5. A parrot saying "Polly want a cracker"	✓	
6. A young lioness stalking prey with her mother	✓	
7. A woodchuck going underground to hibernate		✓

In your textbook, read about habituation, imprinting, and learning by trial and error.

For each item in Column A, write the letter of the matching item in Column B.

	Column A	Column B
c	**8.** You stay with relatives who have a clock that chimes every hour. The first two nights, the chimes keep you awake, but after that you no longer notice them.	**a.** imprinting
a	**9.** A boy receives a day-old duckling as gift. It soon follows the boy wherever he goes.	**b.** trial-and-error learning
b	**10.** A young woman takes up archery. At first, her arrows don't hit the target, but after a week of practice, she is hitting the bull's eye fifty percent of the time.	**c.** habituation

---

Name _____ Date _____ Class _____

Reinforcement and Study Guide

Chapter 33

Animal Behavior, *continued*

Section 33.2 Learned Behavior, continued

In your textbook, read about conditioning and insight.

Determine if the statement is true. If it is not, rewrite the italicized part to make it true.

11. Learning by *repeating something over and over* is known as conditioning. association

12. In Pavlov's conditioning experiments, the *innate reflex of salivating* was the stimulus that the dogs learned to associate with food. ringing bell

13. Once conditioned, Pavlov's dogs would salivate at the sound of the bell *even when no food was present.* true

14. A child figuring out how to use a chair to reach a cookie jar is an example of *trial and error.* insight

15. Insight is learning in which an animal uses *previous experience* to respond to a new situation. true

In your textbook, read about the role of communication.

Use each of the terms below just once to complete the passage.

behavior	communication	information	innate	language
meanings	odors	pheromones	sounds	symbols

Through various forms of **(16)** communication, animals exchange **(17)** information that affects their **(18)** behavior. Animals can communicate with visual signals, by touching each other, and by producing **(19)** sounds, some of which can be heard over great distances. Communicating with **(20)** odors is another strategy; **(21)** pheromones are species-specific odor chemicals that can have a powerful effect on behavior. Some types of communication involve both **(22)** innate and learned behavior. Human **(23)** language has evolved as a way of communicating with written and spoken **(24)** symbols that have specific **(25)** meanings.

Reinforcement and Study Guide

BioDigest 9 Vertebrates

In your textbook, read about fishes, amphibians, reptiles, birds, and mammals.

FISHES

Complete the chart by checking the correct column(s) for each characteristic of fishes.

Adaptation	Jawless	Cartilaginous	Bony
1. Jaws		✓	✓
2. Gills	✓	✓	✓
3. Lateral line system		✓	✓
4. Paired fins		✓	✓
5. Skeleton made of cartilage	✓	✓	
6. Swim bladder			✓

AMPHIBIANS

Complete the following sentences.

7. Amphibians are __ectotherms__, which means that their body temperature depends upon the temperature of their surroundings. These vertebrates also carry out gas exchange through their __skin__. Amphibians live on __land__ but reproduce in __water__. Almost all amphibians go through __metamorphosis__, a radical change between the form of the young and the form of the adult.

REPTILES

Complete the table by describing the advantages that reptiles have because of certain adaptations. List one advantage for each adaptation.

Adaptation	Advantage
8. Scaly skin	reduces loss of body moisture on land
9. Amniotic egg	no longer dependent on water for reproduction; egg provides nourishment to embryo and protects it from drying out

---

Reinforcement and Study Guide

BioDigest 9 Vertebrates, *continued*

BIRDS

Flight affects almost every system in birds. Explain the flight adaptations in each system listed here.

System	Adaptation
10. Bones	are hollow for lighter weight
11. Respiration	air sacs supply oxygen when bird inhales and exhales
12. Body covering	feathers streamline body and shape the wings
13. Legs	consist mostly of skin, bone, and tendons, for lighter weight
14. Wings	shape and size determine type of flight a bird is capable of

MAMMALS

Various adaptations of mammals serve certain functions. In the space provided, write the letter of the adaptations that perform the function. Any letter may be used more than once.

Function	Adaptation
	a. hair
	b. sweat glands
	c. four-chambered heart
	d. diaphragm
	e. canine teeth
	f. mammary glands
	g. small ears
	h. body fat
	i. molars and premolars
	j. hibernation
	k. estivation

15. protection from low temperatures
    __a, g, h, j__

16. protection from high temperatures
    __b, k__

17. feeding young
    __f__

18. stabbing or holding food
    __e__

19. grinding or chewing food
    __i__

20. providing large amounts of oxygen
    __c, d__

Name _____ Date _____ Class _____

Chapter 34 Protection, Support, and Locomotion

Section 34.1 Skin: The Body's Protection

In your textbook, read about the structure and function of the skin.

Complete the table by checking the correct column for each description.

Description	Epidermis	Dermis
1. The outermost layer of skin	✓	
2. Contains connective tissue, glands, and muscles		✓
3. The thicker, inner layer of skin		✓
4. Partly composed of dead, keratin-containing cells	✓	
5. Contains pigmented cells that protect against the sun's rays	✓	
6. Hair follicles grow out of this layer		✓
7. Site of continual mitotic cell divisions	✓	
8. Richly supplied with blood vessels and nerves		✓

Answer the following questions.

9. Describe the change that takes place in your skin when you get a suntan.
Exposure to sunlight causes an increase in melanin production in epidermal pigment cells, and the skin becomes darker.

10. How does skin help regulate body temperature?
When capillaries dilate, blood flow to the skin increases, and excess heat is lost to the environment. When blood vessels constrict, body heat is conserved. Sweat produced by sweat glands in the dermis also helps cool the body by evaporation.

11. List three other functions of skin.
(1) serves as protective layer; (2) functions as a sense organ; (3) helps to maintain chemical balance

---

Name _____ Date _____ Class _____

Chapter 34 Protection, Support, and Locomotion, *continued*

Section 34.2 Bones: The Body's Support

In your textbook, read about the structure of the skeletal system and joints.

Identify the following as being part of the axial or appendicular skeleton.

appendicular	1. the tarsals, metatarsals, and phalanges in your foot	appendicular	4. the bones in your shoulder
axial	2. the seven vertebrae in your neck	axial	5. your lower jaw
axial	3. your rib cage	appendicular	6. the humerus in your arm

For each answer below, write an appropriate question.

7. **Answer:** They are bands of connective tissue that attach muscles to bones.
   Question: **What are tendons?**

8. **Answer:** It absorbs shocks and reduces friction between bones in a joint.
   Question: **How does a bursa function?**

9. **Answer:** They connect bones to other bones.
   Question: **What are ligaments?**

10. **Answer:** One allows the bones to move back and forth; the other allows the bones to rotate.
    Question: **How do a hinge joint and a ball-and-socket joint differ?**

In your textbook, read about the formation of bone and bone growth.

Complete each sentence.

11. In a human embryo's skeleton, **cartilage** is gradually replaced by **bone** except in a few places like the tip of the **nose**.

12. Some cells in cartilage are stimulated to become **osteoblasts** . They secrete a substance in which **calcium** **salts** and other minerals are deposited.

13. Your bones increase in length near their **ends** .

14. Even after you reach your full adult height, the bone-forming cells in your body will still be involved in **repair** and **maintenance** .

Chapter 34 — Protection, Support, and Locomotion, continued

Section 34.2 Bones: The Body's Support, continued

In your textbook, read about compact and spongy bone and skeletal system functions.

Answer the following questions.

15. If you cut through to the center of a large leg bone, what bone components (in order, from the outside in) would you encounter?
nerve and blood vessel-filled membrane; compact bone; spongy bone; marrow

16. How do blood vessels and nerves reach individual bone cells in compact bone?
through osteon systems

17. What role does bone marrow play in the functioning of your circulatory system?
Red bone marrow produces red blood cells, some white blood cells, and cell fragments involved in clotting.

18. In what way is the skeleton a storehouse?
Calcium, phosphorus, and other minerals are stored in bone. Fat is also stored as yellow marrow.

In your textbook, read about growth, mineral storage, and injury and disease in bone.

Determine if the statement is true or false.

false	19. Once you have finished growing, your bones no longer change.
true	20. Calcium is both deposited in and removed from bones.
false	21. Calcium removed from bone is rapidly excreted in the urine as an unnecessary body waste.
true	22. As a person ages, his or her bone density usually decreases.
false	23. Because bones in an adult's skeleton are harder than children's bones, adults are less likely to break a bone in a fall.
false	24. Osteoporosis is most common in older women because they rarely include milk in their diet.

Chapter 34 — Protection, Support, and Locomotion, continued

Section 34.3 Muscles for Locomotion

In your textbook, read about three types of muscles and skeletal muscle contraction.

Complete the table by checking the correct column for each description.

Description	Type of Muscle		
	Smooth	Skeletal	Cardiac
1. under voluntary control		✓	
2. striated		✓	✓
3. slow, prolonged contractions	✓		
4. attached to bones		✓	
5. found only in the heart			✓
6. not under voluntary control	✓		✓
7. lines cavities and surrounds organs	✓		

In your textbook, read about muscle strength and exercise.

Determine if the statement is true. If it is not, rewrite the italicized part to make it true.

8. Muscle strength depends on *the number of fibers in a muscle.*
the thickness of fibers and how many of them contract at one time

9. When oxygen is limited, *aerobic respiration* becomes a muscle's primary source for ATP.
anaerobic respiration

10. During anaerobic respiration, *oxygen* builds up in muscle cells.
lactic acid

11. A drop in the amount of lactic acid in the bloodstream indicates that muscular activity has *decreased.*
true

Name _____ Date _____ Class _____

Reinforcement and Study Guide

Section 35.1 Following Digestion
of a Meal

The Digestive and Endocrine Systems

In your textbook, read about the functions of the digestive tract, the mouth, and the stomach.

Complete each statement.

1. The entire process of digestion involves first **ingesting** food, then **digesting** it into simpler compounds, then **eliminating** **absorbing** nutrients for use by body cells, and, finally, **eliminating** wastes.

2. By chewing your food, you **increase** its surface area.

3. Various enzymes play a role in **chemical** digestion, while the action of teeth, tongue, and muscles are involved in **mechanical** digestion.

4. In your mouth, the enzyme **amylase** is released from **salivary** glands to begin the chemical breakdown of **starch**.

5. Your **incisors** are adapted for cutting food, while your **molars** are best suited for grinding food.

Determine if the statement is true. If it is not, rewrite the italicized part to make it true.

6. During swallowing, the epiglottis covers the *esophagus* to prevent choking.
   respiratory tract

7. Food is moved through the digestive tract by rhythmic waves of *voluntary muscle contractions* called peristalsis.
   involuntary muscle contractions

8. The churning actions of the stomach help mix the food with *pancreatic juices.*
   pepsin and hydrochloric acid (digestive juices)

9. Pepsin is a *protein-digesting enzyme* that only works in an acidic environment.
   true

10. The stomach releases its contents into the small intestine *suddenly, all at once.*
   slowly, a little bit at a time

Name _____ Date _____ Class _____

Reinforcement and Study Guide

Section 35.1 Following Digestion
of a Meal, continued

The Digestive and Endocrine Systems, *continued*

In your textbook, read about the small intestine and the large intestine.

Answer the following questions.

11. What role do the enzymes secreted by the pancreas play in the digestive process?
   Pancreatic enzymes break down, or continue the breakdown of, carbohydrates, proteins, and fats.

12. Explain the relationship between the liver, the gallbladder, and bile.
   Bile is produced in the liver and is stored in the gallbladder before being released into the duodenum.

13. Once in the small intestine, what happens to
   a. digested food?
      These molecules enter the circulatory system via blood vessels inside the villi.

   b. indigestible materials?
      Indigestible materials pass into the large intestine.

Complete the table by checking the correct column(s) for each function.

Function	Small Intestine	Large Intestine
14. Water is absorbed through walls.		✓
15. Digestion is essentially completed.	✓	
16. Vitamin K is produced.		✓
17. Nutrients are absorbed by villi.	✓	
18. Contents are moved by peristalsis.	✓	✓
19. Indigestible material is collected.		✓
20. Bile and pancreatic juices are added.	✓	

Chapter 35 — Reinforcement and Study Guide

The Digestive and Endocrine Systems, continued

Section 35.3 The Endocrine System

In your textbook, read about control of the body and negative feedback control.

Complete each statement.

1. Internal control of the body is handled by the **nervous** system and the **endocrine** system.

2. Most endocrine glands are controlled by the action of the **pituitary**, or master gland.

3. A(n) **hormone** is a chemical released in one part of the body that affects another part.

4. The amount of hormone released by an endocrine gland is determined by the body's **demand** for that hormone at a given time.

5. A **negative feedback** system is one in which hormones are fed back to inhibit the original signal.

6. When your body is dehydrated, the pituitary releases ADH hormone, which reduces the amount of **water** in your urine.

7. When you have just eaten and your blood glucose levels are high, your pancreas releases the hormone **insulin**, which signals the liver to take in glucose, thereby lowering blood glucose levels.

In your textbook, read about hormone action, adrenal hormones and stress, and other hormones.

For each item in column A, write the letter of the matching item from Column B.

	Column A	Column B
f	**8.** Determines the body's food intake requirements	**a.** steroid hormones
a	**9.** Made from lipids and diffuse freely into cells through the plasma membrane	**b.** glucocorticoids and aldosterone
e	**10.** Bind to receptors embedded in the plasma membrane of the target cell.	**c.** calcitonin and parathyroid hormone
d	**11.** Produce a feeling called "adrenaline rush"	**d.** epinephrine and norepinephrine
b	**12.** Help the body prepare for stressful situations	**e.** amino acid hormones
c	**13.** Regulate calcium levels in blood	**f.** thyroxine

158   CHAPTER 35   BIOLOGY: The Dynamics of Life   REINFORCEMENT AND STUDY GUIDE

Chapter 35 — Reinforcement and Study Guide

The Digestive and Endocrine Systems, continued

Section 35.2 Nutrition

In your textbook, read about carbohydrates, fats, and proteins.

Complete the table by checking the correct column(s) for each description.

Description	Carbohydrates	Fats	Proteins
1. the most energy-rich nutrients		✓	
2. sugars, starches, and cellulose	✓		
3. broken down into amino acids			✓
4. part of a nutritious, balanced diet	✓	✓	✓
5. normally used for building muscle, but can be used for energy			✓
6. broken down into glucose, fructose, and other simple sugars	✓		
7. used to insulate the body from cold		✓	

In your textbook, read about minerals and vitamins, water, and metabolism and calories.

Complete each statement.

8. **Minerals** are inorganic substances that help to build tissue or take part in chemical reactions in the body.

9. Unlike minerals, **vitamins** are organic nutrients that help to regulate body processes.

10. The two major vitamin groups are the **fat-soluble** and the **water-soluble** vitamins.

11. The energy content of food is measured in **Calories**, each of which is equal to **1000** calories.

12. Despite the claims of many fad diets, the only way to lose weight is to **eat** more calories than you **metabolize**.

REINFORCEMENT AND STUDY GUIDE   CHAPTER 35   BIOLOGY: The Dynamics of Life   157

Name _____ Date _____ Class _____

Chapter 36 — The Nervous System

Section 36.1 The Nervous System

In your textbook, read about neurons–basic units of the nervous system.

Complete the table by filling in the missing information in each case.

Structure	Function
1. **sensory neurons**	carry impulses toward the brain and spinal cord
2. dendrites	**carry impulses toward neuron cell bodies**
3. motor neurons	**carry impulses away from the brain and spinal cord**
4. interneurons	transmit impulses within the brain and spinal cord
5. axons	carry impulses away from neuron cell bodies

Order the steps in impulse transmission from 1 to 7.

__4__   6. A wave of depolarization moves down the neuron.

__6__   7. The Na$^+$/K$^+$ pump takes over again, pumping sodium ions out across the membrane, and pumping potassium ions in.

__2__   8. Sodium channels in the neural membrane open.

__1__   9. A neuron receives a stimulus.

__5__   10. As the wave of depolarization passes, sodium channels close and potassium channels open.

__7__   11. The neuron returns to a resting state.

__3__   12. Sodium ions flow into the neuron, causing the inside of the neuron to become positively charged.

Name _____ Date _____ Class _____

Chapter 36 — The Nervous System, *continued*

Section 36.1 *The Nervous System, continued*

In your textbook, read about the central nervous system and the peripheral nervous system.

Label the diagram of the brain to show the cerebrum, cerebellum, and brain stem.

13. **cerebrum**
14. **cerebellum**
15. **brain stem**

Write the name of the part labeled above that matches each description in the table.

Description	Part
16. Includes the medulla and pons	**brain stem**
17. Controls conscious activities and movement	**cerebrum**
18. Important for keeping your balance	**cerebellum**
19. If damaged, heart rate might be affected	**brain stem**
20. If damaged, memory might be affected	**cerebrum**
21. Ensures that movements are coordinated	**cerebellum**

Complete the table by checking the correct column for each description.

Description	Autonomic Nervous System Division	
	Sympathetic	Parasympathetic
22. Controls internal activities when the body is at rest		✓
23. Increases breathing rate	✓	
24. Tenses muscles	✓	
25. Slows heart rate down		✓
26. Activates fight or flight response	✓	

Chapter 36 — Reinforcement and Study Guide

The Nervous System, *continued*

Section 36.2 The Senses

In your textbook, read about sensing chemicals and sensing light.

Determine if each statement is true or false.

true 1. Impulses coming from sensory receptors in your nose and mouth are interpreted as odors and tastes by the cerebrum.

false 2. All of your tongue's tastebuds respond equally well to all taste sensations.

false 3. The lens in the eye controls the amount of light that strikes the retina.

true 4. On a bright sunny day, the cones in your eyes play a greater role in your sense of sight than the rods.

false 5. Only the left hemisphere of the brain is involved in the sense of sight.

false 6. When you are looking at an object, each of your eyes sees the object from the same perspective.

true 7. Much of what you taste depends on your sense of smell.

In your textbook, read about sensing mechanical stimulation.

Circle the letter of the response that best completes each statement.

8. Sound waves are converted into nerve impulses inside the
a. ear canal. **(b.) cochlea.** c. malleus. d. optic nerve.

9. If the semicircular canals in one of your ears were damaged, you might
a. lose your ability to hear low-frequency sounds.
b. lose your ability to coordinate your neck muscles.
(c.) lose your sense of balance.
d. lose your sense of rhythm.

10. The malleus, incus, and stapes are found in the
a. outer ear. b. eardrum. **(c.) middle ear.** d. inner ear.

11. Your senses of hearing and touch depend on nerve impulses being generated by
a. electrical stimulation. b. sound waves.
c. a change in temperature. **(d.) mechanical stimulation.**

12. In the skin of your fingertips, you might expect to find receptors for
a. touch. b. pressure. c. pain. **(d.) all of these**

Chapter 36 — Reinforcement and Study Guide

The Nervous System, *continued*

Section 36.3 The Effects of Drugs

In your textbook, read about how drugs act on the body, their medicinal uses, and abuse of drugs.

Answer the following questions.

1. Distinguish between a drug and a medicine.
A drug is any chemical that interacts with body functions. A medicine is a drug that can prevent, cure, or relieve a medical problem.

2. What is a narcotic?
a pain reliever that depresses the CNS

3. Compare the effect of a stimulant on the CNS with the effect of a depressant.
A stimulant increases the activity of the CNS. A depressant decreases its activity.

4. What is an addiction?
being psychologically and/or physiologically dependent on a drug

5. How does a person's body develop a tolerance for a drug?
With habitual use, the body becomes less responsive to a given amount of a drug.

In your textbook, read about the classes of commonly abused drugs.

Complete the table by checking the correct column for each example.

Example	Stimulant	Depressant
6. Drugs that cause an increase in heart rate	✓	
7. Alcohol		✓
8. Nicotine	✓	
9. Drugs that increase neurotransmitter levels	✓	
10. Barbiturates		✓
11. Drugs that cause vasoconstriction	✓	
12. Opiates		✓
13. Hallucinogens	✓	

Name _____ Date _____ Class _____

Chapter 37 Respiration, Circulation, and Excretion

Section 37.1 The Respiratory System

In your textbook, read about air passageways and lungs.

Circle the letter of the choice that best completes the statement or answers the question.

1. During the process of respiration,
   a. oxygen is delivered to body cells.
   b. carbon dioxide is expelled from the body.
   c. oxygen is used in cells to produce ATP.
   (d.) all of these.

2. When you swallow, your epiglottis momentarily covers the top of the trachea so that
   a. you can swallow more easily.
   b. you can breathe more easily.
   (c.) you don't get food in your air passages.
   d. you can cough up foreign matter.

3. The cilia that line your trachea and bronchi
   a. produce dirt-trapping mucus.
   b. help in the exchange of oxygen and CO_2.
   (c.) move mucus and dirt upward.
   d. only beat when you inhale.

4. The first branches off the trachea are called
   a. bronchioles.
   (b.) bronchi.
   c. arterioles.
   d. alveoli.

5. Inside the alveoli, carbon dioxide and oxygen
   (a.) are exchanged between air and blood.
   b. are transported along microscopic tubules.
   c. are produced inside cells.
   d. are exchanged for other gases.

6. Which is the correct sequence for the path of oxygen through the respiratory system?
   a. nasal passages, bronchi, trachea, bronchioles, cells, blood, alveoli
   b. cells, blood, alveoli, bronchioles, bronchi, trachea, nasal passages
   c. nasal passages, blood, alveoli, bronchi, cells, trachea, bronchioles
   (d.) nasal passages, trachea, bronchi, bronchioles, alveoli, blood, cells

In your textbook, read about the mechanics of breathing and the control of respiration.

For each statement below, write true or false.

false	7. Homeostasis in respiration is controlled by the cerebrum.
false	8. As you exhale, the bronchioles in the lungs release most of their air.
true	9. When you inhale, the muscles between your ribs contract.
false	10. Relaxation of the diaphragm causes a slight vacuum in the lungs.
true	11. Air rushes into the lungs because the air pressure outside the body is greater than the air pressure inside the lungs.
false	12. Relaxation of the diaphragm causes it to flatten.

Name _____ Date _____ Class _____

Chapter 37 Respiration, Circulation, and Excretion, *continued*

Section 37.2 The Circulatory System

In your textbook, read about your blood, ABO blood types, and blood vessels.

Answer the following questions.

1. What cells and substances would you expect to find suspended or dissolved in plasma?
   red and white blood cells; platelets; carbon dioxide and other gases; hormones; enzymes; proteins; inorganic salts; antibodies; nutrients

2. How is carbon dioxide transported in blood?
   About 70% combines with water in the plasma to form bicarbonate; the rest is carried by hemoglobin and/or dissolved in plasma.

Complete the table below by checking the correct column for each description.

Description	Red Blood Cells	White Blood Cells	Platelets
3. Contain hemoglobin	✓		
4. Fight infection		✓	
5. Lack a nucleus	✓		✓
6. Help clot blood			✓
7. Transport oxygen	✓		
8. Comparatively large and nucleated		✓	

For each statement below, write true or false.

false	9. Your blood type can be changed with a blood transfusion.
false	10. Different blood types result from different antibodies being present on the membranes of red blood cells.
true	11. If you have type B blood, then you have anti-A antibodies in your plasma.
false	12. Risks involving incompatible Rh factors are greatest for a woman's first child.

Chapter 37 Respiration, Circulation, and Excretion, *continued*

Reinforcement and Study Guide

Section 37.3 *The Urinary System*

In your textbook, read about kidneys, nephrons, and the formation of urine.

Answer the following questions.

1. What is the major function of kidneys?
   to filter wastes from blood in order to maintain fluid homeostasis

2. What role does the bladder play in the urinary system?
   It stores the waste solution, urine.

3. What are nephrons?
   the basic filtering units in kidneys

Order the following steps in the filtration of blood from 1 to 7.

4 4. From the Bowman's capsule, fluid flows through a U-shaped tubule.

2 5. Under high pressure, blood flows into capillaries that make up the glomerulus.

7 6. After being stored in the bladder, urine exits the body via the urethra.

6 7. Fluid moves from the end of the nephron's tubule to the ureter.

1 8. Blood enters the nephron from a branch of the renal artery.

5 9. Water, glucose, amino acids, and ions are reabsorbed into the blood.

3 10. Water, glucose, amino acids, wastes, and other substances move from glomerular capillaries into a Bowman's capsule.

In your textbook, read about the urinary system and homeostasis.

Complete each statement.

11. **Ammonia** and **urea** are two toxic nitrogenous wastes that your kidneys constantly remove from your bloodstream.

12. The kidneys also help regulate the blood's **osmotic** **pressure** , **pH** and **(or) sodium level**.

13. Individuals with diabetes have excess levels of **glucose** in their blood.

Chapter 37 Respiration, Circulation, and Excretion, *continued*

Reinforcement and Study Guide

Section 37.2 *The Circulatory System*, continued

In your textbook, read about your heart, blood's path through the heart, and inside your heart.

Label the parts of the human heart in the diagram below. Use these choices:

aorta	left atrium	left ventricle	pulmonary arteries
pulmonary veins	right atrium	right ventricle	

13. _____ **aorta**

14. **pulmonary arteries**

15. **pulmonary veins**

16. **left atrium**

17. **right atrium**

18. **left ventricle**

19. **right ventricle**

20. Where does blood go from the pulmonary veins? From the right ventricle? From the left ventricle?
    to the left atrium; to the pulmonary arteries; to the aorta

21. What prevents blood from mixing between atria and ventricles?
    one-way valves

In your textbook, read about heartbeat regulation, control of the heart, and blood pressure.

Determine if the statement is true. If it is not, rewrite the italicized part to make it true.

22. The surge of blood through an artery is called *the cardiac output.* **pulse**

23. The pacemaker initiates heartbeats *by generating electrical impulses.* **true**

24. An electrocardiogram is a record of *the strength of each heartbeat.*
    the electrical changes in the heart

25. The *atrioventricular node,* along with sensory cells in arteries near the heart, regulates the pacemaker.
    medulla oblongata

26. *Diastolic pressure* occurs when the heart's ventricles contract. **Systolic pressure**

Name _____ Date _____ Class _____

Chapter 38

Reproduction and Development

Section 38.1 Human Reproductive Systems

In your textbook, read about human male anatomy and hormonal control.

Answer the following questions.

1. What are the primary functions of the male reproductive system?
to produce sperm and deliver them to a female

2. How does the location of the scrotum affect sperm?
Being outside the body core, the scrotum maintains sperm at the cooler-than-body temperature conditions that they need to develop normally.

3. How many sperm can the average mature male produce in one day?
300 million

Order the steps in the formation and transportation of sperm from 1 to 6.

4 4. Mature sperm enter the vas deferens.

2 5. Newly formed haploid sperm cells pass through a series of coiled ducts to the epididymis.

6 6. Sperm leave the body via the urethra.

3 7. Sperm mature in the epididymis.

1 8. Cells lining tubules in the testes undergo meiosis.

5 9. Sperm travel along the ejaculatory ducts and into the urethra.

Complete each sentence.

10. When a young man's voice "changes," he is probably entering **puberty**, a time when he will develop other secondary **sex** **characteristics**.

11. A hormone released by the **hypothalamus** stimulates the **pituitary** gland to release **follicle**-**stimulating** and **luteinizing** hormones.

12. FSH regulates **sperm** production, while LH controls the production of the steroid hormone **testosterone** by the testes.

Name _____ Date _____ Class _____

Chapter 38

Reproduction and Development, *continued*

Section 38.1 Human Reproductive Systems, *continued*

In your textbook, read about human female anatomy and puberty in females.

Determine if each statement is true. If it is not, rewrite the italicized part to make it true.

13. When an egg cell is released from an ovary, it moves down the oviduct *by gravity*.
peristaltic muscle contraction and beating cilia

14. As is the case in human males, a woman's *hypothalamus* produces FSH and LH.
pituitary gland

15. *FSH* stimulates follicle development and the release of estrogen from the ovary.
true

16. In females, *luteinizing hormone (LH)* is responsible for the development of the secondary sex characteristics.
estrogen

17. Long before a woman is born, cells in her ovaries that are destined to become future eggs undergo several *mitotic divisions*.
one meiotic division or a partial meiotic division

In your textbook, read about the menstrual cycle.

Complete the table by checking the correct column for each event.

Event	Phase of Menstrual Cycle		
	Flow	Follicular	Luteal
18. LH stimulates the corpus luteum to develop from a ruptured follicle.			✓
19. Estrogen levels are at their peak.		✓	
20. A cell inside a follicle resumes meiotic divisions.	✓		✓
21. Progesterone levels are at their peak.			✓
22. The uterine lining is shed.	✓		
23. LH levels rise abruptly.		✓	
24. Ovulation occurs.		✓	
25. The uterine lining becomes engorged with blood, fat, and tissue fluid.	✓		
26. FSH begins to rise.			✓

Chapter 38 Reproduction and Development, *continued*

Reinforcement and Study Guide

Section 38.3 Birth, Growth, and Aging

In your textbook, read about birth.

Answer the following questions.

1. What are the three stages of birth? **dilation, expulsion, and the placental stage**

2. Describe the action of oxytocin. **Oxytocin stimulates contraction of the uterine muscles and dilation of the cervix.**

3. After the placenta is expelled from a woman's body, what effect do continued uterine contractions have? **Continued contractions constrict the uterine blood vessels and prevent hemorrhaging.**

In your textbook, read about growth and aging.

Complete each sentence.

4. Your growth rate, as well as the type of growth you undergo, varies with both your **age** and your **sex**.

5. **Human growth hormone**, abbreviated **hGH**, regulates growth.

6. hGH exerts its effects primarily on **bones** and on **muscles**.

7. LGH works by increasing **protein synthesis** and **skeletal fat metabolism**.

Complete the table by checking the correct column for each description.

Example	Childhood	Adolescence	Adulthood
8. Your growth rate continues at a steady rate.	✓		
9. Lines develop on your face, especially around your eyes and mouth.			✓
10. You reach maximum physical stature.		✓	
11. You begin to reason.	✓		
12. You may have a sudden growth spurt.		✓	

Chapter 38 Reproduction and Development, *continued*

Reinforcement and Study Guide

Section 38.2 Development Before Birth

In your textbook, read about fertilization and implantation, and embryonic membranes.

Use each of the terms below just once to complete the passage.

amnion	blastocyst	chorion	chorionic villi	embryo
implants	oviduct	placenta	umbilical cord	zygote

Usually in the upper part of a(n) (1) **oviduct**, an egg and one sperm unite to form a(n) (2) **zygote**. This single cell divides repeatedly to form a(n) (3) **blastocyst**, which (4) **implants** in the uterine wall. Part of the blastocyst becomes the (5) **embryo**, which is surrounded by a fluid-filled, membranous sac called the (6) **amnion**. The embryo is connected to the wall of the uterus by its (7) **umbilical cord**. The amniotic sac is enclosed by the (8) **chorion**, which later forms the (9) **placenta**.
Nutrients and oxygen from the mother and wastes from the embryo are exchanged in the (10) **chorionic villi**.

In your textbook, read about fetal development and genetic counseling.

Complete the table by checking the correct column for each event or example.

Event/Example	Trimester		
	First	Second	Third
11. Fetus can survive outside the uterus with medical assistance.		✓	
12. Fetus weighs more than 3000 grams.			✓
13. Embryo is most vulnerable to outside influences.	✓		
14. Embryo becomes a fetus.	✓		
15. Fetus can use its muscles to move spontaneously.		✓	
16. Fetus becomes oriented head-down.			✓
17. Sex of fetus can be determined.	✓		

Name _____ Date _____ Class _____

Reinforcement and Study Guide

Chapter 39 Immunity From Disease

Section 39.1 *The Nature of Disease*

In your textbook, read about what an infectious disease is, determining what causes a disease, and the spread of infectious diseases.

Answer the following questions.

1. Why is a disease like osteoarthritis not considered an infectious disease?

   Infectious diseases area caused by pathogens that invade the body.

2. What is meant by Koch's postulates?

   a series of experimental steps, developed by Robert Koch in 1876, used to identify

   infectious pathogens

3. In terms of disease, what is a reservoir?

   a source of pathogens

Complete the table by writing in the method of transmission for each example.

Example	Method of Transmission
4. While exploring a cave, a person breathes in fungal spores that cause a lung infection.	airborne
5. A person contracts Rocky Mountain spotted fever after being bitten by a tick.	vector
6. After having unprotected sex, a person contracts syphilis.	direct contact

In your textbook, read about what causes the symptoms of a disease, patterns of disease, and treating diseases.

For each statement below, write true or false.

true	7. The toxin produced by a particular microorganism might be far more destructive than the direct damage the microbe does to its host cells.
false	8. Endemic diseases often disappear in a population, only to resurface unexpectedly many years later.
false	9. If you catch the flu during an influenza epidemic, your best hope of recovery is to take antibiotics.
true	10. It is important for researchers to try to discover new antibiotics because many types of bacteria are becoming resistant to the ones now being used.

Name _____ Date _____ Class _____

Reinforcement and Study Guide

Chapter 39 Immunity From Disease, *continued*

Section 39.2 *Defense Against Infectious Diseases*

In your textbook, read about the innate immune system.

Determine if the statement is true. If it is not, rewrite the italicized part to make it true.

1. Healthy skin is a good defense against the invasion of pathogens because it is *free of bacteria*.

   a physical barrier that prevents the entry of pathogens into the body

2. In your trachea, *saliva* traps microbes and prevents them from entering your lungs.

   mucus

3. Macrophages migrate *into the bloodstream* when the body is challenged by a pathogen.

   out of body tissues and into infected areas

4. Phagocytes at the site of an infection or inflammation destroy pathogens by surrounding and engulfing them. ___ true

5. The third line of defense against infection is the consumption of pathogens *by neutrophils*.

   monocytes that mature to become macrophages

6. Interferon is produced by cells infected by *pathogenic bacteria*.

   viruses

In your textbook, read about acquired immunity.

Circle the letter of the choice that best completes the statement.

7. The human lymphatic system is important in
   a. filtering pathogens from lymph.
   b. keeping body fluids constant.
   c. resistance to disease.
   (d.)all of the above.

8. Tissue fluid is found
   a. in lymph vessels.
   b. in the bloodstream.
   (c.) around body cells.
   d. in lymph ducts.

9. The main function of lymph nodes is to
   a. store red blood cells.
   (b.)filter lymph.
   c. filter excess fluid.
   d. trigger an immune response.

10. A reservoir for lymphocytes that can be transformed into specific disease-fighting cells is the
   (a.) thymus gland.
   b. thyroid gland.
   c. pituitary gland.
   d. pancreas.

Chapter 39 Immunity From Disease, continued

Reinforcement and Study Guide

Section 39.2 Defense Against Infectious Diseases, continued

In your textbook, read about antibody immunity and cellular immunity.

Complete each sentence.

11. **Acquired immunity** is the building up of a **resistance** to a specific pathogen.

12. Two types of immunity that involve different kinds of cells and cellular actions are **antibody** immunity and **cellular** immunity.

13. The presence of foreign **antigens** in the body triggers the production of **antibodies** by plasma cells.

14. A **B cell** is a lymphocyte that, when activated by a **T cell**, becomes a plasma cell and produces **antibodies**.

15. Cellular immunity involves several different types of **T** cells.

16. A **killer T cell** releases enzymes directly into the **pathogens**.

Complete the table by checking the correct columns for each example.

Example	Type of Immunity	
	Cellular	Antibody
17. Involves the protection of antibodies		✓
18. Simulated by antigens in the body	✓	✓
19. Clones of killer T cells produced	✓	
20. Memory cells produced so the body can respond quickly to a second attack	✓	✓
21. Key role played by antigen-antibody complex		✓
22. T cells destroyed by pathogens directly	✓	

Chapter 39 Immunity From Disease, continued

Reinforcement and Study Guide

Section 39.2 Defense Against Infectious Diseases, continued

In your textbook, read about passive and active immunity to infectious diseases.

Answer the following questions.

23. Distinguish between active and passive immunity.
Active immunity develops as a result of direct exposure to antigens; passive immunity results from acquiring antibodies through inoculations, or via the placenta or breast milk.

24. In what two ways can passive immunity develop?
(1) naturally, when antibodies are transferred from mother to fetus or nursing infant; (2) artificially, via injection

25. What is a vaccine?
a substance made up of weakened or dead pathogens, or parts of pathogens that, injected into the body, will cause active immunity

In your textbook, read about AIDS and the immune system.

For each statement below, write true or false.

true 26. The virus that causes AIDS—Human Immunodeficiency Virus—is well-named because it attacks the immune system.

false 27. HIV can be transmitted by air.

true 28. A child born to a woman who is infected with HIV is at high risk for being infected, too.

false 29. HIV destroys a person's resistance to disease by attacking and destroying memory T cells.

false 30. In a blood sample from an HIV-positive person, you would expect to find most of the viruses existing free in the blood, rather than being hidden inside cells.

false 31. If a person is infected with HIV, he or she will usually develop AIDS within about a year.

true 32. The cause of death for a person with AIDS usually is some type of infection that the body's weakened immune system can no longer fight off.

true 33. The majority of persons infected with HIV will develop AIDS.

T264   ANSWER KEY   BIOLOGY: The Dynamics of Life

REINFORCEMENT AND STUDY GUIDE

Name _____ Date _____ Class _____

Reinforcement and Study Guide

The Human Body

In your textbook, read about skin, bones, and muscles.

Skin has four functions: (1) **protects tissues and organs** , (2) **helps regulate the body temperature** , (3) **produces vitamin D** , and (4) **contains many sensory receptors** . These functions help maintain homeostasis in the body.

Complete the table to describe the role of bones.

Support for	5. **softer, underlying tissues**
Place for	6. **muscle attachment**
Protects	7. **vital organs**
Manufacture of	8. **blood cells**
Storehouse of	9. **calcium and phosphorus**

This diagram shows the various steps involved in the respiratory process. In the space provided, describe the steps as indicated.

Step 1: Oxygen enters the lungs when you inhale.

Step 2: (10) **Oxygen passes from the alveoli in the lungs to the bloodstream.**

Step 3: Oxygen passes from blood to the cells.

Step 4: (11) **Oxygen breaks down glucose to produce ATP for cells and to release CO2.**

Step 5: (12) **Carbon dioxide passes from the cell to the bloodstream.**

Step 6: (13) **Carbon dioxide passes from the bloodstream to the alveoli in the lungs.**

Step 7: Carbon dioxide leaves the lungs when you exhale.

LUNG

Bloodstream

Bloodstream

Cell
O2 + ATP
Glucose CO2

Name _____ Date _____ Class _____

Reinforcement and Study Guide

The Human Body, *continued*

In your textbook, read about reproductive, endocrine, and lymphatic systems.

14. The endocrine system is a communication system; its messages are hormones. They are produced by glands and travel in the **bloodstream** to **target tissues** . There they **alter the metabolism of the target tissue cells** .

15. The structures of the male reproductive system—the scrotum, **testes** , epididymis, seminal vesicles, **prostate gland** , bulbourethral gland, urethra, and **penis** —are involved in **producing** and maintaining sperm cells and **transferring sperm cells** into the female reproductive tract.

16. The structures of the female reproductive system—the **ovaries** , oviduct, **uterus** , and vagina—produce and maintain **egg cells** , receive and transport **sperm cells** , and support the development of the **fetus** .

Explain how these systems of the body interact with each other.

17. Skeletal system ⟶ Circulatory system ⟶ Muscular system
Possible answer: Skeletal system manufactures blood cells that travel through the circulatory system to bring oxygen and nutrients to the cells of the muscular system.

18. Digestive system ⟶ Circulatory system ⟶ Urinary system
Possible answer: Circulation system carries waste products from food breakdown to the urinary system to be eliminated.

19. Endocrine system ⟶ Reproductive system
Answer should reflect: Hormones secreted by glands in the endocrine system alter the metabolism of target tissues in the reproductive system.

20. Respiratory System ⟶ Circulatory system ⟶ Cell ⟶ Circulatory system ⟶ Urinary and Respiratory systems
Answer should reflect: Oxygen supplied by respiratory system is carried by circulatory systems to cells; waste products from metabolism are carried by circulatory system to urinary and respiratory systems for excretion.

21. Circulatory system ⟶ Lymphatic system
Answer should reflect: Fluids from capillaries of circulatory system bathe the cells and then are absorbed by the lymphatic system.